Duquesne Studies - Philological

Series 8

LAMENTS FOR THE DEAD IN MEDIEVAL NARRATIVE

DUQUESNE STUDIES

PHILOLOGICAL SERIES

8

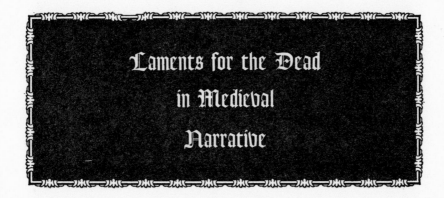

Laments for the Dead
in Medieval
Narrative

by

VELMA BOURGEOIS RICHMOND

DUQUESNE UNIVERSITY PRESS
Pittsburgh, Pa.
Editions E. Nauwelaerts, Louvain, Belgium

DUQUESNE STUDIES

PHILOLOGICAL SERIES

Library of Congress Catalog Card Number 66—29691

For my parents

PREFACE

This book is a result of my interest in the relation of medieval narrative and Elizabethan tragedy. Since "laments for the dead" is my own phrase, I should explain that I use it to refer to an extensive body of material that has not previously been recognized. Both the essay and the anthology demonstrate that a convention of laments for the dead not only existed, but also was important and effective in medieval narrative. It provided many of the most impressive scenes in medieval narrative and offered to the Elizabethan dramatist a complex and meaningful tradition after which strikingly dramatic scenes could be modeled. I hope that my study will provide some insight to the way in which a traditional rhetorical form persists in different genres over a period of several hundred years, and that it will also suggest something of the resources of a too much neglected part of medieval literature.

My research on this theme began while I was a graduate student at the University of North Carolina, working with Professors Robert A. Pratt and Ernest W. Talbert. For their continued interest in the work and encouragement I am deeply grateful. As a Fulbright scholar at St. Hugh's College, Oxford, I worked with Miss Helen Gardner, who supervised my B. Litt. thesis. Her advice, not simply about critical evaluation but also about scholarly writing, has been inestimably valuable; and I can scarcely do justice to my indebtedness to her. The present study is really a revised and expanded treatment of the thesis I did with her in Oxford. Finally, I wish to acknowledge my indebtedness to my husband for his unfailing interest and encouragement of the writing of this volume.

V.E.B.R.

CONTENTS

11

Chapter I

INTRODUCTION

Medieval narrative fiction has not been very extensively or seriously studied as a means of commenting on human experience, apart from the usual generalizations about the escapism of romance. Scholars have, of course, considered rather widely the courtly elements and the relations of myth and legend in medieval narrative; and there have been extensive studies of some attitudes toward death in the Middle Ages. But no attempts have been made to study the ways in which death was treated in medieval narrative. I do not wish to concern myself here with attitudes toward death as it was considered in theological or philosophical treatises or in observations of individual writers who stop their main arguments to make expository comments, but rather to show the way in which a writer telling a story makes his characters react to the fact of someone's death. In short, my interest is literary. Medieval narrative is not important merely for linguistic study or entertaining complexities of plot or a multiplicity of curious details; it is a literature which enjoyed enormous popular appeal and thus, of necessity, must contain insights about human behavior. Death, obviously, is a crucial and pivotal experience, so that a consideration of the attitudes of writers toward moments when death is recognized can offer suggestions about evolving literary skills. Even the more primitive medieval narratives illustrate a conscious awareness of the necessity for particularizing, for understanding, for assimilating, basic and inevitable parts of the human experience; they recognize the value of using the occasion of death for exploiting resources of emotion, for revealing something of the complexity of individuals and their relations to other persons and the world in which they live. The results of this study reveal an established tradition of "laments for the dead." This is the name which I give to passages that are, quite simply, what is said when someone is dead or is believed to be dead. Only brief and casual comments on the importance of laments for the dead in medieval narrative have been made,[1] and there has been no systematic collec-

[1] An example is in E. K. Chambers' essay on "Malory." Professor Chambers suggests that Lancelot is Malory's protagonist, and part of

tion or analysis of the material, which is both extensive and impressive, for it provides a focus for observing the evolution of literary awareness. In laments for the dead we observe writers of narrative going beyond the telling of stories to investigate a fundamental and universal experience which allows, indeed necessitates, a consideration of some complexities of the motives and behavior of the human personality.

The medieval lament for the dead is important not only as a significant element of narrative, but also as a traditional form of expression which offered many suggestions to early Elizabethan tragedy. Since Elizabethan tragedy, unlike Greek, presupposes that tragegy is "about deaths," a consideration of this aspect of the 'medieval heritage' seems particularly pertinent. It is usually accepted that romances had their greatest influence on drama—we need only recall that romances are frequently coupled with plays for condemnation—but specific studies of this relationship are either non-existent or limited to general borrowings of plot. Laments for the dead are a distinguished part of medieval narratives, for they are the basis for many of the most effective and dramatic scenes. Thus it seems likely that writers of early Elizabethan tragedy were influenced to emphasize scenes of death because many of the most memorable scenes of medieval narrative had been those in which a death was commented upon. Both the idea and the techniques of treating death were immediately and popularly available.

A commonplace of criticism of early Elizabethan tragedy is that its rise is partially a consequence of interest in and imitation of "Senecan" tragedy in the third quarter of the sixteenth century. Professor Tucker Brooke's introductory comments are typical:

> Though tragic narrative, as illustrated in the *Fall of Princes* and *Mirror for Magistrates,* had a great hold on readers, there was hardly any tradition of tragedy on the English stage when Elizabeth came to the throne. Thus, although Seneca was acted at schools and original tragedies in Latin were produced at the universities ... there appears to have been no popular interest in English tragedy till after 1580. Up to that time such tragedies as appeared in the vernacular were exotics, quite unlike in that respect to the early comedies. . . .

---

his argument is: "But it is relevant that it is on him [Lancelot], and not on Arthur, that the threnody, which forms its epilogue, is spoken." In *English Literature at the Close of the Middle Ages* (Oxford, 1947), p. 198.

Early Elizabethan tragedy is Senecan tragedy . . . translation of Euripides' *Iphigeneia at Aulis* . . . argues no direct contact between the English stage and the art of Greece. Nor is it likely that the tragic implications of medieval nondramatic writings, lately well analysed by Professor Farnham, would have found outlet in the theatres if the remarkable interest in Seneca between 1559 and 1581 had not prepared a channel for it. During these years the entire canon of ten tragedies ascribed to Seneca was translated by different hands, and in 1581 they were published together in an impressive volume.[2]

The only suggestion that this view may be too absolute is a last entry in a footnote: "Howard Baker, *Induction to Tragedy* (Baton Rouge, 1939), doubts the extent of Seneca's influence."

The present study arose then, on the one hand, from an unwillingness to accept the attitude which is typified in Professor Tucker Brooke's estimate, and on the other, from a desire to consider an aspect of medieval narrative which has been largely neglected. The laments which appear in this anthology have sufficient intrinsic merit to warrant critical analysis and discussion, and they have an extrinsic significance because they suggest a basis for a reconsideration of early Elizabethan tragedy. Many of the passages have real literary merit, for writers of narrative, in general, give to laments a precision and subtlety which are often absent in the mere recounting of events. On the occasion of a death, they make a revealing attempt not only to elucidate a human problem but also to evolve a literary technique, a form, which is capable of conveying, in a distinguished style, a multiplicity of ideas that have both a universal significance and a crucial function within the narrative itself. Further, such elaborately studied laments provide a substantial tradition for Elizabethan playwrights who were evolving an individual variety of tragedy, which terminates with death, and needed examples of dramatic and intense interrelations of characters in moments of crisis.

There can be no doubt of the immense popularity of medieval romance. The collection of Robert Thornton (1440) is characteristic. Perhaps no other secular literature was so much enjoyed in the fourteenth and fifteenth centuries, and certainly early printers like Caxton were simply perpetuating popular taste. Even later in the sixteenth century the vogue continued, for although medieval romances were somewhat supplanted after about 1575 by a new stock

[2] In *A Literary History of England*, ed. A. C. Baugh et al (New York, 1948), p. 460.

of romances imported largely from Spain through French, many older favorites persisted. Both *Guy of Warwick* and *Beues of Hamtoun,* for example, remained in circulation in the seventeenth century.[3] In short, the appeal of narrative is enormous and constant, so that there was an appreciative and large audience who grew accustomed to scenes of death that were distinctive and clearly among the most sophisticated and impressive literary achievements of a popular genre. Thus Elizabethan writers of tragedy may have been influenced to focus attention upon scenes of death through a wish to imitate this material which was distinguished by its penetration into human character and actions, which receive ever greater attention with the emerging Renaissance interest in personality. Further, laments in romances often show evidence of conscious rhetorical skill. Those who make claims for borrowings from Seneca place much emphasis upon the "rhetorical element" in Elizabethan tragedy. Therefore, a good beginning for a reconsideration of the origins of Elizabethan tragedy is a study of "rhetorical" treatment in death scenes of medieval narrative, for the similarities of subject matter and forms of expression are many and varied. Thus in the native popular tradition there are ample precedents for both an interest in death scenes and a technical skill in their execution. This sustained tradition of several hundred years provides a more plausible source of conventional material than the sudden interest in Seneca for a period of twenty years at the end of the sixteenth century. One of the most obvious problems in dealing with a form, like laments for the dead, which springs from a universal idea, is deciding just wherein lies the tradition of the form and where mere inevitable similarity of material must occur. The distinction between a literary setpiece consciously produced and a lament more spontaneously developed by the mere logic of circumstances is not always clear. With a recognition of this possibility of two ways in which the passages may have been composed, and of course a third way which would have been a combination of the two, a valid analysis may be attempted.

First it is perhaps necessary to justify, or to document, the lament for the dead as a form, particularly since the phrase is not part of the vocabulary of literary criticism. Death is one of the most fundamental parts of human experience, so that there has always been an attempt to understand and assimilate the event. It is not surprising to find in the Middle Ages many comments about death; this is true

[3] Ronald Crane, *The Vogue of Medieval Chivalric Romance During the English Renaissance* (Menasha, Wisconsin, 1919).

in any age; however, it is somewhat unusual and quite significant that the lament for the dead was a recognized and accepted form of expression at that time. There is too much evidence of conscious composition of laments in narrative, and there are too many explanations of how to go about composing laments, for it to be possible to deny that medieval writers were writing with an established genre in mind, and not making chance utterances. Lamentation, being exclamatory, is rhetorical in its essential nature, so that treatises and manuals of rhetoric are the most obvious sources for explanations of the form, and with these we may begin to find evidence for a tradition of laments for the dead.

Unquestionably the best evidence is Geoffrey de Vinsauf's lament for Richard I in *Poetria Nova* (Anthology, pp. 132–35).[4] Karl Young[5] indicated something of the importance attached to the lament:

> ... in the later Middle Ages, this particular passage in the *Nova Poetria* had exceptional vogue as a literary gem. Even in its place as part of an extended didactic poem, this lament was conspicuous as the longest of the literary "examples" in the treatise and was, in some manuscripts, furnished with rubrics or glosses drawing attention to its structure and significance.[6]

His article published for the first time a fifteenth-century manuscript (Br. Mus. MS. Cotton Cleopatra B-VI, fols. 8[r]–9[r]) which divides the piece into five sections according to the apostrophes which are made. He further quotes a thirteenth-century manuscript (Br. Mus. MS. Add. 37495, fol. 7[v]) which observes six divisions in the composition and has a marginal gloss on rhetorical *colores*. Thus he concludes:

> Clearly, then, Vinsauf's lament for King Richard was treated with respect as a forcible and finished literary production and as a significant illustration of superior rhetorical practice.[7]

He supports this view with other appearances of the lament in books of rhetorical instruction. The most striking evidence of its fame,

---

[4] When the text of a lament is included in the Anthology, references will be given in parentheses.

[5] Karl Young, "Chaucer and Geoffrey of Vinsauf," *MP*, XLI (1944), 172–82.

[6] Young, "Chaucer," p. 172.

[7] Young, "Chaucer," p. 176.

however, was its circulation independently, apart from the *Poetria Nova* and purposes of instruction. It appeared, for example, as "Planctus de morte Regis Ricardi Cuir de Lyon" in an anthology compiled in the thirteenth and fifteenth centuries (Bodl. MS. Add. A. 44 (30151), fols. 7ᵛ–8ᵛ), and it was the chief literary adornment used by Nicholas Trivet in his life of King Richard in the *Annales*.

Geoffrey's lament was written as a model of proper rhetorical embellishment, so that it is much more elaborate than less self-conscious passages. The apostrophe which immediately precedes Richard's complaint is for times of prosperity and warns against complacency, for grief always comes hard upon happiness. England's glory rested in her King Richard, who, like a mirror, gave pride to those who looked in, was a star which gave splendor, a column which supported, a thunderbolt which frightened the enemy, a glory almost to the height of the gods. But quickly a mirror may be broken, a star eclipsed, a column broken, a blow of thunder cease, a princess become a slave. A reversal from quiet to anxiety, from laughter to tears, from wealth to poverty, comes swiftly. Death is an augur; astrologists are to be done away with. Man may know the present, but God alone knows the future. The die of fate changes in a brief time, as examples of former fortunes show.

The complaint for Richard is an apostrophe for times of sorrow. His empire is addressed and told to testify grief in a lament—to weep, grow pale, twist fingers, make a clamor in the heavens—for the death is Normandy's, not Richard's. This is followed by an apostrophe to Friday, the day on which Richard died. Then there are rhetorical questions about what soldier dared to do this against Richard. More apostrophes follow, "O dolor! O plus quam dolor! O mors! O truculenta/ Mors!" Death is first wished dead and then asked whether it knew whom it was ravishing. This leads to praise of Richard, master of weapons, glory of kings, delight of the world, so wonderful that Nature could not add anything to what he was. And this is why Richard was taken away. The next apostrophe is to Natura, who was pleased to stretch out her hand and recall it, to give thus and to take the marvel back. The return of Richard or one like him is demanded imperatively, but this is not possible, for with him the supply of the wonderful and precious was exhausted. As much happier as Richard's empire was before, so much more wretched is it now. Finally the poet apostrophizes God. He asks why One Whose omnipotence could have prevented Richard's death has let the king die. Richard is praised for his godly deeds, and the lament concludes with a final statement of the idea that the tears of the world are as long as laughter is brief.

Even this cursory summary indicates the elaborate care with which Geoffrey wrote a lament for the dead. He is more interested in careful verse, repetition, and clever figures, than in ideas. He does, however, make specific certain ideas, which are typical in laments in medieval literature—grief, changing Fortune, accusations of treason, loss of honor, questioning about reasons for the death, extensive praise. As an apostrophe for sorrow the lament is introduced naturally after one for prosperity. Obviously the position of this lament as a "literary example" in a rhetorical treatise means that it cannot be discussed as a passage integrated with a narrative.

It would be absurd to suggest that most laments for the dead in medieval literature are as intricate and elaborate as Geoffrey's. But Geoffrey's lament indicates a definite recognition that a lament for the dead is a literary form. In view of this, Chaucer's treatment of laments for the dead is very striking. There can be no doubt that Chaucer knew Geoffrey de Vinsauf's *Poetria Nova*. Notes in a standard edition [8] always make this point in explaining these lines in *The Nun's Priest's Tale*:

> O, Gaufred, deere maister soverayn,
> That whan thy worthy kyng Richard was slayn
> With shot, compleynedest his deeth so soore,
> Why ne hadde I now thy sentence and thy loore,
> The Friday for to chide, as diden ye?
> For on a Friday, soothly, slayn was he.
> Thanne wolde I shewe yow how that I koude pleyne
> For Chauntecleres drede and how for his peyne.
>
> (B, 4537–44) [9]

And the point of Karl Young's article is to add to the conventional attitude that Chaucer's reference is derisive, an argument that some helpful suggestions, if not a specific source, of the general moralistic element (the dangers of pride and instability of earthly happiness)

[8] F. N. Robinson, *The Works of Geoffrey Chaucer*, 2nd ed. (Cambridge, Mass., 1957), p. 754.

[9] Arabic numbers in my text, either following a quotation or in the discussion, are used to refer to lines of verse and pages in prose narratives. Large Roman numbers refer to parts of the narrative, and small Roman numbers are for volumes of the edition quoted. References to manuscripts are given when this is necessary to avoid confusion, but generally an edition has only one version.

of the tale may be found in the *Poetria Nova*. We can be certain
that Chaucer and his audience were well acquainted with the lament
for Richard I, which he ridiculed. Only a well established tradition
is characteristically singled out for travesty, and the single reference
to "Friday" is chosen to recall details of Geoffrey de Vinsauf's lament
and to suggest the absurdities of excessive lamentation.

Having seen such definite objections to Geoffrey's excesses, we
are not completely surprised to find that Chaucer did not use laments
for the dead on several occasions when he might have been expected
to. In *Troilus and Criseyde* laments might have been most suitably
made at Hector's death (V, 1554 ff.), but since Chaucer's interest
is in the two principles, an omission is understandable. It is more
disconcerting to find that Troilus' death receives only a stanza of
narrative comment (V, 1828–34), and we must conclude that Chaucer
in his greatest romance narrative did not write a proper lament for
the dead. The other striking opportunity which he does not use is
the death of Arcite in *The Knight's Tale*. Here there is rather extended narrative description, but only nine lines of lamentation (A,
2835–36; 2843–49), most of which is a statement of the consolation
that all which lives must die. Perhaps Chaucer was so struck by
the absurdity of Geoffrey's lament, which he later ridiculed so capably, that he did not want to risk any similarity. He differs, then,
from most writers of medieval narrative, even though he is most
explicit in his knowledge of a tradition of laments for the dead. His
skill in writing a variety of memorable scenes perhaps made it unnecessary for him to use the more obviously exploited occasion of
a death.

The most notable exception of Chaucer's antipathy to laments is
his earliest work, *The Book of the Duchess*. There Chaucer most
specifically and very capably writes in a tradition of laments for the
dead. In the opening section Alcyone makes quite a reputable lament
for Seys when he is lost (90–94), and exclaims "Allas!" (213) when
she knows definitely that he is dead. This episode prepares for the
main narrative. The first complaint of the man in black is creditable:

> "I have of sorwe so gret won
> That joye gete I never non,
> Now that I see my lady bryght,
> Which I have loved with al my myght,
> Is fro me ded and ys agoon.
>   Allas, deth, what ayleth the,

That thou noldest have taken me,
Whan thou toke my lady swete,
That was so fair, so fresh, so fre,
So good, that men may wel se
Of al goodnesse she had no mete!"

(475–86)

Here we have a genuine expression of grief, exclamation of "Allas,"
an apostrophe to death, a wish for death, and conventional praise
of the lady. The long explanation which the man in black makes of
his grief (560–709) is much more than an ordinary lament for the
dead. He begins by saying that nothing can lessen his grief, listing
classical expedients which will not help, and he wishes earnestly for
death. With an exclamatory "Allas," he describes his sorrowful state,
which is a reversal of all former happiness. False Fortune is given
as an explanation of his distress. He describes her evil changeability
and tells how he lost the game of chess he played against Fortune.
He does not, however, blame Fortune, for he would have made the
same winning play had God willed it so. Then he cries out, "Allas,
that I was born!" and repeats a wish for death because his sorrow is
so absolute. With this the man in black is overcome and stops speaking. The protagonist answers this outburst with reminders that suicide
results in damnation, and his companion speaks again. Praise of the
dead lady is made obliquely when the man in black describes his
lady and her many attributes, physical and moral. After hearing an
account of the progress of their love, the protagonist asks where
the lady is. The man in black again cries, "Allas that I was bore!"
and declares, "She ys ded!" His questioner simply says, "Is that
youre los? Be god, hyt ys routher!" (1310), and there is no further
lamentation. *The Book of the Duchess,* which is almost purely an
elegy, is unlike most medieval narrative, so that it is difficult to
discuss it as part of the main tradition. It is, however, very interesting to find within an elegiac narrative passages which are distinguishable as laments for the dead. And these laments provide a good
deal of dramatic interplay between personages; further, they are the
principal means by which the action is moved forward. Thus Chaucer
seems to have been willing to rely upon this form of expression in
his earliest work, though he discarded—and indeed ridiculed it—in
his later, more sophisticated narratives. Perhaps we might argue that
this first use of laments for the dead in *The Book of the Duchess*
is so comprehensive and successful that Chaucer could do no more

with the form—except the final travesty. Certainly there are many writers, not least importantly Marlowe and Shakespeare, who suggest this pattern of early reliance and subsequent rejection of rhetorical effects of lamentation.

Finally, it should be noted that Chaucer has several laments in *The Monk's Tale*; and in *The Legend of Good Women,* which also has the formal structure of a *De Casibus,* he enriches three of the legends with laments. Paradoxically, in comparison with other such works, for example Lydgate's *Fall of Princes*, this is a high number, since passages of lamentation tend to be merely set-pieces in the form of *envoys,* rather than the expressions of characters within the narratives. The evolving interest in interplay of characters, suggesting a new complexity of personality observable in crucial scenes of many medieval narratives, would have detracted from the significance of the great man and his subsequent fall which so sharply contrasts to his previous eminence.

In contrast to Chaucer's overall paucity of laments for the dead, we find in *The Tale of Beryn,* which was written as an addition to *The Canterbury Tales,* that laments are vital to the narrative. The only death in the tale is that of Beryn's mother, but she is lamented no less than four times. Actually all Beryn's misfortunes are explained as a direct result, not so much of his gambling, but of his initial failure to lament his mother's death. Here, then, the writer not only includes a lament for the dead, but also he uses an established belief in the importance of laments for the dead as a mainspring for the action of his story and the chief didactic point. Here we are struck by the use of laments for the dead as an obvious means of expanding a narrative effort. Confronted with the problem of writing this additional tale, the author turns to the lament, a genre which is well recognized and popular in its appeal. The early play *Locrine* or Marlowe's *Tamburlaine, Part II* are splendid illustrations of the same inventiveness. The lament because it is a form which offers possibilities for variation in expression is used by each of these writers, and its function as a part of humanity's experience is of such universal significance that it cannot be avoided. Indeed it can become so central that it is the *raison d'être* for this whole series of works of literature, not simply a striking feature.

Gower, who is interested in pure narrative, makes little use of the artistic embellishment of laments for the dead. In the *Confessio Amantis* he has only one example, and this is not particularly distinguished. The scene is a good one, for the mourner is Thelegonus, who has just unwittingly slain his father Ulysses (VI, 1714–22). Gower uses many conventional ideas, such as exclamations of "Alas, that I was born," a wish for death, actually an invitation for someone to kill him, and a protest against "unhappi destine," so that there can be little doubt of his awareness of the traditional lament for the dead. The passage, however, has no intrinsic significance; it is simply an adequate expression. The opportunities for a mourner to lament are not lacking in the *Confessio Amantis,* but Gower seems not to have liked the form. He wrote only a few love complaints which were even more appropriate to his stories. Thus we can perhaps conclude that these forms of rhetorical embellishment were not in keeping with his intention. Indeed lamentations would probably be somewhat awkwardly placed in the simplicity of expression and short line of the *Confessio.* Further, Gower seems to limit exchanges of dialogue that suggest dramatic interplay to the framework of his Confessor and Amans.

Quite a different attitude toward the embellishment of rhetorical laments is to be found in *Sir Gawain and the Green Knight,* which has one very impressive example. When Gawain leaves to keep his appointment with the Green Knight, all:

> Carande for þat comly: 'Bi Kryst, hit is scaþe
> Þat þou, leude, schal be lost, þat art of lyf noble!
> To fynde hys fere vpon folde, in fayth, is not eþe.
> Warloker to haf wroȝt had more wyt bene,
> And haf dyȝt ȝonder dere a duk to haue worþed,
> A lowande leder of ledeȝ in londe hym wel semeȝ,
> And so had better haf ben þen britned to noȝt,
> Hadet wyth aluisch mon, for angardeȝ pryde.
> Who knew euer any kyng such counsel to take
> As knyȝteȝ in cauelaciounȝ on Crystmasse gomneȝ!'
>
> (674–84)

There is no actual death in the romance, but on this occasion there is a genuine fear that the hero will be killed, so that his companions make what may be called an "anticipatory" lament. The main ideas are praise of Gawain and questioning the wisdom of a king's judgment. Naturally feeling is less intense because only a feared, not an actual loss, is being lamented. What is significant is that the poet stopped his narrative to have characters within the story make a lament, indicating an understanding of the form and its usefulness in conveying emotional distress. Such recognition is

the more important because there is no obvious occasion for this
kind of expression in this romance. Here a poet of real excellence,
one who has literary finesse and sophistication, regards the lament
for the dead as an effective form, one which he can adapt to his
individual purpose. He has, then, the advantages of a conventional
form but does not lose the initiative. In the hands of a superior
writer the lament, used discreetly and imaginatively, fosters originality
and enriches the narrative texture.

Thus for various reasons the finest narrative poets of the fourteenth
century made little use of laments for the dead. Chaucer evidently
knew the form but, in general, considered it an unsatisfactory embellishment; Gower is not interested in embellishment, but only in
advancing his narrative; the author of *Sir Gawain* had no real opportunity for a lament for the dead, but on the one occasion when
there was an opportunity for this kind of embellishment, he adapted
the form to his own purpose. Even these few illustrations, however,
suggest the rich potential of laments for the dead. In the narratives
of somewhat lesser poets, who rely more obviously upon traditional
material, we find laments for the dead in abundance. Though many
lack distinction, many others have real excellence. The opportunity
afforded by the occasion of a death scene characteristically inspires
even lesser writers of narrative, who recognized at least partially its
many advantages.

Perhaps the most striking indication that laments for the dead were
an accepted tradition occurs in two laments in which the mourners
make it clear that they know they are following a convention. In the
Laud Troy Book after Hector has refused to stay at home, Andromede says:

> For I wot be me drem to-nyȝt:
> If thow to-morne gos to fyȝt,
> With-oute the deth may thow not passe;
> Then may I say for the "alas!
> That I was borne!" for care & sorowe.
> Be-leue at hom, my lord, to morwe ...
>
> (10,017–22)

This lady clearly knew what was expected of her, for she has well
in mind the most acceptable opening line of a lament for the dead.
Andromede is aware of a tradition which not only insists upon a
mourner's making a lament for the dead, but also provides a specific
formula to be followed. A hero like Hector must be properly

mourned, and the conventional utterance of grief by his bereaved wife is accepted automatically. The emotional effect of such lamentation is clearly recognized by Andromede, who uses the familiar words of despair in an attempt to dissuade her husband from beginning a fatal venture. This is her way of intensifying the revelation of her dream of Hector's impending death. Fuller exploitation of the dramatic potential of such situations of wifely anxiety and foreknowledge comes later in a character like Shakespeare's Calpurnia, but the passage in the *Laud Troy Book* shows the way.

The other illustration of a mourner who explicitly recognizes that he is following a convention of laments for the dead is in *Eger & Grime.* Here one character consciously creates a lament to win the sympathy of another character in the story. Grime pretends that Eger is dead and produces a suitable lament (1314). Everything that Grime does, he does to help Eger win the vain Winglayne; and he takes the occasion of announcing Eger's death to further his friend's love-suit. Grime plans his lament carefully. He first announces the death, heightening grief by explaining that Eger was wounded when he left, and then turns against Winglayne, who, with her ridiculous refusal to wed anyone who has not won every battle, is responsible for the slain knight's undertaking. He neatly turns the conventional phrase into "alas *that* eu*er* shee was borne!" and concludes with traditional praise of "the best k*n*ight *th*at eu*er* was in the world." It is this lament which prepares for Eger's happy and 'victorious' return and leads to his marriage. This self-conscious adaptation is further evidence of the acceptance of laments for the dead within a tradition of medieval narrative. We have gone beyond a poet's simple use of a lament to win pity or sympathy or to advance the action. Now a poet is making a character within the narrative recognize the utility of laments and effectively produce an appropriate one to gain the sympathy of a fierce antagonist and precipitate the story. Clearly this is an exploitation of the form for ingenious and subtle effects. The complex levels of awareness indicate a literary finesse which is not typical of much medieval narrative. Again the conventional form is not only known, but also altered ingeniously as a means of influencing feeling. Here, as with Andromede in the *Laud Troy Book,* we have a character resorting to a lament for the dead because he knows that it is a means of gaining sympathy.

These examples support the claim that a lament for the dead is a recognized and developed form of expression. It seems possible, then, to establish a tradition of rhetorical laments in medieval literature before "Senecanism" produced Elizabethan tragedy. I have made a cursory examination of much medieval literature in which it seemed likely that laments for the dead would appear. There is a marked prevalence of the form, and several examples occur in almost every type of medieval literature. Secular medieval drama might have offered the most pertinent examples, but unfortunately there is so little record of this drama that it is almost useless to look for a tradition of laments there. We can do no more than regret, for example, that we do not have all parts of *Dux Moraud* where there might well have been a mourner's lament. Folk plays offer an occasional suggestion, but they are hardly "tragedies." Revivification in the St. George plays, for example, precludes the possibility of extensive lamentation. Medieval religious drama is not without encouragement, for the *planctus Mariae* is a kind of lament for the dead. Certainly many of the ideas expressed by mourners in secular literature are used in religious writings, for example in the York *Christ Led Up to Calvary.* The Bodley *Burial and Ressurection* is also a *planctus,* the highest development of dramatic *planctus* in English, for it is a play in itself. Similarly, there are sometimes laments in the lives of saints, but since the death of a saint is always joyous, lamentations, if they appear, are of a rather different quality. Sometimes, of course, a religious drama, like the twelfth century *Adeodatus,* contains a lament which is very similar to what may be found in secular literature. Several of these laments from religious literature are included to show their similarities with secular laments, on which our principal focus is placed.

Laments for the dead are fairly widespread as independent lyrics. There are many separate *planctus Mariae,* and there is a sizeable number of independent secular lyrics which are essentially laments for the dead. These include political songs, such as the *Elegy on the Death of Edward I* or *Lament for King Edward iiijth.* An example which has real literary merit is Dunbar's *Elegy on the Death of Bernard Steward, Lord of Aubigny* (Anthology, pp. 135–36). Here we find exclamations of "Alas," high praise with conventional epithets such as "the flour of chevalrie" and "prince of knychtheid," rhetorical questions about death, and religious consolation in prayer. All these ideas are characteristic of laments for the dead in medieval narrative, and it is a pleasant change to find these commonplaces handled by a true poet. Neither Dunbar's metrical skill nor brilliance of language contributes to a larger pattern as a lyric is a separate entity. Thus independent lyrics, in general, are not included. They are outside the scope of the present study, which has as a primary purpose the demonstration of an evolving literary form that is notable for its distinctive appearance in long narratives. Without the larger context and characteristically a blending of dialogue and narrative comment, laments cannot be used as a means of revealing the complex interrelations of characters and of heightening the emotional intensity of scenes which relieve the monotony of endless and often repetitive adventures.

Similarly laments for the dead which appear in chronicles are largely isolated, for they are usually set-pieces. A prose account of the life of Edward II in Fabyon's *Chronicle* is stopped for Edward's verse lament on ill fortune and prayers to God. This passage uses many of the same ideas which are found in laments for the dead, and it is an interesting blend of secular and religious motifs, but it is not so much a part of the narrative account as a literary embellishment. The narrative account is stopped for a literary embellishment and resumed when this is over. No real attempt is made to interrelate narrative and lament. In contrast, a chronicle like Laȝamon's *Brut* has laments for the dead which are an integral part of the story. There they are what one character says about another, and a definite relation is established between the embellishment and the narrative. Such laments, then, are included in the present discussion.

A third kind of set-piece includes laments in a work like Lydgate's *Fall of Princes*, where they are made as part of a rigid scheme of *envoys* and ghosts. The same is true of Sir David Lindsay's *Papyngo's Second Epistle to Brethren of Court,* which has extended commentary on deaths and falls, but no attempt is made to fix these observations as part of the story. A similar criticism may be made of most of Chaucer's *Monk's Tale,* but not of the *Legend of Good Women.* One of the traditional interpretations of *The Pearl* is that it is an elegy. Certainly this reading has validity, and it is of interest to us. But the poem has the same quality as an independent lyric. It must stand as a separate and complete whole, so that it is not a lament which forms part of a narrative. Thus it is not really within the tradition considered here.

The purpose of this study has been to discover whether there existed in the centuries before Elizabethan tragedy began, a tradition of laments for the dead as a quasi-dramatic device. Since early Elizabethan tragedy is secular, I have begun by not including the bulk of medieval religious literature because it is less immediately applicable. The body of medieval secular drama is not sufficient to prove anything; independent lyrics have no larger context so that their dramatic quality is limited to certain aspects within their brief scope; much the same is true of set-pieces in chronicles; verse written in a formalized style with *envoys* or ghosts has no opportunity for flexible dramatic handling. Thus there remains one large body of medieval narrative where laments for the dead which are primarily secular can be handled as an integral part of the story with definite dramatic qualities—medieval romances—and most of our examples, both verse and prose, have been selected from this material.

Approximately one hundred twenty-five romance narratives, a complete list of which appears in the bibliography, have been included. They begin with the earliest extant English romance *King Horn* and include romances up to about 1535. The terminal date has been selected because it is late enough to include all the work of William Copland. Caxton, de Worde, and Copland printed only romances which were "medieval," that is, they printed only the old verse romances of the fourteenth and early fifteenth centuries and more recent prose translations, some of which they made themselves, from French. Since Copland added no new texts, but simply drew from de Worde, 1535 is a satisfactory terminal date. To go beyond this would stretch the "medieval" classification, and since the date is late enough to include not only Malory and Caxton, but also Lord Berners and Henry Watson, this seemed the best solution. In this group of romances I have found about five hundred passages which may be called "laments for the dead." Of these, about sixty-five have genuine artistic merit, and these are the ones which are used for most of the discussion and included in the anthology. Written in a wide variety of styles, these laments show great diversity of ideas and attitudes about death. Thus they provide insight into one important facet of the medieval mind: its relation to a basic and universal experience. When they are discussed in the context of the narratives in which they appear, the laments are often shown to be nuclei for significant scenes in which narrative writers create moments of complex confrontation between human personalities with skill and discretion. In these ways they look forward to the work of the Elizabethan tragedies, and they also provide substantial evidence of literary sophistication in the mass of medieval narrative which has been so much neglected as aesthetically naive.

Chapter II

GENERAL CHARACTERISTICS OF
LAMENTS FOR THE DEAD

A lament is simply what is said when someone is dead, or is believed to be dead, and consequently the ideas expressed are not the result of elaborate mental deliberation. Laments for the dead in medieval narrative differ in only one important way from those which anyone would make in life. They are artistic, though admittedly often in a very rudimentary form, so that they contain some slight flourish, an 'Alas, that I was born!' at least. Otherwise, the typical lament expresses the same ideas which occur to anyone when he learns of a death. Thus we find in laments for the dead as well as straightforward statements that the person is dead, expressions of grief, praise for the deceased, or scorn and dispraise, self-accusatory comments, assumptions of responsibility for the death, resolutions to do something about the death, and cries for revenge in chivalric manner (the idea perhaps least familiar today). Further we find various moralizations on particular deaths; accusations of treason in the slaying, assertions that the death is justly deserved, cries against Fortune, religious questioning, prayer, consolation, and considerations of the future of the public weal, such as how the kingdom will continue, either collapsing without those who are dead or going on with some kind of substitute, the loss of the king's honor when his knights are slain, and rather futile wishes to give up riches, relinquish kingdom and kingship, to have the dead person alive again.

Laments for the dead almost always contain some stylistic embellishments, such as exclamations of "Alas" and "Waileaway" or elaborate apostrophes and metaphors. Frequently care is given to using parallel or balanced phrases, and repetition of words and sounds is another way in which a passage may be unified. Other rhetorical devices, such as descriptions, both moral and physical, of the person, digressions of narrative explaining the sorrowful nature of a person's death because it occasioned personal grief, was sudden, contrasted sharply with a successful life, emotional appeals for pity and sympathy, and so on, are not infrequent.

We may also distinguish in many laments for the dead qualities which may be called "dramatic," that is, characteristics which make a lament not simply a rhetorical piece set into a narrative, but rather a passage of lamentation which is an integral part of the story. Thus we find interplay among characters who learn of a death. Some laments are made by more than one person, with alternating comments rather like a small scene in a drama. Further, there are examples of elaborate anticipations of a lament, occasions when the poet carefully prepares the scene, establishing a setting and feeling so that a lament follows, as it were, inevitably, providing the only satisfactory comment within the situation.

It goes almost without saying that any lament which has a complex of ideas, or elaborate stylistic qualities, or a dramatic function, will probably be rather long, perhaps fifteen lines or more, because it would be difficult for the poet to develop any of the three aspects in less space. Thus it is these longer passages which are of most significance and interest in a study of laments for the dead in medieval narrative. Laments illustrating each aspect will be considered in later chapters. Here we shall simply introduce some of the possibilities by considering shorter or less important passages which suggest ideas, stylistic techniques, or dramatic situations, but lack the fullest unfolding or development.

The simplest kind of lament is the brief statement that someone is dead, but even here some further idea is usually suggested. There is a good example in *Sir Orfeo*:

> 'O,' quaþ þe steward, 'now me is wo!
> Þat was mi lord Sir Orfeo.
> Allas! wreche, what schal y do?
> Þat haue swiche a lord ylore!
> A way! þat ich was ybore!
> Þat him was so hard grace yȝarked,
> And so vile deþ ymarked!'

$$(542\text{--}48)$$

The use of several traditional ideas, such as 'What shall I do?', 'Alas, that I was born!', great sorrow, reference to the kind of death, and exclamations, but without development of any idea, anticipates the longer, more elaborate kind of lament. Here we have simply a statement of several ideas but no distinctive analysis. Instead the poet relies upon traditional rhetorical exclamations to convey the steward's grief over the loss of Sir Orfeo. And since the listener is Orfeo himself, there is a dramatic overtone which is developed later. The disguised Orfeo is actually testing his steward, who expresses a genuine and intense grief that is wholly desolating and involves no hint of a wish for personal advancement. Thus Orfeo is reassured of his integrity and names him successor to the kingship. The *lai* is, of course, a brief narrative, so that fuller lamentation would destroy its artistic balance. But the author, like writers of longer medieval narratives, knows the effects which can be gained by a lament for the dead. He uses the form to add a poetic flourish to his narrative, to advance the action, and to achieve a subtle relationship with his audience who recognize the irony of having Orfeo hear his own death lamented by the steward. Such complex relationships are more fully exploited in longer works, but the basic characteristics of laments are present here.

Not infrequently a single passage contains laments both for a specific person and for many persons. One of the better examples of this is to be found in the fourteenth-century *Le Morte Arthur* when Arthur laments the knights who were slain when Launcelot took Guinevere away:

"Ihesu cryste!   what may I sayne?
  In erthe was neuyr man so wo;
Suche knyghtys as there ar slayne
  In All thys worlde there is no mo.
Lette no man telle Syr gawayne,
  Gaheriet hys brother is dede hym fro,
But weilaway!   the reufulle Rayne,
  That euyr launcelote was my fo!"

(1974–81)

Here an introductory exclamation and rhetorical question gain immediate attention, and the "weilaway" at the end echoes the initial emotional outburst. Several ideas—grief, praise, concern for the public weal through reference to Gawayne, and a comment on the general situation—are introduced, but none is developed. The lament is too brief and generalized to be really distinctive, but it is one of many laments that contribute to a pervasive sense of loss throughout the romance. Further, it reflects the need to make a comment upon a death, to stop the quick flow of narrative to particularize this basic human experience.

The type of lament which for convenience may be termed anticipatory does not technically satisfy my definition of a lament as a passage expressing grief for a person who is dead or believed dead, but since it is what is said when a person is believed to be unable to escape death, the anticipatory lament is quite an interesting variation as we noted in *Sir Gawain & the Green Knight*. When Clariodus rides out, the people of Belvelladonn lament:

> Fair weill, our confort and all our joy!
> Fair weill, our cheif protector out of noy!
> Fair weill, the gentillest Knicht and maist worthie
> In all the warld that beine aluterlie!
>
> (III, 1855–58)

The main ideas are commonplaces in medieval romance; without Clariodus the people are helpless, and they praise their knightly protector accordingly. The passage is carefully written, as is indicated by repetition of the initial "Fair weill," followed by balanced phrases of praise in the conventional idiom. Placed almost in the middle of the narrative, this lament serves primarily to reiterate the value and importance of the knight Clariodus, who has accomplished much and will continue his victorious adventures. The poet uses the lament form, rather than a simple statement of praise, because it is more highly charged emotionally and lends vitality to the scene.

One kind of anticipatory lament is peculiar to the Troy legend. This is the prophetic warnings of Cassandra. These passages may be justly regarded as laments for the dead because they anticipate, and accurately, the mass deaths which are to come, and the presentation of ideas is very much the same as that found in more straightforward laments. Cassandra's comments are characterized by an attempt to assist the public weal, and she consistently advises the Trojans to send Helen home and frequently upbraids them for having made mistakes such as sending Paris or failing to sue for peace. As we observed earlier, the idea of a fall from high place is an important theme, especially in Lydgate. Lydgate is terribly tedious, but the first few of Cassandra's thirty-seven lines indicate the manner:

> And seide, "allas!" ful ofte, & "wellawey!"
> "O woful wrecchis þat ȝe be þis day,
> Vnhappy eke, and graceles also,
> Infortunat and inly wo-be-go!—
> How may ȝe suffre þe grete harmys kene
> Which ȝe are likly her-after to sustene . . .
>
> (III, 2251–56)

The picture of total death and destruction is indeed a grim antici-
pation, and Cassandra's wailing lamentation adds immediacy to Trojan anxiety and gives her some distinction as a character.

Yet another kind of lament which is not actually a lament for
the dead, but very like one, is the lament which is made for a lost
person. These are passages which lament as though he were dead
a person who has been lost, stolen, or captured. They occur fairly
frequently because romantic narratives often begin with a loss, that
is, the sequence of events follows from a young knight's setting out,
usually without permission, on a series of adventures. The greatest
variety of ideas in a lament for a lost person occurs in the *Foure
Sonnes of Aymon* (574) when Reynard leaves. Two of the brothers
lament alternatively with numerous cries of "Alas" as punctuation.
Alarde begins by saying that they are left in sorrow and that it would
have been better for Reynard to slay them than to leave them in
a state of nothingness. When Alarde swoons, Richard continues by
asking how they can possibly go on. Then he is grieved, first for
the loss of honor which the departure brings, and secondly because
Reynard is not replaceable. There is not his like under heaven; thus
all joy of the world is now gone. The poet manages to give the
rather commonplace ideas of this lament more interest by having
two brothers speak, separating their comments by action when Alarde
swoons. There is, in short, some sense of dramatic possibility. A
lament spoken as dialogue by two mourners offers a variation in
the narrative flow. It provides a minimal human confrontation and
presentation of familial relationships. Obviously the scene is not really
successful, but it attempts what is brilliantly done in a more elaborate
passage like Alexander's death scene (Anthology, pp. 179-80).

Women are far less important in medieval romances than men are,
but occasionally they are the persons lamented. Naturally, the virtues
for which women are praised are somewhat different from those
praised in men, so that laments for women offer new ideas. Further,
deaths of women occur in circumstances which are obviously different
from those in which men die, for example childbirth. The most effective of these laments is that made by Florence for his wife Clariet
in *Huon of Burdeux*:

> 'a, my ryghte dere louer, in an yll oure ye were borne; for your
> sake I had forgoten all payne, and thought to haue liued in rest
> with you/ me thynke ye be rauysshed & stollen awaye fro me/
> a, false deth, *tho*u arte hardy to take fro me that thynge that

I louyd best/ the most fayrest, most trewest, and most swetest creature leuynge'/

(691)

Here may be seen the typical themes of praise; the lady is best, fairest, truest, and sweetest. The lover shows grief for his loss and anxiety for his future without the lady. It is the image of death as the ravisher which is noteworthy. The idea is not particularly original, but it does illustrate the kind of variety of thematic matter which may be introduced in laments for women. Here, as in laments for men, although rather obvious ideas are used, they are chosen with some care to gain interest. Such laments are part of the narrative writer's attempt to go beyond mere statement by confronting the implications of an event. They reflect the need to particularize human experience and the choice of an image of death the ravisher is especially appropriate in a lament by a husband for his wife.

Although laments for the dead are not especially appropriate to Malory's intention, he does reserve the full force of a lament for the dead for one woman, Gwenivere, and it is Launcelot who utters it (1256). The tone is quite subdued, for at this point in the narrative the passion of feeling and action has been spent. Now that all have taken some kind of religious vow, it is most fitting that Launcelot begin by making an apology, hoping that he is not displeasing God by making the lament and avowing that he is not rejoicing in his sin but confessing his sorrow. It is significant that Launcelot does not lament the Queen alone, but speaks of her with Arthur, even in commenting on *their* beauty; and the image of the two lying together in death is well chosen to emphasize the guilt which Launcelot now feels. The conclusion of the lament is an assumption of responsibility; Launcelot accuses himself of pride and the fault which has brought them all low. Inevitably, he concludes that he is not able to sustain himself in the face of self-accusation and condemnation. Thus the lament serves as a summary of the previous action; it is a comment upon the moral values which have been examined in the romance. Launcelot is noble and praiseworthy, but his excellence has to be judged in light of the complexity of his character which involves wrongdoing as well as admirable behavior. These last lines have an additional purpose; they also serve as a transition into the conclusion of Malory's work, Launcelot's own death and Ector de Maris' eloquent lament (1259) which summarizes his knightly excellence. Launcelot's lament for Gwenivere with Arthur is an explicit recognition of the sanctity of their marriage. This admission adds to his stature; his recognition of his own failings and acceptance of responsibility counterbalance his wrongdoing. Malory, then, uses laments for the dead to make explicit the argument of his work; and thus Launcelot is clearly seen as a tragic character, a complex human being whose excellencies of personality and achievement are coupled with serious wrong actions. He is, in short, a character who might well appear in an Elizabethan tragedy.

From this use of laments for the dead in the most tragic situation, we turn briefly to a group of laments which have quite different objects. This is a very curious variety of lament in which although the same ideas appear and the same stylistic devices, the object is no longer a man, not even a woman, but rather a horse, or greyhound, or even a boar. These passages may be regarded as strong proof of the importance of a horse to a knight, but objections to sorrowing for something less than a knight do appear in a later romance. Although the number of laments for animals is less than for men, the variety and many characteristics are not dissimilar. Some express only grief, others a desire for revenge. In the *Wars of Alexander* several lines of narrative, describing the sorrow and weeping of Alexander, introduce his lament for Bucephalus:

> Bucifalon þe bald stede · þat he for bale dies.
> þe berne blischis oñ his blonke · & seȝes breth faile,
> Sighis selcuthly sare · & sadli he wepis,
> For he had standen hi*m* in stede · in stouris full hard,
> Woñ hi*m* wirschip in were · fra many wathe saued
> Þe kynge to þis carioñ · he castis his eȝen,
> Said, "far*e* wele, my fair*e* foole · þou failid me neuir*e*!
> Sall now þi flesch her*e* be freteñ · wi*th* fowlis & wi*th* wormes,
> Þat has so doȝtyly done? · nay, driȝtin for-bede!"
>
> (5582–90)

The alliterative quality of the verse ties the themes tightly together, and the selection of ideas is good. The brief farewell, praise, and resolution that the dead one will not be forgotten, are quite adequate to make the lament potent. Alexander's anxiety about what will happen to the body is noteworthy, for he gives orders for the construction of a tomb. Such concern is reserved usually to the most distinguished heroes, for example Hector in the Trojan narratives. Since Bucephalus was such a valuable horse and his prowess has been emphasized in much detail, Alexander's sorrow does not seem exaggerated or misplaced. The *Wars of Alexander* is, unfortunately, a fragment which ends with the details of Bucephalus' death. Other complete Alexander romances, which have much elaborate lamentation upon the death of Alexander, lead us to speculate that the treatment of Bucephalus was to serve as a kind of preparation. If a king's horse is so honored and praised, how much greater must be the lamentation and grief for the death of the king himself.

Not all medieval narratives express such concern over the death of an animal; other romances have a reversal of the attitude. Some offer only consolation; the horse is dead, but only the great deeds of the knight are important, and there are lots of other horses to replace the lost one. A more complex lament for a horse occurs in *King Athelstone* (345–404). The messenger's steed falls dead on London Bridge, and his master begins with a conventional "Allas þat I was born!" and continues to lament by praising the horse's virtues and finally ascribing a monetary worth of one hundred pounds. The archbishop chides the messenger for such complaining and demands concern for the more important issues, for human beings, but he does not fail to promise remuneration to the messenger. *King Athelstone* is a narrative with many threats and impending catastrophies, but these are all averted. However, the author still manages to use the rhetorical death lament in the scene on London Bridge. It is appropriate that the animal who has been crucial for carrying messages and accelerating the action be thus commented upon, but the horse is not treated as though it were a human being.

An animal which is much more essential to the narrative and the occasion for elaborate lamentation in the boar in *Sir Eglamour*. When the giant finds the boar's body, he begins with an "Alas," proceeds to praise the faithful animal, and declares he will revenge him (542–45). The giant tries to carry out this promise by charging into the castle, calling to the traitors that he will pull down stone walls and hang the culprits with his own hands (551–55). Finally he challenges Eglamour, assuring him that he will pay dearly for the slaying (573–76). This kind of progressive lament through the narrative is a treatment of ideas very like that accorded the worthiest of knights. Eglamour's slaying of the boar, and subsequently Morrasse, are only part of his many adventures undertaken to win the fair Cristabelle. The narrative writer uses laments for the dead to advance the action; they signal progressive stages of the giant's response to the loss of his favorite and thus give a distinctive quality to the account of the second feat demanded of Eglamour. In fact,

Morrasse's grief and laments precipitate his fight with Eglamour and thus prolong the second feat. Thus the author of *Sir Eglamour* strengthens his narrative by distinctly varying the conventional three-fold tasks. The slaying of the boar is itself a complicated action, and the giant's laments continue to enrich the texture of this part of the narrative, so that the episode is one of the more memorable adventures in medieval romance.

Turning from the objects of lamentation to a specific consideration of the ideas which are typical, we find the most constant is, of course, grief. Few laments, as has been noted in many examples already cited, fail to have at least an "Alas, woe." Thus a discussion of grief would have to include practically every lament if it were to be complete. One type emphasizes loss; for example, the Greeks' lament for Achilles in Lydgate's *Troy Book:*

> "Fare wel oure trust, now Achilles is dede!
> Fare wel oure hope, & holly al our spede!
> Fare wel oure Ioye, & oure chef diffence,
> Þat had in manhod so gret excellence!
> Fare wel, allas! oure souereyn assuraunce!
> Fare wel in knyȝthod al oure suffisaunce,
> For now, allas! vnlikly is þat we
> Shal euere wynne or geten þis cite—
> To vs, allas, so frowarde is fortune!"
>
> (IV, 3237–45)

Here the ideas are presented through a series of panegyric apostrophies, each prefaced by "Fare wel." Thus there is a very obvious stylistic design which is in keeping with the very careful arrangement of ideas in the lament. All the apostrophies except the non-commital "oure Ioye," are directed toward one thing—the fate of the public weal. The predominant idea is certainly one of loss, but this loss produces not so much personal grief as public fear. The Greeks are grieved that Achilles is dead, but chiefly because in losing him they lose much of their capacity for taking the city. To blame Fortune is a characteristic solution or explanation of Lydgate, as has been noted in several previous laments. Again the poet uses a lament for the dead to make a significant comment upon the action and to embellish the style.

Concern for the future is an idea very often developed from an initial expression of grief. Quite often a lament is centered on the question "What shall I do?" The *Buik of Alexander* affords a fine example in Emynedus' lament for Cassamus:

"Quhat sall word of vs, Drychtin deir?
Quha sall vs now gif counsall,
Or quha sall help vs in battall!
Now is heir, with worship, deid
Bounte, largenes and manhede,
And all gude sikkerly alsua!"

(IV, 10,804–809)

Here the order has been reversed, first questioning about the future
and then praise of the deceased, but the effect is still the same. A
sense of desolation is made emphatic through repetition and rhetorical questions which give the passage urgency.

The question "What shall I do?" is very often answered with a
wish for death, which in romances seems to be characteristically
feminine. Women who are distressed by loss of a father, mother,
or even a cousin, often want to die as a solution to their grief, but
most frequently the desire springs from loss of a lover. In *Clariodus*
(I, 914–29) Meliades begins her anticipatory lament for Clariodus
with energy:

Saying, O [wofull] Death I thé defy,
What may thy cruell dairt doe me moir paine
Nor have him with a cruell lyoun slaine,
Whom I luif better nor I do my lyfe!

(I, 914–17)

She then questions whether anyone can help her lover in his fight
with Death. She wonders whether her present grief is the "joy" of
love. This is followed by a more docile acceptance when Meliades
says she will forgoe the "world's bliss." She concludes by praising
Clariodus and bidding farewell to the company of men, for after a
man so gracious and gentle as her lover no other will serve. Again
we see a lament for a probable death used to heighten the importance of a knight, but here the emphasis falls upon the lady's de-
pendence and need. These attitudes are appropriate since so much
of medieval romance narrative tells of feats accomplished by knights
to safeguard or in honor of their ladies.

Finally there are laments of grief cut off by someone's offering
a consolation, or more frequently, chiding the bereaved for unnecessary lamentation. A good example is Floripas' retort: "Lordes, in
the honour of god, leue your lamentyng and sorowe: we knowe
not yet the trouthe of the mater." when the French lament Richard
of Normandy (in *Charles the Grete*, 154). This statement is signifi-

cant because it shows a recognition that laments for the dead can be protracted, and it emphasizes the necessity for reserving such utterances to appropriate situations. Thus we have a rudimentary critical evaluation of the form.

Just as it is difficult to find many laments without some expression of grief for the person who is dead, so is it difficult to find passages which do not have some praise for the dead. Almost every lament mentioned so far, especially those with panegyric apostrophes, illustrates the idea. Perhaps the greatest praise ever made of a knight is that of Sir Ingraham Umphraville of Sir David Brechin in Barbour's *Bruce;* he is willing to abandon his country to prove the depth of his feelings. Robert the Bruce has Sir David hanged for treason, for failing to report the plot in which he did not participate. Sir Ingraham protests against seeing the disgrace of one so noble (XIX, 76–81); then he asks to leave Scotland (XIX, 95–108) because his heart makes him no longer want to live in a country where so worthy a knight, so chivalrous and so vigorous in war, so accomplished in manhood, so renowned in worship, was so cruelly killed. Sir Ingraham's renunciation is at great personal cost, and it is an ultimate expression of his admiration for the deceased knight. It is to the Bruce's credit that he grants permission. Thus the lament functions on a variety of levels. It distinctively characterizes Sir Ingraham and also adds to the stature of Robert the Bruce, who subtly makes distinctions in matters of loyalty and justice; and it is, furthermore, a statement of praise.

At the opposite extreme are laments which express dispraise, but there is also a variety of lament which is a pivot between praise and dispraise, actually neither the one nor the other. Guy of Warwick's lament for the steward Berard whom he has slain is illustrative:

> And seyd, 'a, thow Duke fellown,
> Now nere-hand a[r]t thow for-lorne.
> Alas the tyme that thow were boren!
> A bolder kny3t was neu*er* lyvand,
> Ne neu*er* dow3tyer man of hand.
> Ne haddist thow be trayto*ur*, be seynt Richere,
> In all the world ne had bene thy pere.'
>
> (Caius, 9975–81)

The first three lines offer conventional comment, but the concluding lines present a new idea. Guy makes a moral judgment about his

slain foe. Berard did not lack any of the qualities which make a
worthy knight, except the important one which would have led him
to use his excellence for good, the quality which could have kept
him from being a traitor and let him realize his fine personality.
Later Guy holds Berard up as a model to Tirri. Counselling him
to be advised by the fall of the steward, Guy warns against pride,
envy, false taking of inheritance, and urges Tirri to think on the
loss of heaven and the shame which result from a traitor's failure
as a person. He concludes with a prayer that God keep Tirri from
care.[1] This lament, then, is important primarily as a comment upon
the potentiality of human personality. Guy is struck by the failure
of the steward to direct his strength and resources to good. The
fascination of good and evil in conflict is clear, and we have a
suggestion of tragic possibility. Guy's didactic comments to his
friend Tirri are a fuller exploitation of these ideas and show his
complex awareness; they are part of his progress to the spiritual
awareness with which the romance concludes.

In contrast to the mixture of praise and dispraise, there are laments which try simply to discredit the person slain. Most frequently
these are brief scornful comments made by an enemy of the person
who is slain, usually as he is striking the death-blow or just after.
Some of these are quite witty. The villein in *Arthur of Little Britain*
(219) casts the cook into a caldron and says: "Thou shalt sethe
without salte, tyl thou be ynough; and yf thy flesshe be harde soden,
I shall broyle the on the coles." There is sometimes a similarly
macabre joke about a slain person's going into the earth. The best
of these is in Laȝamon's *Brut* when Uther slays Pascent:

> Passent liȝ nu þer.
> nu þu hauest brutlond.'
> al bi-tald to þire hond.
> Swa þe is nu iræd.'
> Þer on þu aert ded
> wikien ȝe scullen here.'
> þu and Gillomar þin ifere.
> & brukeð wel Brutlōd.'
> for nu ic hit bitaeche inc an hond.
> þat ȝit maȝen to-ȝere.'
> mid us wunien here.

[1] This long, didactic passage is in both manuscripts: Caius, 10250–69
and Auchinleck, stanzas 230–31.

ne þurue ȝe nauere adrede.'
wha eou scullen feden.

(Cott. Calig. A XX; ii, 335)

Uther's scorn and triumph are vividly clear, and the final macabre touch is a neat conclusion. Here we see yet another range in laments for the dead; they provide an opportunity for acid cleverness. Thus an additional triumph is achieved over a fallen enemy and further strength is shown by the victor.

After the person who is lamenting has accepted the fact of death and expressed grief and praise (or dispraise if he is an enemy), the next response which we might expect is that he would want to do something about the death. In medieval narrative this means revenge, for the immediate emotional reaction is to cry out against the slayer and seek to hurt or kill the person who has inflicted the pain of loss. Fundamentally the idea of revenge is "We sal evin that is od, or end in the pane!" (*Golagros and Gawain,* 734). Often it leads to a suggestion for specific action, a plan for attack, or it may be an incentive for a wounded knight to recover. Very frequently a wish to revenge a fallen companion is accompanied by a desire to discharge an obligation of honor. Sometimes the mourner is more interested in alleviating his sorrow. Naturally revenge is very often mentioned when the avenger confronts a slayer, so that a little dramatic scene is built up. The narrative poet gives vitality to a lament by having the bereaved speak defiantly to his antagonist. One of the best examples is in *Morte Arthure* when Sir Florent slays Feraunt, whose cousin immediately laments:

"Thowe has killede colde dede   þe kynge of all knyghttes!
He has bene fraistede on felde   in fyftene rewmes;
He fonde neu*er* no freke,   myghte feghte w*ith* hym one.
Thow schall dye for his dede   w*ith* my derfe wapen,
And all þe doughtty for dule,   þat in ȝone dale houes!"

(2773–77)

As always the alliterative quality of the verse tends to bind the ideas more closely together, and having only two ideas—king of all knights and revenge—concentrates the feeling of the passage, which would be much less effective if other ideas, say concern for the future or even sorrow, were introduced. Economy in the lament is not absolute, for there is detail which lends potency. The significance of the dead knight is made clear with three adjectives—"*alle* knyghttes," "*fyftene* rewmes," and "*no* freke"—each of which concentrates on the singularity of the person who is being lamented. The only other adjectives, *"colde* dede" and *"derfe* wapene," heighten the two themes of death and revenge; and the *"alle"* of the final line echoes the *"alle"* of the first line to make the unity of the lament complete and to reiterate the quality of the knight. Here a panegyric of the "king of all knights" was given immediacy because it evolved into a defiant vow for revenge and was dramatically staged. Confrontation of individualized antagonists adds distinction to the combat. Resolutions to revenge a death are not always made facilely; they are sometimes the result of serious moral deliberation. Then the idea is no longer an immediate emotional response but instead has become a reasoned, morally justified conclusion.

Sometimes, of course, a bereaved person blames himself, feeling and thinking that he is responsible for the death. Indirect responsibility for deaths is more typical in romance narrative than direct responsibility; that is an individual does not actually kill, but does something which leads to a death. For example, there are several laments made by women for whom knights have given their lives, trying to rescue them or competing in tournaments for their favor. A king may accuse himself because knights die fighting for his honor. Similarly, a leader sometimes blames himself for not deploying his men properly, lamenting those who were slain as a consequence. Finally, there is another type of negative responsibility when one member of a family neglects others so that they die of grief. Thus Blanchardyne sorrows because his parents died of grief at his departing:

'And yet (quoth he) how vnnaturall was I to forsake them whome nature charged me to loue and obey! now I may iustlie accuse my self of the murther of these my louing parents: alas! I cannot excuse my selfe, neither can I plead ignoraunce that I knewe not that my departure would be the finishing of my parentes ioyes, and cause of their death, which now (to my open shame) I finde most true. And should I, nay, could I, suffer my selfe to be led and carried away with such vaine fantasies, as leaue them comfortles to whom I was the greatest comfort. Die, *Blanchardine,* die! and the rather die, that art the cause of thy parents death: alas! to kill a man is hainous murder: but to murder my parentes, a sinne against Sanctitie: all creatures haue care to foster those that gaue them life; and I, careles in killing my father. The Storke, when he seeth his sire olde & redy to die with famine, taketh him vpon his shoulders, and feedeth him by his trauaile: But I, insteede of feeding, haue famisht, and in place of trauelling, haue traiterously ouerthrowne my parents.'

(214)

This is certainly a penetrating analysis. Blanchardyne recognizes his failure to carry out his responsibility, and he goes further in admitting that he realized what would happen before he left. His honest evaluation of his actions adds to his stature, and a character who is aware of the implications of what he does certainly shows an advance in imaginative writing of medieval narrative. Thus Blanchardyne's wish for death is carefully prepared for; it is the result of relentless and logical argument, not a simple emotional reflex. The dramatic phrasing of his conclusion is suitable introduction to the fine metaphor of the stork with which the lament concludes. This use of imagery is a sophisticated stylistic embellishment that is appropriate to the intellectual complexity of the ideas presented in the lament.

Of course, there are also accusatory laments which are directed at people other than the speaker. Very often such passages ignore the dead person and concentrate merely on condemning the slayer. A striking example is the violent outburst which young Beues of Hamtoun, after a preliminary "Allas! Allas!", directs at his mother:

'Vile houre!   þe worst to-drawe
    And al to-twiȝt!
Me þenkeþ, ich were þer of ful fawe,
For þou hauest me mader slawe
    Wiþ mechel vnriȝt!

Allas, moder, þe faire ble!
Euel be-comeþ þe, houre to be,
    To holde bordel,
And alle wif houren for þe sake,
Þe deuel of helle ich hii be-take,

    Flesch and fel!
As o þing, moder, i schel þe swere:
ȝif ich euer armes bere
    And be of elde,
Al þat haþ me fader islawe

And ibrouȝt of is lif dawe,
    Ich schel hem ȝilden!'

(Auchinleck, 301–18)

There is brief mention of praise and revenge, but the chief interest
is in placing blame where it is due. The poet does not fail to make
the most of a dramatic situation of a young boy defying his adulter-
ous mother, and we think immediately of Hamlet's antipathy to
Gertrude. Even the disturbing sounds of revelry made by Devon
and the false queen are analogous, and they precipitate the young
boy's outburst, which gains immediate sympathy. Beues' moral indignation is emphasized by heavily connotative words and exclamatory outbursts; the vigor of language is extraordinary, one of the
really distinguished qualities of the romance. Beues is less grieved
for his father than he is disturbed by the loss of honor which results
from his mother's perfidy. His violent reaction precipitates, of course,
his being sold into slavery and thus introduces the complex series
of adventures that make up the narrative. Even in this early scene
Beues shows the strength of conviction and courage which suggest
that he will mature into a powerful and brave knight, whose popularity was second only to that of Guy of Warwick. Throughout the
narrative Beues' integrity is emphasized, so that this lament early
establishes his high principles and relentless determination to live
in a proper moral order. Thus this lament for the dead is not simply
an embellishment, but the center of a highly dramatic scene in
which intense emotional interplay occurs between human beings who
are intimately related; further, essential traits of character are established and the action advanced.

Concern for loss of honor is common among kings, especially
Charlemagne, whose laments express not personal grief for the loss
of his peers, but a more selfish concern for his own well-being.
His egoism and anxiety in lamenting are a crucial revelation of his
character. In contrast, there are kings, like Alexander, who are not
selfish in their attitudes. Instead of conveying distress because of
loss of prestige or threats to kingly honor their laments declare that
they would give up all or portions of their riches and perogatives
to have their brave knights alive again. Anxiety about the future
of the public weal, however, is perhaps a more frequent theme, for
even if the fairest flower of knighthood is lost, the kingdom must
go on. After considerations of grief, praise, revenge, accusations,
and so on, a more permanent situation must be sought. Frequently

it is necessary that reconciliation be achieved to prevent further destruction. This situation leads to a kind of lament which almost ignores the person who has been slain and instead pleads for a cessation of strife. The most striking examples occur in the Arthurian romances, where personal feeling and conflict are strongest. Launcelot is in the unhappy position of realizing that he is responsible for the war within the kingdom and has accidentally killed Gawain's brothers. He pleads desperately with his council to sue for peace. Quite naturally the opposite attitude, wishing for more knights so that a fiercer battle might be fought, is also present. Thus reactions to a death vary from utter despair to practical plans for carrying on with what can be salvaged after death's destruction.

The initial emotional reactions are grief and despair, immediate praise or dispraise, personal assumptions of responsibility and cries of revenge, and practical considerations about how those who remain alive will now continue to live. When they have been realized, then there is time for moralization, for a more intellectual analysis, an attempt to understand more fully the reasons and meaning of a death. Laments for the dead in medieval narrative offer many suggestions. Human rationalization makes almost inevitable a placing of blame on someone other than the beloved. Thus there are many moralizing laments which assert that the death came about through treason. Laments made by Trojans after the betrayal of the city are of this type. Not every rational analysis of a death, however, results in a conclusion that the person should not have died. Quite often the person lamenting calmly notes that the death was justly deserved. Thus Gawayne argues that his brothers were warned against fighting Launcelot, whose superior skill could not fail to destroy them, and Robert the Devil coldly slays his men because they will not repent their evil deeds as he has done.

This clarity and sharpness in making a judgment are typical. Strong opinions and feelings, not delicate nuances, characterize medieval narrative. Perhaps the most interesting examples are in *Titus and Vespasion* where the deaths lamented are suicides, the worst possible death. The two men lamented are Pilate and Archelaus, who helped Pilate. Thus the Christian viewpoint is especially pertinent, and the full judgment of Christendom falls heavily. Archelaus dies first and the Emperor calls him a traitor who got what he deserved, but still argues that he should be buried as a king (3837–42). Vespasian is even harder and harsher in his evaluation when Pilate kills himself:

"To fouler deth myght he not goon
Þan sleen hym with his owne hand;
For wors was noon, I understande,
Whil he livede, noo moo lorn,
Þat ever was of moder born;
For he assentede, by a wickede rede,
To doon Jhesu Crist to deed,
He myght not with worse hand
Have ben slayn, I understande.
I vouche wel sauf he dyede soo,
Right as he dede, soo lete hym goo."

(4396–4406)

Here again there is an aridness of style that is appropriate to the
ideas expressed. Not emotion, but straightforward statement of facts
most fully damns the man who committed the most infamous deed
in history. Suicide is a suitable end for the man who so fully deserves dispraise, and a bare recognition of this is sufficient comment. There is no need for elaborate argument, but a bold statement
is appropriate.

Moralizations which blame Fortune for causing death are much
less frequent than might be expected. It is true that much medieval
narrative verse contains passages which discuss Fortune, but it is
rare that a character within the narrative speaks of Fortune. Lydgate,
whose interest in Fortune is exemplified throughout the *Fall of
Princes,* provides the most impressive lament for the dead with
moralizing on Fortune. Telegonus' accidental slaying of his father
offers a splendid dramatic opportunity for lamentation, and in the
Troy Book Lydgate has the son cry out:

"Allas!" quod he, "þat eu*er*e was I born!
For cursid is my woful destine
And my fortune, which I may nat fle!
Cursid my sort, cursid my auenture!
And I, refus of eu*er*y creature,
Forwaried eke my dispocisioun,
And cursid is my constellaciou*n*—
Cursed also and infornate
Þe hour in whiche my fader me [be]gat!
So wolde God, wi*th*-oute lenger red,
—Taquiten hym anoon—þat I were ded,
To leie my lif for his deth to borwe!"

(V, 3244–55)

Here the conventional "Alas, that I was born!" functions as much more than an introduction; it sets the dramatic idea of being piti-lessly taken up by Fortune. Everything about the young Telegonus is cursed from the hour of his begetting; references to Fortune and the stars reveal his explanation of his destiny and make his wish for death more urgent. Although Lydgate's verse is full of observa-tions on and addresses to fortune, this is the only time when he puts this favorite idea into the mouth of a character in the story, and the immediacy and vitality thus gained are noteworthy. Usually he simply stops the narrative for a long, didactic moralization. This lament is altogether more dramatic and impressive. The repetition of "cursid" emphasizes the basic helplessness of Telegonus' position and is the stylistic device that holds the passage together. Like Blanchardyne, Telegonus is guilty of patricide; but his situation is more pitiable, since he kills his father with a direct blow in the fury of combat without being aware of what he is doing. Thus he appropriately explains his action in terms of 'destine' and 'fortune.' Lydgate gives these concepts unusual reality in this scene because he has established a concrete situation in which a human being is seen committing an act which is not the result of an understood, reasoned decision. Indeed Telegonus does exactly what he would have avoided had choice been his.

Closely related to the idea of Fortune is the Fall of Princes theme, which appears several times in laments in Laȝamon's *Brut;* for ex-ample, when Leir laments change in the fortunes of kings (i, 145), or when Merlin notes that kings may not live long (ii, 291). A dramatic use is made of the idea when Arthur slays Colgrin and Boldulf (iii, 476–77). The young king tells his slain foes to lie where he has struck them down, for they climbed too high. He indulges in traditional boasting and ironic comment, declaring that he now gives into the hands of his enemies the lands they sought. Having tried to ascend into heaven they can now descend into hell, where they will meet many of their kindred. These are to be greeted and all may live together, while Arthur's people live in bliss in his land, praying for their souls. Fundamentally the passage is an elabo-rate insulting lament of dispraise, and the judgment is heightened because Arthur gives a moralizing explanation for his victory—the pride and excessive ambition of his foes. Here, as in Telegonus' lament for Ulysses, we find a dramatic use of the idea of a fall from high place which is made integral with the narrative, not extraneous as a piece of didactic comment. Thus again we find a writer who uses laments for the dead to enrich the texture of his narrative.

They provide a basis for dramatic scenes with dialogue and direct confrontation of personalities, and they also serve as a means of giving vitality to an abstract idea to gain greater understanding and sympathy. Such use of a literary form to emphasize a reasoned concept indicates an evolving skill that is both stylistic and intellectual.

Much more characteristic than laments which turn on the ideas of pagan Fortune or the Fall of Princes, are those which have a moralization that involves the Christian God. These passages are not only more numerous and widespread, but also they are more varied. *Le Morte Arthure* offers a fine example of Christian religious lamentation when the Archbishop finds Launcelot dead:

> "Allas!   syr bors, that I was borne!
> That euyr I shuld see thys in dede!
> The beste knyght hys lyffe hathe lorne
> That euyr in stoure by-strode A stede.
> Ih*esu* that crownyd was w*ith* thorne,
> In heuyn hys soule foster and fede!"
>
> (3890–95)

Here the principal idea is to give a soul to God and to ask His mercy, but the lament is organized so that the idea is much more significantly put than it is in barer statements. The first lines preserve the conventions of initial emotional reaction of grief and the traditional rhetorical phrases; then the Archbishop praises the dead Launcelot, and finally he most fittingly prays that his soul may be fostered by Christ. The result is a most effective lament, succinct and well organized, but not lacking in intensity of feeling. The worth of the knight is made clear, but this is placed in a perspective of eternality, so that praise is not mere rhetoric. Further, belief in heaven serves as consolation for the loss of a beloved person. This is a type of lament peculiarly appropriate to the Archbishop of Canterbury, a religious authority who speaks with some objectivity as well as feeling. There are other laments of this type in which the person particularly recommends the soul to God because he feels responsible for the death. Pagans, in contrast to Christians, frequently turn against their gods who failed to preserve the lives of those lamented. Laments which turn on moralizations are, then, yet another important part of the tradition; they are used to give dramatic qualities, immediacy, to fundamental truths.

Closely related to these laments are those spoken by individuals who are moved to become hermits or nuns or do some kind of penance. Their laments reach a climax in a statement of this intention to lead a religious life. A good example of the basic idea is Bedwere's lament at Arthur's tomb in *Le Morte Arthure:*

> "Ermyte," he sayd, "wi*th*-oute lesynge,
>   here lyeth my lord that I haue lorne,
> Bold arthur, the beste kynge
>   That euyr was in bretayne borne.
> yif me som of thy clothynge,
>   For hym that bare the crowne of thorne,
> And leue that I may wi*th* the lenge,
>   Whyle I may leue, And pray hym forne."
>
> (3550–57)

Here again the directness and careful organization of ideas which characterize this romance make the lament memorable. Alliteration gives unity to the passage; the "l" sounds are particularly effective in conveying a sense of loss, and the long vowels suggest a plaintive tone of resignation. The style, then, echoes the meaning, for laments of this type are used to express a calm resolution. Acceptance of the death of a loved one is expressed through a renunciation of worldly involvements; thus the beloved gains some consolation from a closer union with God.

With this resolution there can be no further lamentation; grief is transcended and death accepted positively. Thus we have reached the last possible phase of any lamentation which expresses a universal, natural range of attitudes and situations promoted by the fundamental experience of death. The brief examples discussed here necessarily display only the basic characteristics of laments. Longer passages will offer more complex statements of these ideas, fuller exploitation of elements of style, more elaborate dramatic qualities, and many different combinations of all these details as we shall see in the next chapters.

Chapter III

CHARACTERISTIC IDEAS IN

LAMENTS FOR THE DEAD

No single lament, however long, contains all of the ideas which may be assembled by examining over five hundred pertinent passages, but there are many laments in which perhaps half a dozen ideas are combined. It is difficult to arrange these more involved laments for discussion, either according to the hypothetical "natural" pattern which was suggested in chapter two or according to the character of the person being lamented or of the person lamenting. But, in general, the first arrangement is more satisfactory and will be used, although this will be altered when another arrangement will make comparisons and contrasts more pointed.

Near the end of the narrative *Sir Ferumbras* (Anthology, p. 136) Charles makes a lament for his knights in which grief is the pervasive idea; thus the passage may serve as a good beginning. Charles' tone is more pitiable and subdued than usual, and he is less a presumptuous man than we have learned to expect from his previous action. The heavy sprinkling of exclamations of "Alas" indicates something of his distress. Here Charles does not, as in another romance, dare God to take away his douzepeers. They have already been killed; and when Charles realizes the enormity of his loss, he is reduced to a state of abject misery and heplessness. Thus we can read the line "Alas! ... þat y euere y ȝut croune bar" and feel convinced that this is not merely rhetorical convention. A little of the more characteristic—and unpleasant—Charles is evident when, after expressing grief, he thinks next of his personal loss of honor and repute. Quite naturally this concern evolves into a wish for death. As usual, Roland is singled out as the most valuable knight; Charles would not have lost his honor had Roland lived. Finally Charles blames himself, admitting that he has had to sustain the loss because of his own folly. This, he concludes, is cause enough for woe. His grief is such that he swoons even as he sits on his horse. Although Charles still has selfish interests most at heart, he does emerge a

51

little less a boor because of this lament which is handled in such a way that the idea of grief, not selfishness, pervades. Regardless of the reason for grief, we still feel some sympathy for one so bereaved. Thus in the same way that a lament can damage Charles' character by being too aggressive or selfish, it is also possible for the narrative poet to build up sympathy for the character by having him lament as one overcome with grief, bereft of his most valued followers and hopeless, it would seem, to help himself.

Arthur is a consistently more attractive figure than Charles, and this appears very strikingly in the way he laments his knights. A good example comes almost at the end of *Morte Arthure* (Anthology, pp. 136–37). He begins by admitting graciously that his kingship comes through the courtesy of his men who do everything to maintain him, his dignity, and his office. Such largesse of sentiment adds immeasureably to the king's stature; he is obviously worthy of his position because of his noble characteristics. Because Arthur owes so much to loyalty and values the trait so highly, he feels with special intensity the sadness and horror of losing his men through a traitor. The contrast between the rich blood of the Round Table which has been shed and the rascal who is responsible for his sorrow, is used to intensify Arthur's grief; thus "rewthe es the more!" In the beginning of the lament there is, then, a real intensity of feeling, conveyed by such evocative phrases as "the riche blude of the rownde table" which is repeated in "þe Bretons blode." The lament reaches an emotional climax in Arthur's metaphor of himself as a widow who wants her children. The analogy makes the king's personal involvement with his peers explicit; they command the most intense human attachment. "I may werye and wepe, and wrynge myne handys," has, then, two levels of meaning: it continues the metaphor and introduces a return to Arthur's lament as a king who has lost "wyt" and "wyrchipe." Finally Arthur renounces his lordship, not because he is afraid to continue in a world without his old prestige, but because without his noble knights he no longer wants to go on. His grief is a personal rather than a professional one, and thus immediately more appealing. In one day's fight the best of Breton blood has been shed, and it is this loss which makes Arthur no longer want to live; all his joy has ended. Indeed his life is almost ended, for in less than one hundred lines the narrative concludes with a fulfillment of Arthur's wish for death. Thus in addition to being a memorable indication of Arthur's character, this lament for the dead serves to prepare for the king's death; it fosters a mood of grief and emphasizes the sense of loss. Further, it provides an opportunity for elements of literary style which are admirable and distinctive even in a medieval narrative that is notable for its excellence of expression.

Such control and balance are lacking in the lament which Eglentine of Brehaigne makes for her father. She is less restrained in expressing her feelings about the loss of the king slain by the Saracens in *Partenay* (Anthology, p. 137). "Alas," she exclaims, her parents are dead and she has no comfort. She asks what she, a pitiful orphan, shall do. She can foresee nothing but destruction of her royal realm and repeats, "what shalt thou now don?" Saracens are certain to lay waste the whole country, and Eglentine invokes God's curse upon them. Aside from this, she does not know what to do. She thinks that she will be forced to accept Saracen law completely. From the very beginning Eglentine's dominant idea is "What shall I do?"; she does not swerve from it, as the repetition makes clear. Only her first two lines concern anything other than herself, and even they are directly related because they explain how her present woeful situation came about. The same may be said of the lines about anticipated destruction of her kingdom. Earlier we have noted, especially in the Charlemagne cycle, that laments which are focussed solely on personal anxiety about the future or loss of honor are less sympathetic than those with a less selfish outlook. It is curious, then, that this lament having only an idea "What shall I do?" and distress about loss of a kingdom, seems far less objectionable and even provokes some sympathy. The reason for our reaction is obvious: Eglentine is a woman, and women in medieval narrative are in no position to alter circumstances, so that mere emotional concern seems inevitable. Thus Eglentine's feelings of inadequacy and despair are pathetic rather than contemptible. Just as Guy of Warwick did not think he could blame Felice, because she was a woman, for causing the destruction of his men, so we cannot blame helpless Eglentine for feeling hopeless and crumbling before what seems to be impossible opposition. The family relationship is stressed by her calling herself an orphan, but she also expresses anxiety about the fate of the kingdom and her future spiritual life, so that the lament goes beyond the most immediate emotional desolation even though this is primary. Within the romance of *Partenay,* which has so many complex family situations, Englentine is richly characterized by this lament. In a later scene (2308–33) her uncle the King of Alsace offers consolation, arguing that revenge has been accomplished and honor maintained. But Eglentine reiterates her initial attitude:

"Ha, sir," she said, "good lord souerain,
  My gentile uncle, and my ful swet frend,
When I me bethenke on my fader slayn,
  A-non my hert with*in* wepingly is tend."

(2325–28)

This unwaveringly feminine response heightens our awareness of the woman's vulnerability and thus strengthens the importance of Raynold who champions her cause against the Saracens.

Slightly more complex is Emenedus' lament in *Hay's Buik of Alexander* (Anthology, pp. 137–38) which couples self-blame with a wish for death. Emenedus' lament is both for himself and for his slain knights. Because of pride and arrogance he acted according to his own will rather than according to Alexander's orders and caused many knights to perish. Now he wishes earnestly that his life might be forfeit. Only in the last lines is Emenedus' sense of guilt mitigated. Then, before expressing a final regret that he bore arms (a neat variation of the more conventional "Alas, that I was born" with tragic possibilities), he declares that he was ordained a "hard fortune." Repetition of the phrase "I am the caus" emphasizes that the dominant idea is self-blame, and it also ties the passage together. Again what we have is a lament with a single idea, but the greater length makes possible a more complete consideration. The opening lines with their series of "adew" apostrophes are conventional and too formal to convey genuine feeling of an intensely personal nature, but they appropriately express Emenedus' relationship to Alexander. He can use only a tone of humility in praising the noble king whose orders he disobeyed because of pride. The mode of rhetorical repetition which is thus introduced gains potency as the lament develops, and self-blame is reiterated as the crucial idea. Having got beyond a somewhat stilted beginning, Emenedus does reveal depth of conviction and sincerity in his almost merciless self-accusation. This is softened by the somewhat ambiguous statement that "hard fortoune vas ordand me beforne." Thus in this lament for the dead we see an emerging self-awareness. Emenedus recognizes his subservient position to Alexander, admits his pride and guilt, blames himself absolutely, and finally recognizes a force outside himself. His regret that he bore arms, that he participated in the active world of daring rather than choosing a more contemplative life, suggests elements of the medieval view of tragedy. Here, then, we have a lament that serves not only to add to the impressiveness of Alexander, but also to characterize interestingly one of his officers by suggesting a wide range of attitudes and feelings.

As noted in chapter two, the idea of Fortune is not frequently presented in laments for the dead in medieval narrative, but there are two notable exceptions, in *Melusine* and *Partenay,* one in prose and one in verse. The occasion for the two laments is the same. Raymond(in), Amery's adopted son, is out hunting with his uncle and misdirects his sword when trying to kill a boar, giving Amery a mortal wound. Raymondin's lament in *Melusine* (26) is the less significant. He begins by crying out against Fortune and speaks of the love which he had for his uncle. But after this initial reference, which is at most lip-service, Raymondin turns to "god fader almighty," asking where a sinner such as he can find refuge. Although he believes he deserves judgment and condemnation for his treasonous act, he fears them. Thus he beseeches the earth to open and devour him, for he wants to fall into hell with the darkest angel who was once fair. Finally Raymondin repeats his self-accusation and asserts that he deserves hell. Quietly thoughtful for a moment, he recognizes the irony of his situation. Amery had just told him that should a man slay his sovereign lord this could lead to his becoming a man more honored than any of his lineage. Now Raymondin thinks himself the most miserable and dishonored of men, and again he blames himself. He will turn away from his home, seeking the adventures promised by his uncle and accepting what God sends, doing penance for his sin.

Raymond's lament in *Partenay* (Anthology, pp. 138–139) is quite fundamentally different. Here the idea of Fortune is more than merely introduced. Raymond not only addresses false Fortune, accusing her of treating him badly, but also declares that anyone who trusts Fortune is more a fool than a dumb animal. Fortune is ever changing, helping some and hurting others, making rich poor and poor rich. Fortune aids some and destroys others, and Raymond protests that he is one of those destroyed. Thus defeated, he addresses himself to "iseu crist, the charitable god hye/ the trew, the swete, the piteful, of mercy," and asks for pity on his soul. With this he swoons and is quiet for an hour and then, again seeing his lord dead, resumes his lament. Now there is no hesitation; "Come, deth!" is Raymond's dominant idea. He argues that death should not wait, for he has lost both soul and body now that his uncle lies dead before him. He pleads that death come to him, or he will slay himself. This would be a terrible thing, for God, condemning

despair, has willed that no Christian should slay himself. He laments
that he was not born dead, for then he could not have damned
himself. Raymond's despair and self-blame and contempt are such
that he counts himself less worthy than a Saracen who believes in
Mahoun.

This lament is much more satisfactory than the one in *Melusine,*
not only because the breadth of ideas is greater, but also because
Raymond's assimilation is more satisfactory. Whereas in the prose
version pagan and Christian ideas are confused, in this Raymond
moves from the conception of Fortune to faith in Jesus Christ. The
final two lines of the first part of the lament prepare for the second
part. Raymond's discussion of suicide makes clear his wish for death
but simultaneous realization that to kill himself, to give way to despair, would be disobedient to God. A conflict exists between what
he knows is right and what he wants to do. Raymond does not give
way to despair, but he wants to kill himself; thus although his body
does not sin, his mind does. This sin, coupled with the slaying of
his uncle, makes him value himself as no more than a Saracen.
Because he is not properly true to his Christian ideal, Raymond
counts himself a pagan. In his presentation, no less than in his
analysis of Catholic doctrine, Raymond shows himself well-informed,
isolating Fortune's salient characteristics in his discussion. This lament is one of the most purely intellectual in medieval narrative.
There are only three exclamations of "Alas" in thirty-six lines, and
these do not obtrude as rhetorical embellishments. The syntax is
untortured, direct so that the fairly involved ideas are readily grasped.
The ideas have nobility, for Raymond's personal concern is spiritual;
his anxiety is for his soul, not for worldly repute and prowess. Thus
we see in a lament for the dead a subtle statement of an orthodox
idea, which emerges from a deeply emotional reaction by means of
a careful reasoning.

A similarly overwhelming despair is felt by Clariodus when he is
told of Meliades' death, and he reacts violently enough to substanti-
ate an assertion that men become as distraught as women when they
lose their loves (Anthology, pp. 139–40). Clariodus tries in his
frenzy to leap from a window, but he is restrained and begins to
think of revenge. His lament begins "What shall I do?" Now that
he is alone, there seems to be no point in anything. All everyday
activities, such as walking, riding, sleeping, seem aimless. Thus he
cries out, "O Death, cum slay me cative in distress," believing that
this is most to be sought since he will never again have a day of

happiness. The poet breaks into Clariodus' lament to note how painful it was to observe his grief. Then the grieved man continues with a prayer to God to save him from utter despair, that is from killing himself. He pleads by Christ's five wounds that he may not destroy his soul, recognizing that the intensity of his grief has bereft him of intelligence. Clariodus prays God to have mercy on the soul of his lady Meliades, whom he loved honestly and who was falsely slain through treason. He asks God to comfort and succour her through the grace of Christ's wounds and to take her among the angels. There is here an admirable development in Clariodus, and his lament points a moral lesson. He begins his lamentation as many do, distraught about his personal situation, anxious because he feels incapable of living without his lost beloved. In fact, he gives way to such utter despair that he pleads with Death to take him. But from this excess of passion and grief comes a strength. Clariodus is so beside himself that he recognizes he is losing control, that he does not know exactly what he is doing. Thus he is frightened, and in his fear he turns to God for help. For himself he asks only that he may have strength and enough balance of mind not to kill himself. And we see this prayer answered, for Clariodus grows calmer; and as he does, he becomes more detached from his personal anxiety. Thus he is able, at last, to pray for Meliades' soul. He asserts his belief in God's goodness and justice, and he entrusts his love to God. Very quickly Clariodus is rewarded with a restored intelligence, so that he is able to marshall his men, find the traitor Sir Thomas, and make him confess his treason. When Meliades' reputation is cleared, Clariodus is somewhat consoled, and he begins his journey home. Here, then, rather dramatically, by the contrast between an initial movement to leap from a window to self-destruction and the quiet acceptance of God's will, the poet has demonstrated something of the effect of prayer on the chaotic consciousness of a man who felt only futility. This change is clear not only in the intellectual development of the lament but also in its rhetorical pattern. Exclamatory expressions such as "Alleace!" and "O" and the reiterated interogatives "quhair" and "quhairto" reflect the mental agony of Clariodus' first reaction. The second part of the lament lacks such rhetorical vigor; questioning is replaced by invocation, such as "Have mercie, Lord," and "I ask thé mercie, sweit Redemer myne," and "Be thow hir ressait."

In contrast to these variations of feeling and attitude, Deyanyra's lament for Hercules in the *Recuyell of the Historyes of Troye* (Anthology, pp. 140–41) is consistently saner and calmer. But she is much more culpable and concludes by commiting suicide for complex reasons. Deyanyra begins her lament with the question "Alas, what shall I do?" Then she praises Hercules as the greatest of men, on earth and in the sky. Next she considers her own responsibility in causing his death. Quite rightly she both accuses and acquits herself. In fact she did give her husband the poisoned shirt, but she did not know its nature. This leads to a repetition of her initial praise in which Hercules is regarded as a hero in the technical sense, that is, he is both man and god. Deyanyra follows this definition with specific illustrations of his prowess: he was a wise man, a subduer and destroyer of monsters of the sea, hell, and earth, a corrector of tyrants and a humbler of the proud and exalter of the meek, valuing virtue, not treasure. Having subdued all with his club, Hercules might have been ruler of the world. Deyanyra cries out "Alas" that through her this mighty prince, this "glorye of men," was slain. Never will another equal him. Now she questions whether she ought to live after Hercules, and immediately answers "Nay," fearing that she would be derided by other ladies or punished by strong hands for her culpability. She resolves to kill herself, and as she plunges the knife she cries out her innocence. The idea of praise which we see here is very typical—except for celestial attributes which come from Hercules' divinity—but the idea of self-accusation is treated more originally. Deyanyra's analysis is honest and realistic; she makes no grandiose claims of culpability, nor does she deny cavalierly her error. This rather detached approach prepares for her decision to kill herself. It is significant that she does not kill herself from an excess of grief or feeling of inadequacy. Quite coldly she calculates that her life as Hercules' widow, and in some ways his murderer, will not be a pleasant one. Like Shakespeare's Cleopatra, Deyanyra is not willing to risk certain scorn or potential revengers. She clearly recognizes Hercules' eminence, which will make people react against her because she destroyed him. Thus killing herself is a practical and honorable solution, but Deyanyra cannot forbear reiterating her innocence of spirit even as she accepts the inevitable. There is no use of Christian belief here; Deyanyra is purely in the tradition of pagan widow-suicide.

With elaborate praise Charles, who is similarly disadvantaged, laments Roland more creditably than he does his peers (*Otuel and Roland,* Anthology, pp. 141–42). He begins by praising Roland as the "Noblest warrior" and declares that since he has lost his best knight, he wishes for death. Ten lines of narrative interrupt to describe Charles' swoon, mad cries, tearing of hair, and sighs. He recovers to repeat a wish for death and then begins a more elaborate praise. Roland was as strong as Samson, bold as a lion, and like David for Absalom, Charles will weep for Roland. He contemplates suicide since all hope of future joy is gone. Finally Roland is declared equal to one of the Nine Worthies, Judas Machaebeus. At this point Charles' barons interpose to tell him to stop mourning, realizing that death is unavoidable and that he must take consolation. Again Charles' excesses and limitations are pointed up by the laments for the dead in which he indulges. His grief, which is expressed as a wish for death, is not appropriate to him either as king or Christian, but he does show an awareness and appreciation of his peer Roland as well as personal anxiety. The interest in this lament, apart from its effect of making Charles more sympathetic, lies in its use of specific Biblical allusions, a rare technique in laments for the dead in secular narrative, which points toward uses of the lament in religious narrative. The allusion to David and Absalom is fairly conventional; there is, however, a latent ambiguity in this father-son relationship which we cannot avoid. It raises the question of loyalty which is crucial to the Charlemagne romance. Further the Biblical allusions are all from the Old Testament, possibly because the material offers more heroic possibilities. Certainly the bereaved is dissuaded from suicide more naturally when his values are in a Judaic rather than a pagan tradition. And we cannot resist speculating that the choice of such details, like the subject matter of Archbishop Turpin's lament in *The Sege of Melayne,* reflects something of the religious temper of French Catholicism.

A more straightforward and very effective wish for death is that expressed by Oisel for her lover Tirri in *Guy of Warwick* (Anthology, p. 142). The opening is especially pointed because it uses a detail of physical description, a technique which succeeds consistently in laments for the dead in medieval narrative verse. The ideas in the passage are neatly tied together; the emphasis is exclusively on death. Oisel proceeds quickly from her observation on Tirri's appearance of death to an assumption of responsibility for the death, and then to a firm avowal that she cannot live without her lover. Since he has died for her, she will die for him, even kill herself. The absence of traditional 'alas, woe' exclamations increases the intensity of the lament. The line "þi better neuer was y-born nas" is the only one which has really trite phrasing, and it too is neatly blended with the others; thus it does not lack forcefulness. Being limited to a single attitude, without the usual attempt to include several traditional motifs, this lament affords an opportunity for developing one idea and succeeds very well. Oisel is shown not as a hysterical woman, but as one deeply committed to her love on whom her every thought is focussed. There is a basic irony in the emphasis upon physical characteristics of death, for though he appears to be dead, Tirri is in fact still living and recovers to swear lifelong fellowship with Guy. Oisel's very explicit devotion to her lover, with whom she has eloped, contrasts with Felice's characteristic demands that Guy prove himself the finest knight under heaven. As the lament makes clear, she is a rather attractive heroine because of her love and admiration.

Two laments of pure and elaborate praise form an excellent pair for comparison, together illustrating most of the possible ways of praising a knight, the person most frequently lamented in medieval narrative. It is curious that in both cases the person making the lament is a brother. In the *Buik of Alexander* (Anthology, pp. 142–43) after the defeat of Betys, Alexander marches toward Tars to see Candace and meets an old Chaldean man, Gaudifer's brother, who laments his loss at Gaderis. He praises the brother by declaring him second only to Alexander, very high compliment indeed. The old man does well to single out "bounte" along with knightly prowess and courteous traits, for largesse was a virtue much esteemed in medieval narrative, as is indicated by didactic romances like *Sir Cleges*. The knight endowed with these virtues has distinct eminence, so that it is not surprising to find other complimentary adjectives— wise, debonaire, hardy, kind, and fair—to describe his attributes. The mourner shows his sincerity by calling the gods to witness his praise. The gods are well chosen here. Venus and Mars are exactly what we would expect to judge love and war; Neptune is known for his bounty, and Mercury attests alertness and swiftness. Thus the last two lines actually summarize the whole passage.

Coupling the virtues of Venus and Mars is certainly the idea of Ector de Maris when he laments Launcelot (Anthology, p. 143), the knight who, with perhaps only Tristram as a competitor, most clearly combines prowess in arms and excellence in love. Launcelot is praised as the best of Christian knights, strong in arms, courteous, a true friend to man, a kind lover of women, stern in battle against men, meek and gentle in hall with women. It is significant that neither Venus nor Mars is given a stronger or higher place in this final estimate; an excellent knight had to be subject to both. Here the lament admirably fulfills its purpose; it summarizes the career of Launcelot.

Thus we see in these two laments the types of praise most frequently employed. In both the praise is very enthusiastic but somewhat generalized. In the lament for Launcelot almost equal attention is given to love as to war, wheras the lament for Gaudifer mentions love only in the reference to Venus and essentially we receive an impression of a knight who was generous and excelled in battle. Launcelot is, of course, a much more crucial personality in Malory's narrative, so that we can understand this more complex presentation. The lament recalls Launcelot's fundamental conflict between martial valor and his love for Gwenivere. Further, Malory gains immediacy through his more rhetorical style. Repetition of "thou were" unifies the lament; it serves to suggest Launcelot's eminence and, as in an *ubi sunt* lyric, to emphasize that this is now lost. Both passages are, then, appropriate final comments upon the careers of worthy knights, and they show ways in which praise is essential to the lament for the dead.

One of the most impressive types of lament for a dead knight is that which summarizes his career. Of these the most striking is in *Guy of Warwick* when King Athelstone reveals Guy's identity (Anthology, pp. 143–44). The actual scene is handled with remarkable restraint. Felice, who arrives just before Guy dies, is given but one word "Allas" (Auchinleck MS., 294), and the narrative has only three lines which describe her kissing the body and wringing her hands. The fine touch is that Guy's body produces a sweet breath, a sign of heavenly blessing such as we find in the accounts of Hector in the romances of Troy. Guy's dying, however, is not so simply accepted as the death scene might suggest. The King of England, Athelstone, delivers a long lamentation, having come some distance to the hermitage where Guy died. Athelstone's emphasis is upon Guy's saving England, his modesty, his renown, and his honesty. He recalls how Guy fought for him at Winchester, slew a dragon in north England, twice saved England with his might. Guy has no peers. Had he wanted honor he might have been an emperor, for he was offered the daughter and lands of the Emperor for whom he fought against the Sowdon of Babylon and his thirty kings, slaying them all. "The flower of Christendom," Guy also killed the paynim Ameraunt, Duke Otoun of Pavia who was treacherous, and the giant Berrard. The gentle Guy went all through the world, constantly waging war against falsehood, ever a true knight. Athelstone explains how Guy made him swear at Winchester not to reveal his identity for twelve months. Now that time has passed, Athelstone concludes with a prayer for Guy's soul.

Here the dominant idea is to summarize Guy's career, and by so doing to praise him; thus the speech is curiously dispassionate, a factual summary of the hero's life. By having King Athelstone speak the lament, the narrative writer emphasizes Guy's importance, and the many details document the significant points of his career. There is no attempt to inspire admiration; indeed it is simply accepted that Guy was the "flower of Christendom." Further, there is no frantic outpouring of feeling. The restraint which characterized Felice's meeting with her husband after so many years of separation is repeated here. The muted tone reflects the shift in the manner of the romance which occurs about half-way through when Guy renounces his own renown and adventures to become a pilgrim. Although Guy still fights as a knight in Christian causes, the glory-seeking which was the original motivation has disappeared. Thus his loss is accepted with resignation, vividly underscored by the fact that none can move his body. Again the hero has lived his life to the proper conclusion, and the lament for the dead indicates the acceptance of this in the romance world. In contrast to many laments, for example those made by Arthur and Charlemagne, this lament for Guy of Warwick has a detached quality. Like the narrative in which it appears, it is episodic; the cumulative effect from a summary of adventures is memorable and provides a minimal preparation for the splendor of St. Michael's bearing Guy's soul to Heaven.

Laments are usually spoken by a knight's king or friend or beloved. However, the device of having an enemy praise the person slain is often used effectively. A good example is the lament for Gawain in *Morte Arthure* (Anthology, pp. 144–45). No one doubts that Gawain is frequently the hero of the Arthurian cycle, and Arthur's laments for him are perhaps the best known in medieval romance. In the *Morte Arthure,* however, there is another striking lament which carefully prepares for Arthur's. The poet devotes half a dozen lines of narrative to praising Gawain, the good man of arms who guided many others. Then King Frederick of Fres asks the identity of the slain knight (Gawain), describing his arms and declaring that he was a most redoubtable foe. Modred, the enemy of Arthur and his knights, identifies Gawain and laments with fulsome praise. Gawain was peerless—most gracious, hardy in arms, charming in hall, lordly in conduct. Modred assures King Frederick that had he known Gawain, who was such a good knight, he would sorrow for his death all his life. Even a traitor like Modred weeps for Gawain, and he goes away lamenting that the fates wrought such woe. The effect here is similar to that gained from having Agamemnon make a lament for Hector in the Trojan romance. Here Gawain is lavishly praised by his opponents; thus even Arthur's extravagant last lament, which is one of the finest and most exalting in medieval narrative, seems fitting. We do not fail to recognize conventional excess and rhetorical embellishment, but they are not jarring when set into a pattern of elaborate praise which evolves so skillfully. The author varies the tension in this death scene. King Frederick does not know Gawain's identity, and Modred knows him well. Both agree that Gawain was a peerless knight and praise him accordingly. Frederick notes his recent exploits on the battlefield; Modred supplies the background details of his heritage and his behavior at court as "þe hendeste in howle." The inevitable conclusion is that Gawain's death can rightly produce only endless grief for any who have known him, and this conclusion is reached by means of a memorable dramatic scene between bold antagonists.

The devices of summarizing a hero's career and having an opponent praise the slain knight are combined when Hector is lamented, both in the *Laud Troy Book* and in Lydgate's *Troy Book*. Although Lydgate reduced eighty-eight lines to fifty, he has also added some new ideas which are worth pointing out. There are many similarities between the two, which is not surprising since both draw heavily on Guido delle Colonne. What is particularly notable is that it is Agamemnon who makes the lament, and the setting is the Greek council. Thus we might expect dispraise or at least slurring insults, but instead he delivers a pure eulogy. The effect of having an enemy, and one of the most quarrelsome of enemies, enumerate Hector's victories and describe his importance as Troy's outstanding knight, is to make Hector appear even more valuable than he would if a colleague or relative were praising him. Trojan Hector has won praise from Greek Agamemnon by proving his ability and vigor in slaying a host of Greek kings; there can be no doubt or question of personal prejudice in his favor. And not one of the other Greeks disputes what Agamemnon says, so that really Hector is praised by all the Greeks. Lydgate (IV, 14–65) limits Hector's slaying to eighteen kings, but he begins by telling the Greeks that they should give thanks to the gods for granting a victory over the

                                              berer-vp of Troye,
Her full[le] trust, her honour and her Ioye,
Her hool diffence and protectiou*n*,
And vn-to vs deth and confusiou*n*—

                                              (IV, 19–23)

The Greeks could never have had victory while Hector lived; none
could avail against his mighty sword. Agamemnon lists kings whom
Hector slew, and even this abridged version is impressive. Then he
returns to the initial idea, suggesting offerings of thanks to the gods
who by Hector's death increased the Greeks' joy and distressed their
foes in Troy, as will soon be clear. Specifically, Agamemnon wants
to thank Fortune, who with the turning of her wheel has brought
the Greeks into such comfort through the death of Hector, who
oppressed them. Troy can do nothing but await death and destruction. Lydgate's original idea is the characteristic reference to Fortune
which does not appear in the Laud version. He has, however,
weakened markedly the effect which we find in Laud, where a relentless mass of detail serves as a foundation in creating a heroic
figure.

   Agamemnon begins also in the Laud version (Anthology, pp.
145–47) with a reference to the gods, calling upon the Greeks to
glorify them for giving mastery over the enemy who is now slain.
The directness of this beginning is typical of the Laud version, and
it indicates a basic difference, for the earlier version is consistently
more forceful. Lydgate's characteristic tendency to didactic heaviness
leads him to stifle much of the energy which is found in the *Laud
Troy Book*. The earlier version less pretentiously and more successfully points out that while Hector lived the Greeks could not possibly have won; now they can be fairly confident of becoming mas-
ters of the city and all its goods. This idea is repeated in other
words, and Agamemnon declares that it was better to slay Hector
than half the Trojan forces, for he alone slew more than all the
others. Agamemnon can feel confident because the Greeks have a
force of more than sixty thousand. He cannot, however, avoid giving
credit where it is due. Hector's deeds are well known, and they may
not be hidden. Thus Agamemnon lists twenty-two kings by name,
refers to "others mo" and then to "many duk and Amerelles" and
"lordes" whom Hector, who also took away coffers and chests, slew.
At intervals Agamemnon interrupts his list to praise briefly some
of those slain, but he observes that the Greeks were all afraid of

Hector and that no man was his equal. All this contributes to make Hector a brilliant hero whose victories are too numerous to name in their entirety. He who slew Hector, Agamemnon affirms, is blessed, for he brought an end to the shame and evil of the Greeks, who can now master all the other Trojans. And he proceeds to outline the plan he has for an ultimate victory.

This lament in both versions of the story enables the poet to express strong pro-Trojan sympathies. Earlier both the poet of the *Laud Troy Book* and Lydgate had made it clear that Hector was killed through treachery. Achilles attacks Hector not only when he is unarmed, but also from the rear so that he is unsuspecting. Both poets had also stopped the narrative to eulogize Hector themselves, and it is difficult to say which outdoes the other. The poets' grief, elaborate praise, account of the bringing of the corpse into the city, Trojan grief, preparations, building the tomb, embalming the body to preserve it from corruption (perhaps the greatest tribute)—these ideas fill out over three hundred lines in both (*Laud,* 10987–11298 and Lydgate, III, 5424–5764). Lydgate's eulogy, which begins with the interlinear title "The lamentacyon of kynge Priamus for the dethe of Ector," (III, 5422/3) is more consciously artistic. For example, he declares that he cannot call upon the muses to help him because his subject is too "direful"; he must summon Furies from hell, and he asks why Fate cut Hector's thread. Similarly, an interlinear title (11012/3) "Lamentacio Troian*orum pro* morte Ec-toria" shows that the Laud poet is not unaware of an artistic tradition. Such explicit labeling of passages as "lamentation" is a precise recognition of the tradition of laments for the dead. This is rhetorically a more formal acknowledgement than we encounter in most narratives, and it serves appropriately to introduce both rather formal expressions of grief. Both narratives also include brief laments by the Trojans. In Laud this (11029–33) is a token use of the conventional exclamations of "weylaway" and "Alas, that they were born." Lydgate's lament of the Trojan women is more effective:

> "Allas! now shal oure fadris cruelly
> In oure siȝt be slay[e]n day be day!
> Allas þe whyle! & no man shal seie nay!—
> Far-wel oure helpe, now Hector is goon,
> In [whom] þe surnes of vs euerychon
> Was wont to reste: now is he ded, allas!"
>
> (III, 5522–27)

Following upon this preparation Agamemnon's praise is not difficult to accept; it seems judicious and temperate and leaves no doubt that Hector is the hero of the narrative. Thus a multiplicity and variety of lamentation are offered to provide adequate praise for one of the most popular heroes of all time. These medieval narratives miss no opportunity for indicating the worth of Hector and making clear his supreme value to the Trojan cause. By giving the very fullest praise to his enemy they heighten our sense of Hector's worth, but the more characteristic effects of lamentation by a knight's friends are not neglected.

The conventional manner of lamenting is for the men of a slain knight or king to praise him, but there are two striking exceptions to this in the Scottish *Buik of Alexander*. The two laments might be termed "inverted," that is they have as their object dispraise rather than eulogy. King Clarus has fallen, and dispraise is heaped upon him, first by his men and then by an individual follower, his nephew Marcian. The men cry out (Anthology, pp. 203–204) that they must flee since their lord is dead. Here it would seem that the model has been a eulogistic lament for the dead, but all the opposites of the model have been included in the new expression. Every quality which is included is among those listed as not praiseworthy in a king. Clarus fought with all good men, kept deceivers and flatterers as his privy counsellors, who are now fleeing, and now he is beyond any aid. Line 9591 epitomizes the tone of this inverse lament; do not weep, but laugh at this death. He who is dead is despicable and should be despised. Marcian's dispraise (Anthology, p. 204) is a little more subtle. The lament begins with a praiseworthy trait, fighting foremost in battle. But the first characteristic attributed to the dead man is pride, so that this and not courage would seem to have made Clarus choose the vanguard. All the evil qualities of envy, miserliness, covetousness, spoil and rapine, arrogance are typical of Clarus; and his love was of thieves and murderers, not good knights. Death, however, spares none, and thus all greediness and ill-got gains are now useless. This again is a neat inversion. The conventional manner is to console the mourner with the fact that all that lives must die and he should accept the inevitability. Here death is an inevitable conclusion to be accepted gratefully; death is a much wanted destroyer of an evil man. The sentiments of hatred and dispraise in these two passages are stronger and more devastating than any of those spoken by an enemy against his foe. Thus there is a fundamental irony which reflects the narrative writer's subtle awareness of personality. Not content to follow the most conventional style of lamentation, he evolves an individual variation of the form to suggest a distinctive view of human capacity. Death of a leader does not always lead to his followers' grief; instead it may bring to the surface their latent animosity.

There are many passages which, if not so effective, are very like laments of dispraise in tone. These are scornful comments made by an enemy of the person who is slain, usually as he is striking the death-blow or just after. The finest example of a victor exulting over his fallen enemy also occurs in the *Buik of Alexander* (Anthology, pp. 147–48). Gaudifeir slays Corneus and he is elated. He takes a macabre delight in defouling the body, and he revels in the joke of Corneus' keeping the passage safe because his corpse is there. Gaudifeir suggests that had he been well-directed Corneus might have been a man of great bravery, and he pronounces a moral judgment against pride as the cause of his foe's failure. Then Gaudifeir is himself guilty of pride, for he expresses satisfaction in Corneus' inability to stop him. These comments are pervaded by an even tone of scorn, derision, and insult. The vigor of feeling is the same that we noticed in the two laments of dispraise; thus the unusual idea may be seen less as a novelty and more as a natural development. And the author of this particular medieval narrative has what may be described as a characteristic and individual handling of the conventional form of a lament for the dead; he stresses the unpleasant. Again we see a brilliant illustration of literary finesse; the author of the *Buik of Alexander* sees in the lament for the dead an opportunity for expressing definitive attitudes. In short, the potential for originality which is provided by a conventional form is here exploited in a meaningful way.

Cries for revenge are one of the least interesting types of laments for the dead because they are usually purely emotional outbursts and offer little opportunity for developing ideas. There are a few exceptions, however, which are worth noting. One example is in Barbour's *Bruce* when the Bruce learns that Setoun has been betrayed by Macnab, beheaded, and hung by Edward I (Anthology, p. 149). The Bruce begins with self-blame; noble and worthy men die for love of him. This means that he will seek revenge. In characteristic manner Bruce is defiant: the King of England thought the kingdom of Scotland too small for both of them. Bruce is quite willing to agree; *he* will take all Scotland for himself. Having made this patriotic outburst, he returns to the immediate situation, praising

Setoun and grieving that one so noble should die. The passage gives some indication of what may be done with the idea of revenge, for Bruce uses it to consider national honor and the interests of the public weal. He reveals a sense of his own importance and his relations to his knights and enemies. There is a genuine feeling of grief, but this is carefully controlled and indeed is really more a means for the Bruce's personality to emerge than an end in itself.

A more explicit and eloquent vow for revenge is made in the *Morte Arthure*. Just after he has lamented Gawain and seen the body brought for burial, Arthur casts aside his hopeless despair and thinks of retaliation (Anthology, pp. 149–50). He vows firmly to kill Gawain's slayer, even if he has to fight alone against an army. Calling upon both Christ and Mary as witnesses, he promises relentless pursuit. Arthur's personal involvement, his readiness to fight alone, the fervor with which he will pursue Modred to wreake vengeance, letting nothing interfere, and his devout sanctioning by vows to Christ and Mary—all contribute to an effect of sincere dedication and intensity. As a final lament for Gawain and the other knights who were slain, this vow for revenge is appropriate not only in the strength of its feeling, but also in its demonstration that Arthur is a fit king who can take action when it is necessary as well as swoon with grief. Thus he is a very much more significant king than Charlemagne in his actions and in his utterances. Fighting against a force that vastly outnumbers his own, Arthur is triumphant and unswerving in his wish and commitment to killing Modred. Thus we see a particularly pointed vow for revenge which punctuates the action of the narrative and deepens our sympathy for Arthur.

Similarly, Arthur's lament when he learns of Childric's plunder and killing in the south (Laȝamon's *Brut,* Anthology pp. 150–51) combines an idea of revenge with religious attitudes and self-blame. The more traditional use of religion after a death is to pray for the soul of the one who has died. The difference here is that Arthur does not pray that God will have mercy on those slain; he prays that he may be able to revenge the deaths. Arthur's first "Alas" introduces self-accusatory comment. He blames himself for not having prevented the slaughter, for not killing his enemies when he had them in his grasp. Thus he is responsible, and all that he can do now is to plan revenge. He will kill Colgrin and Baldulf, and Childric's people will never again deceive him. This lament is restricted in its scope, being limited almost entirely to the idea of revenge, but other ideas are suggested to emphasize Arthur's desire, so that the single idea is admirably presented, and Arthur's lament emerges as a forceful, almost primitive outcry. He is a worthy king, feeling remorse and responsibility for his men from one end of Britain to the other, and his immediate resolution for action is appropriate. Reacting quickly, Arthur still manages to measure the circumstances and evaluate alternative courses of action; however, the sense of urgency is paramount.

A sharp contrast may be seen between such a vigorous, immediate, emotional reaction and a response made temperate through years. A good illustration of the latter occurs in *Percyvelle of Galles* (Anthology, p. 151). When the youthful Perceval appears at court, Arthur notes a resemblance and laments Perceval senior who has been dead for fifteen years. Arthur follows a typical plan. He begins with the idea "Alas, that I was born." Then he regrets that he has outlived this noble knight, whom he now praises, explaining that he so esteemed Perceval senior that he gave him his sister as wife. Now fifteen years have passed since he was slain; and in all that time, although he consistently tried, Arthur has not succeeded in killing the traitor. The only person who can effect fitting revenge, "the bokes say," is Perceval's son. Again the ideas are simple—grief, praise, a desire for revenge—but they are presented in something other than a conventional lament, for this unique lament establishes a great deal in the narrative scheme. It recalls the opening sections of the romance which dealt with Perceval senior and the red knight, and it both indicates the difficulty of the approaching combat and forecasts young Perceval's ultimate victory over the red knight. It also establishes something of Arthur's character, his humility and dedication to his people. More importantly, the lament contributes to the effect of the dramatic scene in hall by simultaneously prolonging an explicit revelation of young Perceval's identity and emphasizing the obvious noble quality of his heritage. The simple device of having the first line of each stanza repeat the last line of the preceding helps to set this lament apart from the rest of the narrative and provides unity. In addition to a fairly complex stanzaic pattern alliteration is used. The "s" and "w" sounds are especially skillful and suggest a sense of grief that is established by the opening exclamations. Thus Arthur's lament for the dead, which is the only use of the form in *Percyvelle of Galles,* is crucial in a variety of ways and one of the most memorable parts of the narrative. The writer has used the wish for revenge as a starting point for complex development of ideas and situation.

The most striking use of an idea of revenge appears in a speech in Lydgate's *Troy Book* which is not begun as a lament for the dead, but which is essentially just that. Achilles and Hector meet, declare their grievances and express their desires to be revenged. As usual, Lydgate throws his sympathy to Hector, making him reply to Achilles' charges that he acts only in self-defence, trying to save the Trojans from Greek pride and impertinence. It is, however, what Achilles says that is interesting in a study of laments for the dead. Some forty-six lines (Anthology, pp. 152–53) are devoted to his feelings about Patroclus' death, and he expresses many ideas which are in the best tradition of lament. The feeling of friendship, brotherhood, is very like what we find between Amis and Amiloun, Valentine and Orson, Guy and Herhaud, or among the four sons of Aymon, but nowhere is it so fully described. Achilles praises Patroclus as young, manly, and virtuous, declaring that he loved his friend as himself. Thus Achilles regards Hector's killing as a very personal thing. Much of his language is like that used by a lover when he has lost his beloved. He will never forget his loss, being sundered from the person whom he most valued. Now all Achilles can do is seek revenge. He vows that Patroclus' death will be dearly bought, asserting a principle of "deth for deth." Within the year, he vows, vengeance will be taken. At this point there is a shift in feeling, for Achilles changes his role of wronged and bereaved friend to boastful conqueror. He looks forward to world repute as an avenger of his friend. The speaker's awareness of his shift in feeling is indicated by his attempt to justify his attitude. He tells Hector not to blame him for this attitude, for as surely as Achilles wants to slay Hector, so Hector wishes to slay Achilles and conspires to do so. Thus, he concludes, there can be nothing between them but death, and he can only hope that when the time comes Fortune will not let Hector escape. Through this lament Achilles is revealed as a personality of some distinction, for he shows a wide range of feeling and intellectual acumen that go far beyond mere physical prowess. In fact, his defense of his desire for revenge reveals a sophistication of outlook and ingenious self-justification. Thus Hector is opposed by a fierce antagonist whose ultimate treachery is not surprising. Further, the Trojan hero's challenge to single combat to decide the war appears especially worthy and free of selfish ambition in this context of duplicity and pretention. Achilles' grief over loss of Patroclus is, however, movingly stated and his personal involvement seems sincere, so that some ambiguity remains. In short, the lament saves Achilles from being a simply unsympathetic man; we are led to recognize several levels of personality, and we have a poetically effective passage. Thus the lament for the dead is again seen as a primary means of enhancing literary depth. And if such lamentation for a fallen Greek is plausible, then the expressions of grief over loss of Hector can indeed be extreme and elaborate in the next part of the narrative.

As laments which are essentially vows for revenge so clearly indicate, mourners most frequently react violently and then reach a more rational, calmer state. The King of Friesland, however, reverses this process when he laments his wife in *Blanchardyn and Eglentine* (Anthology, p. 153). He begins very calmly, "and is she gon, the comfort of my youth," and then continues with a series of conventional apostrophes of praise. He is not surprised that his wife is dead, for he had suspected that the grief of separation might kill her. But, he argues, all flesh is mortal and nothing under the sun is permanent. Laments are too weak either to recall the dead to life or to comfort the bereaved; thus they are of no avail. After this resigned and moralized acceptance, it is rather startling suddenly to have the King muster his energies, dying as he is, and call upon Jove for revenge. Acknowledging Jove's omnipotence, but accusing the diety of destining him to perpetual misery, the King now prays that Jove will prove a righteous judge and grant him revenge on the infidels who profane the name of Jove and have caused all his woe. Finally he asks that his life may end and that his soul and his wife's may join in heaven where they may enjoy the comfort and consolation which were denied them on earth. Thus the King returns to his earlier tone of resignation, showing that he is well steeped in proper dogma and that even a cry for revenge is related to his religious dedication, which allows for a brief outburst but not for sustained deviation. The contrasting attitudes are made very clear in the lines of narrative description and comment which separate the two parts of the lament. We are told that the King of Friesland finds "his heart ouer charged with an other passion"; thus there is careful preparation for his bold shifts in attitude—from calm resignation to a vigorous request for revenge, to a quiet wish for death and fervent prayer for consolation in the hereafter. There is, in short, a dramatic evocation of conflicting emotions. Although the King of Friesland has some self-pity and momentary presumption in wanting to determine the course of events, his obviously intense feeling for his wife and his belief in and acceptance of the will of god are ultimately unshakeable. Here, then, we have a character declaring that laments for the dead, "sorowful grones and passions," are of no avail in altering circumstances; but the form again provides a writer of narrative with a means of expressing a complex range of human awareness and experience in a manner that is dramatic and vital.

Grief, praise, and revenge are fundamentally reactions of a very personal kind, and they are naturally followed by a concern about the future. Such concern may be entirely personal, as when a lady wonders about her future without her knightly protector, but often the consideration is a larger one. It is necessary that the public weal be considered, for even if the fairest flower of knighthood is lost, the kingdom must go on. Usually reconciliation is attempted, but docile acceptance is not the only way in which concern for the public weal is expressed. The reaction of Bishop Turpin when he learns from Roland that many knights have been slain (*Sege of Melayne*, Anthology, pp. 153–54) is significant. Casting his staff and mitre away, he vows never to wear them again and demands why Mary so rewarded men who fought for her. This passage alone indicates that Turpin is one of the most fascinating characters in the Charlemagne romances. A cleric who assumes a militant role as a soldier, he is presented as a character with more gradations of personality than the white Christian peer of honesty and right or the black Saracen knight of treachery and evil. The priest who has left the church to enter a world of politics and war seems to have been of interest to the medieval narrative poet. Only he pauses to lament the many who have been slain, and his utterance clearly reveals his clerical training. The violence of the utterance, the casting off of priestly garb and the doubt and questioning of Mary, both her right and her power, are significant in establishing the character of Turpin. As a lament the passage is extremely interesting because it contains almost none of the conventional subject matter of praise, revenge, and wishes for death. It is instead a full statement of doubt, a theme which appears frequently in the Charlemagne romances, but the god usually doubted is Mahoun. We have, then, not simply a reaction against the established order of the kingdom, but also an aggressive defiance of the accepted divine order. Turpin is angry because the expected protection and aid from Mary have not been forthcoming. Here a lament for the dead provides for a bold statement of an unconventional attitude by an extraordinary personality. Subsequently, Turpin challenges Charlemagne, calls for a crusade, leads armies, performs miracles, ignores his own serious wounds, and keeps extraordinary fasts; in short, he is the bulwark of the French forces, a dominantly courageous man who is unmitigating in his resolve, and the most interesting person in the romance. The lament for the dead dramatically introduces this individual who brings great vigor and life to the Charlemagne material and suggests the dominance of the Church. There is no other lament like this one in any other romance, and once again the originality of an author is demonstrated by his adaptation of the traditional form to his individual need.

The only passage which may be compared with Turpin's outburst is a lament made in *Firumbras* (Anthology, pp. 154–55) by Charles when he learns that many of his men have been lost. Again there is a limitation of ideas which results in marked intensity of feeling. Charles begins a little plaintively by asking his barons to counsel him and by making a conventional offer to give up his crown for the lives of his peers, but he soon becomes defiant. He prays to God and Mary for the safety of Roland and Oliver, but he vows by God that if they are overcome Christendom is lost. He will never again permit worship in France and describes carefully how he will not only stop religious services, but also will destroy religious properties. Finally, he swears that if his peers are lost, he will never again worship God. This kind of argument, again, is more Saracen than Christian in tone. Defying, and actually challenging, God is quite exceptional. The typical reaction is to leave all to God's will. Here then is another illustration of the lament's being used to express a divergent attitude, and thus characterize an important person in the narrative. In both these laments for the dead the argumentative and independent quality that characterizes French Catholicism is clearly suggested. Charles, being blasphemous here, is less ineffectual than usual, though still hardly an attractive person. He lacks Turpin's vigorous action, but shares his indignation and vengeful fury that divine power has not been on his side.

We return to a more rational attitude with the lament which most strikingly illustrates the idea of treason. The King of France believes that Partonope of Blois has been treacherously slain in his duel with Sornegour, who was aided by a group of heathen knights. Complex sentiments are expressed (Anthology, p. 155). Here there is great ambivalence of feeling. The King begins with a very conventional expression of grief and praise, but he soon turns to questioning why the death should have occurred. The intellectual grasp of the problem is evident in the King's careful recollection of oaths made to fight fairly. He esteemed Sornegour (who was the first to swear to keep the field honestly, in Br. Mus. Addit. MSS. 35288, line 4599) as one most trustworthy, and his manliness was such that he did not need villainy to win. The King's sorrow is heightened by his personal disappointment. He goes so far as to argue that he does not believe Sornegour consented to treason. Here, then, what begins as a conventional eulogy rapidly develops into an extensive moralization, an attempt to understand what appears to have been a betrayal by a man who was as worthy as his antagonist. The restrained language of the passage indicates an interest, not in emotional reactions but in intellectual understanding. Such earnest consideration is appropriate in the context of the narrative where the combat has been elaborately described and indeed the decision to have a duel to decide the issue has been reached with great care. There is a truly Christian integrity of feeling, a genuine wish and attempt to think well of the enemy who is a Saracen king. Thus a crucial experience is made of the combat, which is of only incidental interest in a romance that is primarily focussed on the love of Partonope and Melior. The narrative writer, whose didactic interests are clear, uses a lament for the dead not simply to mark a detail of his action, but to illustrate worthy Christian behavior. His restriction of subject matter and simple conventional language lend cogency to the argument.

A more striking complex of ideas exists in Reynard's lament for Richard in the *Foure Sonnes of Aymon* (Anthology, pp. 155–56) where reflections on treason are combined with a sense of family, praise, and religious ideas. Reynard begins by crying out that his brother's death is a great pity, and this is followed by praise which supports the initial statement. Laments which turn on the theme of promise unfulfilled are surprisingly rare in medieval narrative. Here Reynard makes the claim and is able to praise his brother above Oliver and Roland, and none can dispute him. He deplores the king's treason and confesses that he would never have suspected it. Then Reynard blames himself for causing Richard's death, presumably because he is a leader of the brothers. There is some poignancy in the idea that four brothers are now but three. The emotional appeal of a united family is not lost, and actually it is heightened because the three survivors are wounded and unarmed. The impression which Reynard's comments immediately conjures up is of four strong, brave, and well-equipped knights riding out firmly in the morning and of all beaten through treason, three injured and one dead (it is thought), in the evening. The contrast between the two situations and swiftness with which the loss was accomplished cannot fail to move us. Reynard vows by God that he may not escape since his brother was killed by traitors. He prays that he may wreak vengeance before he dies, promising to devote himself entirely to this end, and God willing, he will accomplish it. This lament in terms of ideas is one of the best in medieval narrative, combining as it does just the right thoughts and sentiments. No one can doubt the sincerity and depth of Reynard's grief, his personal anguish at losing a brother. That Richard was a good knight is not incidental, but it is less pertinent than his being one of a band of brothers. It is perfectly natural for Reynard to want to revenge his brother's death, and he wins our sympathy, first because Richard was lost through treason, and secondly because Reynard makes very clear his belief in God's omnipotence. He calls upon God to assist him in his fraternal duty and wish, but he insists that only with God's will can he be successful, however dedicated he may be. Thus we find in this romance of the Charlemagne group an attitude very different from that expressed in the laments in the other narratives of the legend just discussed. The more orthodox values which emerge in Reynard's lament give a solidity to the personalities who express belief in both divine and earthly order.

Another illustration of fraternal distress is Valentine's lament when he thinks that Orson is dead (Anthology, p. 156). This time it is Fortune who is accused of causing hardship, changing all Valentine's joys into distress, making him lose the man most valuable to him. Orson is lavishly praised for his strength and valiant nature. Valentine blames himself because he conquered Orson in the woods and has kept him in constant danger ever since. There is here a curious hint at the "noble savage" idea. Now, when Valentine had hoped to enjoy comfort and happiness with his brother, he has no tidings of Orson. He vows to God that he will find Orson dead or alive, or die for love of him. These ideas are presented very neatly, and they are held together by repetition of exclamations of "Allas." The passage is typical of many of the laments for the dead in *Valentine and Orson*, for it emphasizes the essential loyalties of family relationships, and such considerations form basic thematic matter in the romance.

One of the most impressive varieties of laments for the dead, then, is that which involves a serious and fundamental moral judgment. Each man has an obligation and responsibility to observe and maintain order in relation to his fellow creatures, particularly the members of his family. We find this basic principle asserted in laments which are devoted chiefly to the exploitation of other ideas. Guy of Warwick's lament for his men, for example, combines many ideas, and it is one of the finest laments for many persons developing into a lament for a specific individual in medieval narrative. The greater length, thirty-eight lines (Anthology, pp. 156–57), makes possible not only the introduction of many ideas but also an interesting development and interrelation of them. Guy begins with a traditional "Alas" and brief praise of those slain, but he turns quickly to an intellectual analysis of the situation. He does not hesitate to place responsibility for the loss on Felice, who has insisted that he must be the finest and greatest knight in Christendom. He argues, however, that because she is a woman, she is not blameworthy. He is not the last to be brought to harm by a woman, and his only wish is that others will be warned by what happened to him. After this general introduction the passage evolves into a specific lament for Guy's best friend Herhaud. This is the most grievous loss, as is apparent from Guy's extensive praise and concern about who will now fight by his side. Guy blames himself entirely for Herhaud's death, and he argues that it is not possible for him to leave the battlefield. He curses the Lombards for not killing him, wishing earnestly that he might have been slain and Herhaud left alive. Guy cannot understand why his own life was spared. He continues his recriminations, lamenting that he did not believe his lord Rohaut. Although advised not to cross the sea, Guy willfully led his followers to death. Thus it is again a kind of pride which produced catastrophe in a medieval narrative—Felice's initial vanity and Guy's proud compliance even when better advised. Guy's fault is the more serious because he refused a father's advice. Indeed he argues that the series of catastrophes which had befallen him stem from his initial violation of order when he ignored his father's superior judgment. And he concludes his lament with a proverb, demonstrating that those who do not believe their fathers relinquish filial privilege. Again we see a family relationship used to intensify a situation, so that a lament for the dead is more potent. The proverb makes explicit the crucial quality of the attitudes expressed. Thus we have an additional argument for the value of a lament for the dead as a means of confronting basic experience.

A similar conflict about self-blame arises in Lydgate's *Seige of Thebes* (Anthology, pp. 157–158). Ipsiphyle leaves her charge, the young son of Lycurgus, to bring the distressed Tideus and his Greeks, who are perishing with thirst, to a river. Although she carefully hid the child before leaving, Ipsiphyle returns to find him killed by a serpent. Already she was in Lycurgus' debt because he sheltered her when, because she spared her father, she was forced to flee by the women who had vowed to kill all men. Thus she laments, "Alas, what shall I do?" She believes that there is no chance of escape if she remains; she must die for her sloth and negligence. The king will certainly accuse her of treason for causing the death of his heir. She expects Lycurgus' grief to turn to rage against her, and the Queen also will have no pity and want revenge. "Alas," she concludes, she deserves death. Ipsiphyle makes no attempt to excuse herself or to justify her action, which she might easily do, and thus she wins our sympathy. She is really far more the object of our attention than the dead child, who simply affords an opportunity for lamenting. Actually Lydgate introduces Ipsiphyle's story, which is from Boccaccio's *Book of Illustrious Women*, as a kind of embroidery; and for once women do not come out too badly. Thus we see a conventional lament-situation used, not to express grief or praise or defiance, but solely to characterize the mourner who is making the lament.

Women are far less important in medieval romances than men are, but occasionally they are the persons lamented, no one more than Helen, daughter of Howell, Duchess of Brittany, who appears in the Arthurian cycle. This fair lady was stolen by a giant who ravished her, so that she died. In every version the setting of the lament is impressive—a lonely spot, approached by a devious and dark route, with an old woman sitting by a low fire. The old woman is Helen's foster-mother, who is herself now the object of the giant's lust. In Laȝamon's *Brut* she begins:

> Wale Eleine.'
> wale deore maide.
> wale þat ich þe uedde.'
> þat ich þe uostrede.'
> wale þat þae wald-scaðe.'
> here þe haveð þus for-uare.
> wale þat ich wes iboren.'
> mine leomen he haueð to-broken.
>
> (iii, 26; MSS, Cott. Calig. A.IX)

Multiple repetitions of "wale" create the effect of a dirge, a keen, that instantly evokes a sense of utter desolation and suggests a feminine quality. This is followed by a narrative of what happened and an account of Helen's fairness and high lineage. In *Merlin* (646) the old woman explains that the lady died before the giant could lie with her, that she has buried her and now watches at the grave, almost going mad for love of her. The alliterative *Morte Arthure* makes the death of Helen an occasion for more than one lament. The Templar is most eloquent when he announces the death to Arthur and breaks into lament in doing so:

> Scho was flo*ur* of all Fraunce   or of fyfe rewmes,
> And one of the fayreste,   that fou*r*mede was eu*e*re,
> The gentileste jowell   ajuggede w*it*h lordes,
> Fro Geen vn-to Geron,   by Ih*e*su of heuen!
> Scho was thy wyfes cosyn,   knowe it if þe lykez,
> Comen of þe rycheste,   that re*n*gnez in erthe:
> As thow arte ryghtwise kyng*e*,   rewe on thy pople
> And fande for to venge them,   that thus are *offendy*de!"
>
> (860–67)

And Arthur (868–79) does not disappoint the Templar, for he begins with an "Alas!" and grieves vehemently for the foul thing that has happened. He would have given the whole of his fifteen year's kingship of France to fight the fiend before he destroyed the lady; he would even have given his life for hers. Now he asks to be shown the way, so that the desired revenge can be executed. The introduction of this striking passage did not involve cancelling the lament of the foster-mother (974–85), who, as in other versions, sits grieving alone by the grave. She protests at the death of the lady, relating the horrors of how she died, grieving that no friends, save the foster-mother of fifteen years, followed after the Duchess, and declaring that she will stay as guard at the grave. Thus several passages combine to make the death of Helen unforgettable; she is a pitiable human being not merely an object involved in a knight's accomplishment of feats of glory.

As he often does, Malory follows the matter of the alliterative *Morte Arthure,* but he fails completely to take the opportunity offered for an artistic lamentation. He is not interested in reproducing the more poetic, stylized passages of earlier romances. He has a husbandman report to Arthur (198), first telling of the tyrant giant, then of his mass slaying and destruction of children, and finally speaking of the Duchess of Brittany, whom he has ravished. Here, however, more than five hundred people followed to aid her; but they could not effect a rescue. The Caxton version adds details of the woman's screams. Finally Arthur is reminded of the lady's lineage and exhorted to take revenge. Again Arthur expresses his sorrow, would have given his kingdom for the lady (an exact verbal parallel here), and asks only to be shown the way to the tyrant in order that he can achieve the revenge sought. The character of the old widow has been altered. She manages a single "Alas" of lamentation before she chides Arthur for talking too loudly and says that not fifty such as he would be sufficient against the giant who has slain the Duchess by forcing her (200). The result is that the dead woman loses significance before the challenge which is presented to the valiant Arthur, and one lament for the dead woman has been practically cancelled out. Thus a comparison of the ways in which various writers handle the same death scene, suggests a clear recognition of the importance of lamentation and the effects that can be achieved by it in medieval narrative.

Not all laments for women are restricted only to "feminine" ideas; some discuss the same ideas which are found in laments for great knights or kings, using familiar themes which are only slightly altered when applied to a woman. Anna's lament for her sister Dido in Caxton's *Eneydos* (Anthology, pp. 158–59), is permeated with unselfish grief and despair and has a special focus of anxiety because Dido took her own life. In the opening "Alas, what haste thou doo/" a prevailing idea is established. Typically Christian is Anna's belief and fear that Dido has condemned herself to eternal perdition, but her wish to have shared her sister's death is more characteristically pagan. Anna's dismay at having prepared unnecessary sacrifices to Pluto is touchingly human and places her wish for death in some perspective. Since Anna thinks almost trivially and without affectation about the sacrifices, we accept her wish for death with her sister as equally natural. Anna's words tumble out just as awkwardly as her ideas seem to be forming. She is aware that she must make a moan, but she does not know quite how to begin. This hesitancy makes her much more human than a mourner who unhesitatingly produces a polished rhetorical lament. Anna's first reaction is puzzlement; she simply cannot understand why Dido has done this thing. It should be remembered that Dido planned to have Barce lure Anna away to prepare sacrifices to Pluto so that she would not stand in the way of her suicide. Thus poor Anna struggles to understand, but she can think only of her lifetime of love and unfailing dedication to Dido. Having abandoned all else to serve Dido, and having always shared in her innermost secrets, Anna cannot grasp the present situation in which all her love and service have been disregarded. What fury, she asks, can have driven Dido to cast her out and not tell her what she planned to do? Willingly Anna would have died too, and now she is left in sorrow with no one to comfort her. All this woe and care, Anna argues, she suffers innocently, having done nothing to bring about such difficulties. This embryonic self-pity evolves into a full-fledged criticism of Dido, who by taking her life has shamed not only herself and her sister, but also the whole city of Carthage. Dido's foul taking of her own life will remain an ignominy to Carthage through all history. This evil state is the more deplorable because the city had previously basked in fair repute; a fall from greatness is always more violent and devastating. By her single action, wilful Dido has destroyed all hope for Anna and for Carthage. Metaphorically Anna and the Carthaginians are sheep without a pastor. Anna concludes with a hopeless suggestion that they look to Dido's wound to determine whether she is absolutely dead. Here, then, we find the person most intimately affected by the death presenting a complexity of ideas as unselfconscious, halting reactions. The technique is essentially that which we find in so many modern novels; a stream of consciousness reveals a character and indeed suggests a pattern of events and attitudes.

It is interesting that, although a woman's, Anna's lament is not heavily charged with emotional frenzy, nor is it like some men's carefully, logically reasoned commentaries. Anna's ideas emerge slowly and tentatively, stemming more from bewilderment than from shame; and although she recognizes and accepts what will happen now that Dido has killed herself, she neither achieves a calm consolation nor gives way to distraught feelings. This is indeed a relief, following upon the mad ravings of Dido, who when Aeneas leaves, grieves and curses as imaginatively and more extensively than anyone else in medieval narrative. After Dido's shrewish cries and threats when she pleads with Aeneas not to leave her and her frantic outburst when he does—invoking of Jupiter and prayers for vengeance on the Trojans, vain boasts that at one time she could have destroyed Aeneas and his men, further invocations to the sun, Juno, Diana, and the furies, a prayer that if it is not yet the hour appointed for Aeneas' death he may at least be engaged in cruel wars and win only defeat and exile to live the remainder of his life as a beggar, a bequest to the Tyrians of an undying hatred of Trojans, and a promise of an avenger (Hannibal) who will make Aeneas' descendants suffer—and her cruel lament just before she kills herself, Anna's moderation is a welcome relief. Intrinsically the passage is meaningful, but seen in context the ideas gain a greater significance and more clearly delineate the characters of the two women. And when we remember that it was Anna who encouraged Dido's love for Aeneas, Anna's complete willingness to share whatever Dido's fate might be, is both more creditable and ironic. Without question she will go so far as to sacrifice her life, but it never occurs to her to blame herself or to accept any responsibility for initiating the disaster. Thus the medieval writer has a curious blend of attitudes: suicide leads to "eternal perdycyon," and loyalty and honor are proper and necessary both in the family and the state, but the individual does not recognize the interaction of personality and event which results in the complications of human experience.

There are, then, certain basic ideas which make up characteristic laments for the dead. These ideas vary with each situation, with the characters of both those who are dead and of those who are lamenting. Some ideas, such as grief and praise, are almost always present; others, such as Fortune, appear less frequently. The most characteristic method is to select about three ideas which are interrelated and combine them to produce a lament which is fairly well unified. Occasionally, of course, a greater complexity of ideas is successfully managed. In the longer laments there is a marked tendency to explore the possibilities of a significant moral question, such as culpability for the death or the ethical implications of suicide. Generally emphasis is placed on the personal reaction of the mourner, but there are also references to broader concerns about the future of the public weal. Our interest is usually greater when the grief of a person lamenting is something more than a personal anxiety, that is, when he not only reacts emotionally but also thinks about some of the implications of the death. His intellectual exploration of these implications gives an insight into human reactions to one kind of personal crisis, for even in conventional medieval narrative there is individuality in the responses which various characters make to death. Often characters really become individuals only when they are confronted with a problem like death. Then their ideas materialize, and as they speak laments for the dead they become not narrative frames but human persons trying to understand and cope with a difficulty. The result is usually increased elegance and vigor of language in a dramatic sense which exploits the subtleties of personality, situation, and intellectual awareness.

Chapter IV

ELEMENTS OF STYLE IN LAMENTS
FOR THE DEAD

Laments for the dead provide the medieval writer of romance with an opportunity to adorn his narrative by the insertion of what is often a kind of set-piece in a more elaborate style than most of his work demands. Generally a writer of medieval narrative is interested in telling his story, recording names of knights, places of battle, numbers slain, duplicity of traitors, and so on. In short, he relates adventures, usually strung together on a loose biographical thread, with almost no attempt to individualize characters or action or embellish his style. The advance of adventures is stopped only infrequently, and almost always this is for one of three kinds of utterance—a welcome to spring ('Merie is the month of May'), a love complaint, or a lament for the dead. The first is pure embellishment with only a minor function of indicating the time of year; the last two are often essential to characterization or unification of plot, or they form a nucleus for a dramatic scene; thus they are the more memorable, usually having at least a dual purpose, and these are often subtle manifestations of the authors' skill. Although style is perhaps the least interesting aspect of laments for the dead in medieval narrative, that is an analysis of style in each lament results in less significant conclusions than analyses of ideas and dramatic situations, there are a few qualities which should be distinguished.

Rhetorical treatises give a fairly definite method of formal arrangement which is suitable for laments for the dead, but it is useless to try to fit all examples from medieval narrative into this pattern. First of all, it is difficult, if not impossible, to distinguish between expressions which are a planned part of a rhetorical system and those which are spontaneous comment. Rhetorical theory, for example, explains that in the first part of an oration, the *exordium*, a speaker should attempt to arouse pity and sympathy among his hearers. The conventional "Alas, that I was born!" fits the formula, but to be sorry that one was born to endure the grief of loss is also a very natural immediate reaction. Since rhetorical theory is, after all, a discussion of methods which have been tried and proved acceptable, such similarities, however, are not unexpected. Occasionally, of course, a lament may be divided into *exordium, narratio, refutatio, confirmatio,* and *peroratio*, but it is not particularly helpful to describe most laments according to this scheme which is too elaborate and best suited to forensic speeches. Generally laments are almost pure *peroratio*, for they are conclusions, summing up the career of a person who is dead, usually to arouse pity and sympathy, but occasionally to incite ill-will.

A good indication of rhetorical theory about laments may be found in the two treatises, Cicero's *De Inventione* and the *Auctor ad Herrenium*, which shared a position of influence and availability in the Middle Ages.[1] Cicero's *De Inventione* has an analysis of the most effective method of lamentation with an enumeration of the topics which should be employed:

> *Conquestio* (lament or complaint) is a passage seeking to arouse the pity of the audience. In this the first necessity is to make the auditor's spirit gentle and merciful that he may be more easily moved by the *conquestio*. This ought to be done by the use of "commonplaces" which set forth the power of fortune over all men and the weakness of the human race. When such a passage is delivered gravely and sententiously, the spirit of man is greatly abased and prepared for pity, for in viewing the misfortune of another he will contemplate his own weakness. After that the first topic with which to evoke pity is that by which it is shown what prosperity they once enjoyed and from what evils they now suffer. The second employs a division according to time, and shows in what troubles they have been, still are, and are destined to be. The third, in which each separate phase of misfortune is deplored; for example, in lamenting the death of a son, one might mention the delight that his father took in his childhood, his love, his hope for the boy's future, the comfort he derived from him, the careful training, and whatever in similar case can be said in bewailing any misfortune. The fourth, in which one recounts shameful, mean, and ignoble acts and what they have suffered or are likely to suffer that is unworthy of their age, race, former fortune, position, or preferment. The fifth, in

[1] J. W. H. Atkins, *English Literary Criticism: The Medieval Phase* (Cambridge, 1943), pp. 14–15.

which all the misfortunes are presented to view one by one, so that the auditor may seem to see them, and may be moved to pity by the actual occurrence, as if he were present, and not by words alone. The sixth, in which it is shown that one is in distress contrary to all expectation, and when he looked forward to receiving some benefit, he not only did not gain it, but fell into the greatest distress. The seventh, in which we turn to the audience and ask them when they look at us to think of their children or parents or some one who ought to be dear to them. The eighth, in which something is said to have happened which ought not, or that something did not happen which ought to have happened: for example, "I was not present, I did not see him, I did not hear his last words, I did not catch his last breath." Similarly: "He died among the enemy, in a hostile land he lay shamefully unburied, long torn by wild beasts, and in death he was deprived even of the honour due to all mankind." The ninth, in which a discourse is addressed to mute and inanimate objects, for example: if you should represent one as speaking to a horse, a house, or a garment, by which the mind of the audience who have loved everything is greatly affected. The tenth, in which one's helplessness and weakness and loneliness are revealed. The eleventh, in which the speaker commends to the audience his children, his parents, the task of burying him, or some such duty. The twelfth, in which separation from some one is deplored, when you are torn away from one with whom you have lived with the greatest pleasure, for example a father, son, brother, or intimate friend. The thirteenth, in which with anger we complain because we are being badly treated by those whom such conduct least becomes, relatives, friends whom we have treated kindly, whom we expected to help us, or by freedmen, clients, or suppliants. LVI. The fourteenth, which is devoted to entreaty: here the only thing is to implore the audience in humble and submissive language to have mercy. The fifteenth, in which we show that it is not our ill fortune which we bemoan but that of our dear ones. The sixteenth, in which we show that our soul is full of mercy for others, but still is noble, lofty, and patient of misfortune and will be so whatever may befall. For often virtue and highmindedness in which there is naturally influence and authority does more to arouse pity than humility and entreaty.

But when the emotions have been aroused it will be advisable not to linger over the *conquestio*. For as the rhetorician Apollonius said, "Nothing dries more quickly than tears." [2]

The *Ad Herrenium* discusses in some detail topics which should be used in a deliberative speech:

The Division we shall make is the following: we shall set forth the things we intend to praise or censure; then recount the events, observing their precise sequence and chronology, so that one may understand what the person under discussion did and with what prudence and caution. But it will first be necessary to set forth his virtues or faults of character, and then to explain how, such being his character, he has used the advantages or disadvantages, physical or external circumstances. The following is the order we must keep when portraying a life:

1) External Circumstances: Descent . . . Education . . .
2) Next we must pass to the Physical Advantages: . . . impressiveness and beauty . . . exceptional strength and agility . . . continual good health . . .
3) Then we shall return to External Circumstances and consider his virtues and defects of Character evinced with respect to these: has he been rich or poor? What kinds of power has he wielded? What have been his titles to fame? What his friendships? Or what his private feuds, . . . bravery . . . motive . . . loyalty, goodwill, and sense of duty . . . What character of man has he been in wealth, or in poverty? What has been his attitude in the exercise of his prerogatives? . . . [3]

Returning to Cicero, we find in the *De Partitione* a pertinent passage which accurately epitomizes a lament for the dead:

. . . this kind of discourse [panegyric] consists in narrating and exhibiting past actions, without employing any argument, and its style is adapted to gently influencing the emotions rather than to achieving conviction and proof. For it does not establish propositions that are doubtful but amplifies statements that are cer-

[2] Cicero, *De Inventione, De Optimo Genere Oratorum, Topica,* trans. H. M. Hubbell, Loeb ed. (London, 1949), pp. 156–63; Book I, lv-lvi, 106–109.

[3] [Cicero], *Ad C. Herrenium De Ratione Discendi (Rhetorica ad Herrenium)*, trans. Harry Caplan, Loeb ed. (London, 1954), pp. 179–83; Book III, vii, 13–14.

tain, or advanced as being certain . . . because virtually the whole method in these causes is directed to giving the audience pleasure and entertainment, in the style employment must be made of those brilliant touches in particular words which are such an extremely agreeable feature, —that means that we must frequently employ new coinages or archaisms or metaphors—, and in the actual construction of the words that we must use frequent repetitions of parallels and similes and contraries and doublets and rhythmic periods not designed to resemble verse but to satisfy the ear with what may be called a suitable verbal harmony. And an even more frequent use must be made of decorative details such as surprising or unexpected events or things foreshadowed by portents and prodigies and by oracles, or what will appear to be occurrences sent by heaven or by fate to the person of whom we shall be speaking.[4]

Of the medieval rhetoricians Geoffrey de Vinsauf is most interesting to us because of his lament for Richard I. Edmond Faral considers Geoffrey's lament a kind of apostrophe and comments on its significance:

Tous sont à étudier de près. Le plus important de beaucoup est la complainte sur la mort du roi Richard, en raison du vaste champ offert par la littérature à l'application du procédé qu'il illustre. La complainte sous toutes les formes, complainte funèbre, complainte sur des infortunes diverses, ruines de villes, défaites, séparations, a été abondamment cultivée, soit isolément et pour elle-même, soit dans des ouvrages où elle n'entrait que comme élément. Or, l'apostrophe y est d'un emploi courant et, à partir du XIe siècle, en constitue une pièce de style: apostrophes aux personnes défuntes ou disparues, apostrophes à des abstractions, personnifiées, la Mort, l'Amour, la Fortune, apostrophes à des objets inanimés, la terre, un pays, une ville, une chambre, une épée, etc. C'est un fait dont les exemples se relèvent par certaines: il est intéressant d'en voir le principe formulé dans les traites d'école.[5]

[4] Cicero, *De Oratore III, De Fato, Paradoxa Stoicorum, De Partitione Oratoria*, trans. H. Rackham, Loeb ed. (London, 1942), pp. 364–65; section xxi, 71–73.
[5] Edmond Faral, *Les Arts Poetiques de XIIe et du XIIIe Siècle* (Paris, 1923), p. 72.

The "colours" of rhetoric are extremely complicated and involved. In the *Poetria Nova*, for example, Geoffrey distinguishes ten tropes, thirty-four figures of speech, and nineteen figures of thought. The scope of our study does not make feasible a discussion of various examples of embellishment in different laments for the dead according to this elaborote rhetorical terminology, and such an analysis would not be particularly helpful in defining laments for the dead as a genre. The style of a lament is largely determined by the narrative in which it appears; and since not all medieval narrative is written in the same manner, not all laments for the dead use the same stylistic devices. Alliterative romances, for example, show a marked interest in style throughout the narrative, and this is also true of laments within the narrative. Romances written in less artistic verse contain laments which are comparably less artistic. Thus it is not really possible to define a style which characterizes all laments, but simply to suggest certain qualities which do, however, appear frequently.

Perhaps the most obvious trait is exclamatory "Alas!" As was pointed out earlier, almost every lament begins with "Alas," and there are several laments which use the exclamation to control the whole movement of the passage. Thus Charles laments Oliver in *Sir Ferumbras*:

> "Alas.' Olyuer, my gude kniȝt.' for þe my herte ys cold.
> Alas.' þe tyme þou scholdest fiȝt. *with* þat Saraȝyn bold.
> Alas.' now buþ myn barou*n*s wyȝt. fro me y-take in hold.
> Alas.' þe tyme þat in mi siȝt. þis mischef falle schold."
>
> (1024–27)

Like alliterative lines, the septenary couplet with internal rhyme is a very careful verse form, so that it is necessary to distinguish the lament from the narrative. Repetition of initial "Alas!" serves admirably. Further, the poet uses the same end-rhyme for all four lines of the lament, and the internal rhymes are also the same. Thus the first, middle, and last words of each line are repetitive. Finally, he uses the phrase "þe tyme" to begin both the second and fourth lines. Neat balance and contrast between halves of the line are devices not infrequently used in septenary couplets, so that when the poet balances the two halves of the first two lines of the lament—noun-adjective: clause:: clause: noun-adjective—he is merely writing as his verse form permits. This lament for the dead, then, is embellished sufficiently to distinguish it from the main narrative, but the style remains appropriate for the basic verse form.

Similarly the poet of *Le Morte Arthure* subtly distinguishes a lament from the narrative by interlinking the stanzas. The Queen makes a general lament (3638–61), blaming herself for all the death and destruction which her love for Launcelot has produced. She praises Arthur and expresses a wish to save her soul. The poet uses a simple device of having the first line of each stanza repeat the last line of the preceding. Thus "As sone As I euyr hym gan see—" becomes "Whan I hym see, the sothe to say," and "Now hathe me sette where I wyll hold" becomes "I-sette I am In suche A place." This technique is not obtrusive, but it does show that some attempt is made to distinguish a lament from the narrative. Gwenivere is very calm and resigned when she makes the lament; thus a sprinkling of exclamations or rhetorical questions would spoil the effect which the poet wants here. The point of the lament is to make clear the Queen's resolve to enter a religious community and, moreover, to analyse carefully the situation which produced this resolve. She is both convincing and moving; the calm which comes from a reasoned decision leaves no doubt of her conviction. Dramatic gestures of the moment are avoided by avoiding stylistic embellishment.

It is often in laments in prose narrative that a lament-style may most clearly be distinguished. Thus in *Valentine and Orson* Clerimond mourns her husband:

> Alas sayde the ladye where may I become whan I haue loste my ioye, my lufe and my comforte, and myne onely hope. Alas my loue Valentyne what haue you thoughte whan you are come to dye so nere me in pouertye, and in so great myserye, wythout geuyng me ony knowledge of you. Alas I haue sene you often in pouertye, colde, and trauayle wythout geuyng you any comforte. Now am I aboue all the moost vnfortuned whan I might not know nor aduyse him that I ought to serue so longe in bytter trybulacyon, as   true and loyall spouse.
>
> (325–26)

Here there are three uses of "Alas" to begin sentences, and they distinguish an expression of grief just as in verse laments. A difference in effect comes because the presence of exclamation attracts more attention in prose than it does in verse. Similarly, balanced phrases stand out more strikingly. This lament, of course, is more carefully planned than the ones previously quoted, containing for example a series of apostrophes, such as "my ioye, my lufe and my comforte, and myne onely hope." Repetition of "my" calls attention to the series and indicates again that the lament is not quite

in the same style as the narrative. Another indication of careful
writing is the parallel syntax of a question followed by a *when*-clause.
And the device of a series is repeated twice, with the two series
linked by repetition of "pouertye."

Even when a prose narrative is written with attention to balance
and qualifying words, a lament is often made in high relief. A good
example is in *King Ponthus and the Fair Sidone* when Genelete sends
false letters to Sidone and her father telling of Ponthus' death (Anthology, pp. 159–60). The form of the lament is conventional;
again "Alas!" introduces grief. The brief passage never loses the
stylized quality with which it begins, for every phrase is paralleled
by another, and the last is slightly extended. This balancing is carried over into the narrative description of grief. Sidone's lament continues the device, for she too begins "Alas!" and praises Ponthus
by crediting him with precisely balanced qualities, intensified by repetition of "so." Her two rhetorical questions, how could God permit
such a thing to happen and what shall she do, reflect a distraught
mind. The "Allas sorowfull wreche!" with which Sidone describes
herself contrasts sharply with earlier hopes based on Ponthus' promise. There is just a sufficient heightening of emotion here to distinguish the lament from the narrative into which it fits. The writer
characteristically includes balanced phrases in the narrative, so that
this alone would not be sufficient; dramatic exclamation and question
are the ways by which he makes a lament for the dead stand out
from the main part of the story.

Unfortunately the opening leaves of the unique English manuscript
of *William of Palerne* are missing, so that one of the most elaborate
and artistic laments for the dead in medieval narrative exists only
in the French original.[6] The narrative begins when a werewolf steals
the infant William; and the Queen, who believes him to be devoured,
laments (Anthology, pp. 160–62). The predominant idea is *ubi sunt,*
and the mass of specific details of physical description is unusual.
The effectiveness of these details comes from a constant awareness
that the child's soft beauty can be devoured violently by the werewolf. This careful enumeration is far more characteristic of love
poetry, but it does not lack force here. Coupled with this rather

[6] The notes and comparisons in Skeat's edition of parallel texts indicate that no consistent pattern of the translator's method may be dis-
cerned; he sometimes followed the French original exactly, sometimes
omitted lines, other times added lines. Thus it seems permissible to consider the French version here.

unconventional aspect are traditional ideas such as reference to Fortune, the failure of the mourner to realize why he must still live, questioning why death has not come to the lamenter as well as to the lost, and general exclamations about mischance. The complexity of the lament is indicated by the resolution which the Queen provides herself. Usually someone else offers consolation, but here the mourner finds her own comfort in the thought that God would not permit the destruction of one so fair. She argues that such cruelty simply cannot be. By including a careful lament for the supposed death of William, the author of the romance succeeds in firmly establishing his hero from the outset. The belief that the werewolf will not harm the child anticipates the later benevolence of the animal who emerges as William's truest and most constant friend and protector throughout the narrative.

The style of this lament is no less striking than the ideas it expresses or its establishment of characters in the narrative. The main emphasis is on William, and this is made clear in the opening address to him, "Son, sweet love." The mother's grief of the Queen is emphasized by her concern about her infant's tender body, which she expects the werewolf to tear apart, and her mention of "tender mouth, rosy colour" introduces the idea. Similarly she asks how this could have happened and calls upon God. In these five opening lines the style is bare, for the intent is to establish ideas which are developed in the rest of the passage. Thus the "Alas!" of line 134 appropriately announces lamentation; and until line 148 when another "Alas!" indicates a shift in intention, the lament is concerned with *ubi sunt*. The distraught mother asks why she lives so long. She repeats the nominative "Son" and asks "Where are ..." calling to mind the lovely body of her son, painfully selecting details of his tender, young beauty to praise and to lament since they are believed to be destroyed now. Repetition of "thy" and "so" (more striking in French "ti" and "li") slows the passage and intensifies the feeling. With line 140 the nominative is changed to "Oh heart!" and the question about loss is repeated. This is followed by another enumeration of physical attributes. Each sentence is carefully balanced with "thy" repeated and adjectives and nouns neatly paralleled. The "Alas!" of line 143 marks another change in thought, for now the lamenter contrasts the infant's destruction with what might have been. Again exact parallels in syntax and repetition of words are stylistic devices. Next the mother cries out, "My child!"; then she begins to refute any idea that her son could be so destroyed, and she places her trust in God. Here where her analysis is more rational and emotional response has lessened, the style of the lament is less elaborate. There are still some balance and repetition, but this is no longer the most striking aspect; ideas are more important.

The three lines of narrative comment indicate, if the lament itself had not already so admirably shown, that the poet recognized a lament for the dead as a traditional form of expression. He carries over the careful balance and repetition to observe that the Queen thus "laments" for her son. Specific labelling of a passage as a lament is rare, as we saw in the *Laud Troy Book* and in Lydgate's *Troy Book*. Thus we have an additional reason for interest and for wishing that we might see how the English translator rendered the passage.

Sometimes the English version is disappointing. An illustration is Charles' lament for Roland in the *Fillingham Otuel* (Anthology, p. 162). George Ellis says in his summary that Charles "uttered many learned and tedious lamentations," and he explains with a footnote that he will not quote the lamentations which are "insufferable in the drawling stanzas of our English translator," but gives instead the French, which is not unentertaining." [7] His selection of the French lament for the dead rather than the English version suggests, if we value his judgment, the extent to which a translator can destroy rhetorical quality. Certainly the French original has stylistic richness; there is much exclamatory enthusiasm, and one epithet of praise follows another to establish the magnificence of the hero. Further, there are many comparisons with figures from the Old Testament, just as we found in Charles' lament for Roland in *Otuel and Roland* (Anthology, pp. 141–42). In short, here we have a splendor of praise which shows greater resourcefulness than we usually find both in achieving varied effects and in sustaining emotional fervor. We can but regret the loss of the English translation, and hope that the poet of *William of Palerne* was more effective at adaptation than Ellis' comments suggest.

Another English version of the Charlemagne romance offers consolation, however, for it profits enormously from the elaborate French lament in *The Fillingham Otuel*. The prose narrative *Charles the Grete* offers perhaps the most rhetorical lament for the dead in all medieval English narrative (Anthology, pp. 162–63). Although it is the style of the lament which is most interesting, the ideas expressed

[7] George Ellis, *Specimens of Early English Metrical Romances* (London, 1805), II, 353.

are not insignificant. Most important is elaborate praise, and half the lament is a series of apostrophes, many of which are almost exactly translated from the French. Roland is addressed as the most honorable of men and valiant of knights, compared to one of the Nine Worthies and to Biblical heroes, and hailed as a Christian defender. Variety of expression prevents the series from becoming tedious. Very carefully Caxton manages to change the syntax before a monotonous effect is achieved. Thus three phrases on the same pattern—"O comforte of my body, honour of frenssh men, suerd of Iustyce"—are followed by two made up of noun with independent clause—"spere that myght not bowe, hawberck that myght not be broken." Then another phrase like the opening three——"helme of helthe" introduces two principal phrases, the second of which doubles the first—"resemblyng to Iudas machabeus in prowesse, samblant to sampson in strengthe, & to Absalon in beaulte!" Next there is a nominative of address followed by adjectives of praise. Then the original pattern recurs—"O destroyer of the sarasyns . . ." and is repeated many times, but again with slight alterations, the fourth phrase having a double object and the seventh and eighth having different prepositions, "without" and "in" for "of."

Charles introduces his self-blame with "Alas!" This leads to a series of rhetorical questions when Charles demands an explanation of his own action and asks Roland directly why he has been left alone. As the lamenter grows more distressed, he twice exclaims "Alas" and asks hopelessly "What shall I do " Now his frenzy has reached its climax, and the distraught style is cast aside. Very calmly Charles finds a consolation in prayer. Here three straightforward declarative sentences explain what he will do—pray to God, angels, and martyrs. The word order of each part of the sentence is: subject, verb, object, noun clause, with one variant, a modifying clause, in the third part. The next sentence, in which Charles assures Roland that he will not be forgotten, also has parallel structure. By beginning with the adverb "alway," Caxton makes the statement more pointed; and we are again aware that a lament is more stylized expression than its narrative. Biblical comparisons here echo those which were used in the apostrophes. With a final "Alas" Charles makes clear the difference between Roland's dying into life and his own continuance in a sorrowful world. One final use of parallel sentence structure contrasts their estates. Charles concludes simply with a declarative sentence containing one transitive and one intransitive clause.

Caxton has managed very skillfully to make the manner of Charles' lament consistent with the matter. When Charles is emotionally distraught, Caxton has him speak in apostrophes and exclamations and ask rhetorical questions; when he is calmer and more rational, he speaks in straightforward sentences. Throughout there is a fine clarity; thus it is never difficult to follow either the ideas or tone of the lament. Caxton does not make the passage sheer rhetorical embellishment. Charles sounds sincere, and we are convinced of his grief as well as of his rhetorical ability when we observe an evolving attitude in a distinctive personality. Thus even the string of apostrophes, which at first seems bombastic, is not unacceptable when read as part of the whole lament; they are crucial in establishing both Roland's importance and Charles' conviction and sincerity. Here, then, we have a lament which exploits the resources of rhetoric with such literary finesse that the dangers of excess are not only avoided but turned to good effect.

In contrast, the lady in *The Squyr of Lowe Degre* is less successful. Her lament is interesting for its rhetorical play, but it lacks any real feeling. The situation is extraordinary. The daughter of the King of Hungary has believed her lover dead and preserved his body for seven years. Now she laments (Anthology, pp. 163–64) that they must be parted because the body has disintegrated into dust. She begins adequately with the traditional "Alas." The phrase "that we should parte in two!" is, however, unfortunate. Circumstances make it either revolting or bathetic, and her next comments force us to decide the latter. The lady's claim that because her lover is now in "small powder" she cannot hold him, uses specific details which cannot be managed successfully. The verse form contributes to the unfortunate effect; rhymed eight-beat lines are too swift and abrupt to give dignity to her observations. It is a relief to learn that the lady is going to bury the body and have priests read and sing. Calling the body her "treasure" is not unacceptable, but the lady's explanation that she buries it to stop thieves again offers a choice of revulsion or bathos. Thus we turn hopefully to her renunciation of "this worldes vanyté." The verse line is admirably suited for the "farewells" to riches, finery, and pleasures; and the next lines are the most satisfactory in the lament. Repetition of "farewell" fourteen times results in a standardization which removes all personal feeling, but the treatment of feeling in the opening lines has been in such bad taste, that we read this more formal utterance with relief. Actually the lines are well written and attractive. The various elements are neatly balanced, and there is enough variety in syntax to keep the passage from being tiresome, but not enough to lose an effect of pleasing monotony which suggests the lady's reaction to the things of this world. Having cast aside the velvets, pearls, and satins of the world, she will now take up the mantle and ring and become an ancress. This turn to religious ideas recalls her promise of priests when she buries the body; and following hard upon her "farewell" renunciation, it is plausible. Her vow always to remain a maiden follows naturally; and her resolution to pray to Christ for her lover's sake, having five masses offered for his soul and giving threepence in token of the Trinity in his honor each day, is an appropriate conclusion. Such systematic orthodoxy might be expected of one who laments so formally. Much of the Lady's initial insensitivity has disappeared. The long series of formalized "farewells" to the world's vanities has introduced a calmness which was needed to offset her almost grotesque involvement. Thus the Lady's rather peculiar behavior and opening unpleasant remarks have been moderated, and she gains some dignity and integrity befitting a heroine. Again we see a lament serving a crucial purpose in presenting an evolution of personality, and the style is essential to signal the change.

A series of "farewell" clauses is also the basic stylistic device for Raymond's lament when Melusine must leave to become a serpent. The poetic version in *Partenay* is almost purely rhetorical (Anthology, pp. 164–65). The first three stanzas are nothing but a series of panegyric apostrophes. Raymond bids "Adieu," calling Melusine every valuable thing that he can think of—lady, glory, pleasure, and so on. There is no particular reason for selecting specific epithets; any which will praise a lovely lady is included. Here the intention is to build up an impression of Melusine's worth, and many expressions are borrowed from love complaints. The formal quality of expression makes personal feeling unlikely. We are simply interested in the variety of conventional praise and in the skill with which epithets are placed in rime royal stanzas. As traditional lover's praise, the passage is quite successful. The use of "Adieu" is the only suggestion that Raymond is making a lament for a lost person, someone who is, in effect, dead. At line 3911, however, all doubt is removed by an exclamation of "Alas!" and the favorite question "What shall I do?" Raymond justifies his grief, blames himself for bringing about his accursed state and declares himself the saddest man alive.

The first three stanzas of Raymond's lament echo exactly the manner and matter of Melusine's parting speech (3830–60), which is four stanzas of "Adieu" to her husband, whom she praises with the same epithets which he uses for her. The appearance of two passages which are almost identical within a hundred lines of the romance, indicates that the poet was consciously embellishing. Both farewells are set-pieces which are too formal to contribute much to characterization, so that they do not function as most laments in medieval narrative do, but merely slow the narrative and artistically embroider the parting of the lovers. Thus it is not surprising that the distinctive quality of the passage is its stylistic richness. Since Melusine is a fairy the impersonality is more fitting than it might be for another person. And again the lament is in keeping with the stanza form, for rime royal is better suited to a series of repetitive epithets than the shorter couplet of *The Squyr of Lowe Degre*. A stilted lament is more acceptable in a stylized stanza than it is in freer verse or prose, and the poet writes with sufficient skill to make his embellishment an asset to the narrative. Raymond's sense of Melusine's worth and his awareness of what he has lost are made memorable in a lament which is chiefly noteworthy for its rhetorical elegance.

It is interesting to see what happens to this lament in the prose version of *Melusine*. Melusine's farewell is cut to a half dozen lines, but Raymond's is developed extensively (Anthology, pp. 165–66). The basic structure of the lament is the same as in *Partenay*, "farewells" followed by mental deliberation about the situation. It is established earlier that a lament is being made, for Raymondin's first word is "Helas." He is calmer, beginning with a statement that Melusine is lost forever and his eternal sorrow is beginning. Next there is rhetorical embellishment. The change from "Adieu" to "Farewell" is a wise one, for it lessens slightly the self-consciousness of what is being said; and since nineteen lines have been reduced to four, greater attention is paid to what is being said. The loss in cumulative effect is made up by sharpness of focus. Here, as in the verse stanzas, a respectable list of traditional aspects is included. Raymondin's praise is intensified, however, because he gives an explanation for it when he credits all the honor which God has given him to his wife's goodness. Then he turns to an accusation of Fortune in which he vividly describes the goddess's method and blames her for making him slay his uncle. "Alas," he continues, Fortune gave him honor and position through his lady and now has taken all away. He curses Fortune's changeability. Then with another outburst of "Alas," Raymondin blames himself; his treason in betraying Melusine is greater because his wife had cleansed him of his first error and guilt in tragically killing his uncle. Exile is all that remains to him.

There are, then, two basic ideas in Raymondin's lament, farewell to his wife and an analysis of Fortune. The idea of Fortune underlies the whole narrative (at the end, for example, the people cry out against Fortune in making their final praise of the lady); thus it is not inappropriate for this idea to be more fully developed than a conventional farewell. The result is one of the most detailed analyses of Fortune in medieval narrative, and a lament which has marked stylistic worth. The devices of repeating "Farewell" and varying epithets, which are balanced in quality, are commonplace. What the author does to make his analysis of Fortune vivid is more striking and difficult. He punctuates his description with "Ha, a" and "alas," so that we never lose a feeling that Raymondin is emotionally involved; and these exclamations slow the analysis sufficiently at crucial points to make us assimilate what has been said. Ordinary matter is cleverly combined with original touches, so that although Fortune is called "falsed and blynd," she is also "aigre, sharp, & byttir." The value of contrast between the top of Fortune's wheel and the depth of her mansion is not missed. A neat balance and parallelism are maintained in the middle of the lament by using pairs—of adjectives, nouns, and verbs—sharpening each comment with extra description and unifying the passage by repeating syntactical constructions. This technique reaches its culmination in the sentences "thous now hatest/ thou now louest, thou now makest/ thou now vndost/" where balanced repetition is used in clauses which accurately describe Fortune's changes, not only through the meaning of the words, but also by the rhythm of the line which, like Fortune's wheel, rocks back and forth. The phrase "no more surety ne rest" continues the manner, and the metaphor of a vane turning in the wind completes the effect. Raymondin's shift from Fortune to his lost love is indicated by "Helas/helas!" which introduces his self-accusation. Even here his manner is not absolutely straightforward, for in addition to using a double nominative, he goes on in a second statement to alter the normal word order by beginning with the adverb "yl," and the first "now" of the final sentence is similarly placed. These final lines, however, are not heavily laden with particular embellishments. Raymondin calmly and directly pronounces sentence on himself. There is, then, a marked distinction between the three parts of the lament which is as clear from the style as from the ideas. Formal rhetorical

flourishes for the initial outburst are followed by balanced phrases
for the reasoned analysis, which leads to a simple statement of the
conclusion. Here, then, is a lament which combines excellence of
style with individuality of ideas, and the speaker of the lament becomes vitally alive—he is a man capable of experiencing and expressing a range of emotion. The style is sufficiently distinctive to
be a focus of attention; but as in all good laments for the dead,
it is inextricably related to the ideas and purpose of the lament.

Alliterative verse might be expected to contain laments with the
most impressive elements of style, and a fine example is Arthur's
lament for Gawain in *Morte Arthure* (Anthology, pp. 166–67). The
basic device of two alliterative staves in the first half-line and one
in the second half-line is maintained. There is no attempt to distinguish the first part of the lament from the narrative. Arthur begins
with a simple nominative, addressing Gawain and describing the grief
which his death has produced. He praises Gawain lavishly, declaring
that he was worthy to be king. The first quality and the muted
emotional effect of the lines make Arthur's sincerity unquestionable.
Thus the failure to begin with traditional "Alas" is, in fact, part
of the design. Arthur speaks directly to Gawain and the lament gains
immediacy which is emphasized by the "k" sounds which suggest a
gasping effort even to begin to speak of so great a loss. This is
followed by elaborate praise which makes explicit Gawain's significance to Arthur. Much of the alliteration uses "w" sounds, and these
provide a keening. A second phase begins with Arthur's exclamatory
"Alas!" Now there is a heightening of emotion, which is indicated
by a series of ejaculations, climaxed by a rhetorical question, with
Arthur's despair and wish for death. Six lines of narrative describe
the king's swoon, quick rising, and kissing the body; and they have
a quality very like that of the lament, for the "s" alliteration suggests
the physical collapse which modulates into vigorous action and se-
vere stress. Arthur's men offer a blunt consolation; they are vehement
when they tell him that his grief is of no avail. An extra alliterative
stave in the line "*th*is es *b*otles *b*ale, for *b*ettir *b*ees it neu*er*!" emphasizes the heaviness which b-alliterative rhymes convey. They accuse
Arthur of acting as a woman and ask him to conduct himself in
knightly fashion, to behave as a king. An appeal for Christ's love
is made as a final emphasis. Such abrupt attempts at consolation
serve only to intensify Arthur's analysis, for he replies that he cannot
be happy again because his sin produced Gawain's death. Four of
six lines have "s" alliterative rhymes, and the sound is carefully

chosen to convey an impression of sorrow, the sighing which is part of an expression of grief. Each line has an additional stave, slowing the pace and increasing this feeling of sorrow, but signalling an acceptance of the death that goes beyond the initial shock and emotional violence.

Arthur kneels and calls upon God to witness his sorrow, and he asserts Gawain's innocence from sin. Repetition of "Down knelis þe kynge" not only indicates the dramatic action but also emphasizes Arthur's growing acceptance of the situation. He preserves the slain knight's heart and makes his vow to Christ and Mary for revenge. Until Gawain's death is avenged, Arthur will forswear his customary pattern of life; he will not enjoy the pleasures of the hunt, or reign, or hold his Round Table; he will resignedly accept God's will. The alliteration in the lines of rejection of worldly activity is strong and vital, like the activities described. In the last lines "d" alliterative staves contribute to a somber tone which conveys a properly mournful manner, one of controlled passion.

This lament is successful, for its range of ideas is wide, and the lines hold together very well. Standard devices of alliterative verse are all that are necessary to make Arthur's lament potent, and the appropriateness of the consonantal sounds is particularly noteworthy. A few other techniques are used—a nominative of address, a single "Alas," an occasional change in the number of alliterative staves and an occasional repetition of the same alliterative rhyme in four lines together. The style here is different from what we find in prose romances where balance and repetition and exclamations are plentiful in laments, but the effect of measured control is the same. We are aware of ideas fitted into a scheme which makes them vivid and of characters who, at least on occasions of death when they are mourners, become more real as participants in a vital dramatic scene. The alternation of narrative description with direct speech clearly indicates action; we have a firm sense of what is happening. We know precisely how Arthur looks, how his movements and expressions mirror his changing attitudes. And he is not alone, for the introduction of other knights and the words of Sir Ewayne add variety to the texture of the scene. Clearly delineated personalities are seen in direct conflict, and the effect of challenging circumstance in altering points of view is clear. The pressure of confronting the experience of Gawain's death forces Arthur into a more precise definition of attitude which leads to an advance in the action, and the narrative writer creates a scene which is memorable because it reveals this tension. A heightened awareness of style reflects such concern and indeed is crucial in expressing it.

Elements of style are important, then, to the tradition of laments for the dead. They signal immediately and obviously that such a formal kind of expression is occurring. The writer of medieval narrative is allowed to embellish his story, to heighten his ordinary style. Thus the style indicates that something unusual, something which warrants special attention and careful treatment, is occurring; and we are led to an explicit recognition of the basic and universal condition of man in confronting death. Theories and manuals of composition provide ample evidence that laments for the dead constitute a genre which was recognized and about which general rules existed. There are some conventional expressions, such as "Alas, that I was born, "Farewell," "What shall I do?" and various epithets of praise. However, elements of style in laments for the dead are not stereotyped; characteristically they are rhetorically an intensification of the general manner of the narrative in whatever the individual style may be. Frequently they are used to indicate precisely the logic of argument within a lament and the evolving emotional pattern. Occasionally a lament has a style that is so repetitive or flamboyant that we lose all sense of argument and situation—or we sense that the narrative writer lacks total control and relies upon flourishes to disguise his inadequacy. The most successful laments for the dead are those in which elements of style are indeed memorably present, but so neatly poised that they serve to clarify and enrich an idea, to add vitality to a dramatic scene. In short, the style, the manner, serves the idea and action rather than obscures and falsifies it. Careful analysis can define and explain how such elements of style function, so that we are startled by the precision of detail which contributes to a significant lament. So perfectly marked an occasion of death scarcely allows us to note the meticulous design, and the narrative writer's literary finesse prevails. Laments are thus a kind of growing point for stylistic awareness in the medieval romances.

Chapter V

DRAMATIC ELEMENTS IN LAMENTS
FOR THE DEAD

Perhaps the most interesting and significant characteristic of laments for the dead in medieval narrative is the use of a lament in creating a dramatic situation. Medieval narratives are largely impersonal, so that characters are usually related only by their presence in the same series of adventures. However, this pattern is changed frequently when there is a pause in the action to mourn someone who is dead or is believed to be dead. Then the writer makes his characters a little more than conventional figures; he has them display feeling and think about the implications of a situation. A lament forms a nucleus around which a scene is built up, a situation in which there is interplay of characters and a quality of drama. Such scenes are among the most memorable in medieval narrative, and they stand out boldly, providing illustration of literary skill and offering examples to the incipient dramatist of the early Renaissance. In these passages we recognize genuine sophistication, for the writer of medieval narrative is evolving a more complex artistic awareness. Just as in painting, we observe a development from a flat surface into one which has levels of representation. In laments that are dramatic we no longer have a simple statement of several ideas, or evidence of careful style, but an awareness of the complexity of human behavior when individuals are caught in demanding circumstances. Thus the narrative writer answers the challenge of the literary process of creation; he works from a basic and real experience, death, to an expression that is art.

Challenges and some cries for revenge provide the most rudimentary dramatic situations, for one character confronts another directly, and there is at least a brief flash of feeling between them. Usually the mourner shouts defiantly three or four lines, kills the slayer, or rides off to find revenge. This basic idea is expanded in the *Buik of Alexander,* when Porrus slays Cassamus and says:

"Here mon thow duell, thow hare auld gray,
And keip this land quhill domisday!

101

Althocht thow hes my father slane,
And thow thairfore hes tholed sic pane,
I the forgeue for euermare,
Thow sall be blamed neuer are
To ioys lufe of lady fre,
Na lede maydin maryit to be!"

(IV, 10243–50)

There is no hearty exultation in accomplishing revenge. Porrus com-
mits Cassamus to the earth, not with a jocular comment but with
a sincerity of religious conviction. He justifies his revenge but simultaneously forgives Cassamus, who will no longer have either sorrow
or pleasure of this world, for killing his father. This lament, then,
gives a deeper insight into a character's attitude than we usually
find. Had Porrus bellowed defiance, he would have been more typical
of romance. The lament serves also as part of the idea of reconciliation between enemies which is peculiar to this section of narrative.
A distinct effort is being made to stop fighting, and Porrus' calmness
and forgiveness of his enemy set a new attitude which carries over
to others in the narrative. The dramatic use of a lament provides
the author with an opportunity for some literary virtuosity.

When Sir Berill is killed in *Morte Arthure* there is a real interplay
of characters. Berill's cousin Cador embraces his body and kisses
him.

Thane laughes the Lebe kyng*e*   and all on lowde meles:
"ȝone lorde es lyghttede,   me lykes the bettyre!
He sall noghte dere vs to-daye.   the deuyll haue [his] bones!"
    "ȝone kyng*e*," said Cador,   "karpes full large,
Because he killyd þis kene;   Criste hafe þi saule!
He sall hafe corne-bote,   so me Criste helpe!
Or I kaire of þis coste,   we sall encontre ones;
So may þe wynde weile tur*n*ne,   I *rewarde* hym or ewyn,
Sothely hym selfen   or sum*m* of his ferez."

(1781–89)

The slayer Lebe exults—in a loud voice—over his victim and recommends his enemy's bones to the devil. In indignation about this comment—which he clearly overhears—Cador objects to vain boasting.
He recommends the soul to Christ and vows revenge. Clearly Cador
and Lebe are both aware of what the other is doing. Voices are
raised, so that boasts will be overheard, and a distinct scene comes

alive. Two valiant knights insult each other in an obvious way. Neither speaks directly to his antagonist, but both make certain that what they boast will be known. The device is like speaking in stage whispers. Individuals reveal very distinctive self-consciousness, for they are concerned with vocal tones and carefully choose their words to produce precise effects. Here, then, is an explicit interplay of personalities. Thus the scene offers an illustration of a technique and a point of view which are popular in Elizabethan drama.

Other kinds of dramatic heightening are provided by messengers. For example, in *Arthur of Little Britain* Emendus laments his faithful friend the King of Mormal (Anthology, p. 167). He commences conventionally with cries of "Alas," praise, moral judgment against the Emperor who slew him, and a wish for death. He is, however, interrupted by a messenger who tells of the Emperor's death. Questioning leads to an explanation that the Emperor died of grief for so many slain and of an old back injury. Emendus concludes that his revenge is accomplished and he does not continue his lament except to say that he would gladly trade the lives of the Emperor and all his followers for the life of his friend the King of Mormal. Thus, as in a drama, a messenger's report stops the action and also gives additional information which makes it unnecessary for the immediate action to continue.

More interesting is a use of a messenger in *Richard Couer de Lion* to announce the death of Wardrewe, son of the King of Germany. The death scene has already filled part of the narrative (740–98); here we are told simply that a knight reports how Richard slew Wardrewe (Anthology, pp. 168–69). Then the King of Germany begins his lament with a conventional "Alas, now haue i non," but swoons before he is able to comment further. His knights try to console him by saying that grief is of no avail. The King asks how his son died, but the knights hesitate, and the Queen has time to come in. Here the writer uses a device of having one character not know what has happened. We and everyone in the scene except the Queen know that Wardrewe is dead. She asks innocently the reason for their grief, and her husband questions sharply whether she knows that their son is dead. Obviously she cannot know, but this quick rhetorical question introduces the King's lament, where he declares how sorrowful he is and that he would like to kill himself. Slowly the Queen realizes that Wardrewe is dead; and in fitting romance-fashion, she almost goes mad, tearing her clothes and hair and posing the futile question, "What shall j do!" Her physical flagellation continues and then, like the King, she asks, "Jn what man*ere* is my sone jlorn?" Then the King says that he was told by the knight beside him, and he orders a retelling of what happened. The knight has Richard's jailor tell what he saw. Thus the episode is repeated (845–70) with heightened effectiveness.

Here, in contrast to the scene in *Arthur of Little Britain,* a messenger is used not to stop the action but to build it up. What interests the writer is not so much the death of Wardrewe or his parents' grief, but the way in which Richard killed him—with a single blow on the cheek. This feat demonstrates Richard's prowess; and since the point of the narrative is to make Richard a hero, the writer wants to repeat it. Thus the lamentations are simply an introduction to a second account of the episode, but they are done skillfully so that repetition will not be tedious. The result is a neat dramatic scene in which there is an element of surprise and careful interplay of characters, as well as a strengthening of the central character.

A messenger is also used in the *Foure Sonnes of Aymon* to announce the death of Charles' son Lohier (Anthology, pp. 169–70). Charles has dreamed that Duke Benes of Aygremount killed Lohier, and while Duke Naymes is trying to convince him that he should not believe his dreams, a messenger comes to say that Lohier is dead. Charles falls to the ground in grief. Tearing his hair and beard, he humbly beseeches God to give him death to end his sorrow. Here, more than in any other sequence, Charles commands our sympathy. He is not a vain king who sorrows at loss of his peers because he needs them to increase his honor, but a father who has lost his son. Naymes tries to comfort Charles. He encourages him to think of his people's grief over their losses, to prepare a noble burial for Lohier, and to make ready to revenge himself on Benes. Charles is sobered and proceeds to do as Naymes has suggested. On the way from Paris, they meet Lohier's bier, and Charles cries "Alas" for his shame. He dismounts and looks at his son's dismembered body, declaring that he will go mad with grief and must seek revenge against Benes. He embraces the bloody corpse, addressing his "fayre sone" with praise and recommending his soul to paradise.

The simplicity of exposition is effective. Charles' first reaction is to pray to God in his sorrow and to wish for death. Then the question of honor is raised, and this leads to thoughts of revenge. When Charles sees Lohier's body, however, he moves quickly to high praise of his son and utters a prayer to God for his soul. The calmness of this final prayer contrasts sharply with Charles' initial desperateness, and it indicates that he has found consolation. A lack of concentration here does not permit fine eloquence like that we saw in Charles' lament for Roland. Slow movement adds to an effect of serenity, but it destroys immediacy. Frequently there is an elaborate introduction which heightens interest and tension, so that a few lines of lamentation may achieve a striking effect. Here the ideas of lamentation are more than adequate, but they are spread too thinly to produce a fine dramatic scene. The interval between the messenger's appearance and Charles' final lament over Lohier's body, is too great. Preparations for departure and beginning the journey distract our attention. There is, then, a good basis for a dramatic scene, but it is realized only in parts. Had the bier reached Charles just after the messenger, there would have been greater unity. As it is, we have to piece together the parts of his lamentation, and we do not have a fully realized dramatic sequence.

Not infrequently a writer of medieval narrative introduces a lament for the dead with elaborate detail, preparing carefully for a character to dominate a scene when he mourns his dead friend or relative or lover. One example occurs early in the narrative and is the only lament in *Ywaine and Gawain* (Anthology, pp. 170-71). The writer has made an effort to create a dramatic scene for the lady to mourn her husband, and we have a specific description of a funeral procession—the lady weeping and wringing her hands, the cross and holy water which are carried by a group of mourners, and a knight in full armour riding beside the body. Having thus established a scene visually, the writer goes on to an aural impression by having Ywaine hear the lamentations, the lady's sad cries and the priest's solemn prayers. Intrigued by what he has heard, Ywaine prevails upon the lady's maid Lunet to let him see the lady from a window. And thus he hears her lament, which is conveniently "lowd." The lament itself is disappointing; the ideas are commonplace (prayers for the dead knight's soul and praise), and there is no stylistic device to embellish. Having so clearly drawn his scene, the writer seems to have been content with rather weak dialogue. What is significant is that there is a sense of the dramatic, a skill in the conception of a scene with vital interplay of characters. The conventional utterances of the lament itself are rather stiffly formalized, but the author of *Ywaine and Gawain* has recognized that a scene of death is a good nucleus for dramatic action, which he creates about the traditional utterance. It is regrettable that he cannot write a lament which within itself has dramatic impact equal to the scene he has created.

A similar criticism can be made of the lament in *Le Bone Florence* (Anthology, pp. 171–72), but the total effect is much more impressive. There is perhaps no more effective introduction of a lament for the dead in medieval narrative. In an attempt to keep both the Emperor's enemies and his daughter from knowing of his death, the body of Florence's father is brought into the city quietly and without many followers. Once inside the city the people raise a standard and banners. The Romans vow revenge against Garcy, who has precipitated the tragedy by seeking to wed Florence, actually killed Emperor Otes in combat, and now is getting ready to lay siege to the city. Florence's maidens tell her that mourners are bringing a bier into the city, but that all is still. Florence looks out and says that she does see men bringing a bier and is sorry. Then as she watches, she recognizes her father's horse Bondynowre, which is being led by a knight. With this recognition Florence begins to realize what has happened, and her suspicion sweeps across all those assembled. She goes alone with Awdygon into the great hall. Without fear she walks to the bier, lifts the cloth, and swoons, so that none can raise her. The writer shows admirable restraint here. He could, for example, have added details about the anxiety of the Emperor's men as they watched Florence approach her father's body, or he might have described the distress of the maidens. Instead with fine clarity and succinctness he gives in a single stanza enough detail to suggest vividly the quick shift of scene from Florence's chamber to the hall, from her first suspicion through verification to immediate collapse.

Florence recovers to lament, "Allas, that y was borne!" She immediately blames herself for causing the Emperor's death and says that she will have to submit to the will of Garcy, a one-hundred-year-old suitor whom she had previously refused and thus brought about the war. Rather than continue Florence's lamentation, the writer returns to a narrative description from which it is clear that she is beside herself. The bystanders fear she will resort to suicide, and there is great wringing of hands. Nobles of the court manage nothing more by way of lamentation than "Allas" and a selfish question about who will provide them with lands and horses and hawks and hounds for the hunt now that the Emperor Otes is dead. This is an unfortunate conclusion, but it does not destroy the fine scene of Florence's recognition and mourning. A helpless woman, Florence, who merely notes that all is lost, gains by contrast with these men who should be virile enough to maintain themselves and manage instead only to lament the loss of their pleasures without any hint of grief at losing a person like the Emperor.

The elaborate descriptive details and the care with which they are introduced, coupled with the brevity of the lament itself, suggest that the author is trying to handle a death scene significantly. He does not rely upon, indeed he rejects, a long and conventional expression of grief by the mourner. Instead he uses his narrative skill to describe the physical situation and emotional states of those present; and he writes dialogue that is pointed and succinct, embellished by no more than the stock phrase "Allas, that y was borne!" There is an attempt, with some success, to fit dialogue and setting in a subtle relationship, and thus we have a scene which is convincing and compelling.

In *Guy of Warwick* not only is the principal mourner unaware that he has reason to lament, but also the slayer does not know the identity of the person he has killed. In a fit of rage Guy killed the Earl of Florentin's son because of a youthful insult made during a hunt. By chance and unknowingly he wandered into the Earl's castle and received his hospitality. Then they hear the town's bells announce a death, and sounds of mourning follow (Anthology, pp. 172–75). The unsuspecting Earl asks the cause of sorrow. Two men carry a body into the hall and lay it on the floor, and the Earl of Florentin slowly recognizes his son. His first comment, "mi sone þis is," indicates an attempt to realize that his son is dead. A conventional reaction follows: the Earl wants revenge, and he wishes that his son's slayer were within his grasp. And in this narrative, of course, this is not a fond wish, for Guy stands beside the Earl. Here we have one of the most striking dramatic situations in medieval narrative. Guy says nothing, but waits tensely. Then one of the few nobles who survived Guy's wrathful slaughter recognizes the man who slew their young master and companions. A fight ensues. Guy kills many more, but he himself is spared by a plea of hospitality, which the Earl cannot refuse. To have his men slay Guy in the hall would be a violation of courtesy and a forfeiture of his honor. He is forced to let Guy, who has slain many of his nobles and his only son and heir, leave unharmed. Thus the old man is left alone amid the destruction in his hall, and he is a very pathetic and sympathetic figure when he makes a final lament. His plaintive "What shall I do?" cannot fail to move us, for without his son his life is over. There is no one else who can succeed to rule his land, and his wish for death seems fully justified; its fulfilment is the Earl's only possible happiness. There is no violent emotion here, no protest against hard fortune, no selfish anxiety about his future; the Earl of Florentin simply and sadly recognizes his age and hopeless position; thus he is reduced to despair and falls over the body of his son in a final symbolic gesture of helplessness.

This scene is skillfully presented, and it is not insignificant in the narrative. In perhaps no other episode is Guy less sympathetically portrayed, for his wholesale slaughter is hardly justified. His only touch of generosity is at the end of the pursuit—the Earl follows him in an attempt to revenge his son—when he spares the helpless old man, although he kills still more of his attendants. The combination of a careless remark of youth and the pain of an old man's loss is one which should not lead to such destruction even from a hero who cannot accept a taunt without violence. The balance of sympathy falls from Guy, who, when he has to plead hospitality to save his life, loses even his position of invincible hero. Possibly it is situations like this one which lead to Guy's renunciation of his bold adventurous life later on. Thus the author is using a scene of lamentation to suggest complexity in the attitudes and experience of his hero. He shows his hero's explicit failings, and the transiency of earthly attainment is seen in the rapid and total loss suffered by the Earl of Florentin. Further, it is the Earl who is presented with a dilemma; honor demands that he revenge his son's death, but it also demands that he not violate the tradition of hospitality. Few characters of romance are given a choice so dramatic, and the scene in the Earl's hall might readily be transferred from the narrative into a play.

An interesting lament occurs in *The Knight of Curtesy and the Fair Lady of Faguell* in one banquet scene (Anthology, p. 175). The Lady's jealous husband, believing an enemy's report, sent the Knight of Curtesy out to seek adventures. He fought bravely, slaying a dragon and many Saracens, but was mortally wounded in a battle at Rodes. Dying, he asked his page to wrap his heart in the lady's yellow hair, which she gave him to wear on his helm when he left, and bring it to her. The husband intercepted the Knight of Curtesy's heart, had his cook prepare it, and gave it to the Lady to eat. Then he explains what he has done. His consolation, "Madame, at the last we all must dye," is scarcely a comfort under the circumstances, but ironically it offers a solution to his wife. When she discovers the horror in which she has unwittingly been a participant, the Lady is stricken with grief—particularly since her love for the knight was chaste and of the most honorable nature, limited to heart and mind. With conventional exclamations of "Alas," she declares that she can live no longer. She retires to her chamber, confesses, and receives the Sacrament. Her lament is continued from her bed, where she lies mourning and waiting for death. Again she begins "Allas," addressing her lover with whose death her joy has gone. She explains that she will carry out her wish for death in a fitting, symbolic manner. She has eaten the heart of her lover, and that meat is the last she will ever eat. Upon it she has received the bread and wine of the Sacrament, and these will be her last nourishment. She will refuse all earthly food. Finally, she accuses her husband of cruelty, asking why he has done this thing and blaming him for her death as well as the Knight's. The last line is as ironically pointed as her husband's consolation, "The hie god graunte to you your mede!"

We cannot fail to recognize the dramatic sense of a poet who has made this scene the climax of his narrative. He manages deftly, without lapsing into excesses of expression which would be cloying on top of the horror which is central to the situation, to make his characters tenable. The husband functions throughout the story simply as a mainspring to start the action. The Lady and Knight command our interest by the unusual nature of their love. Earlier in his death scene the Knight was given an opportunity for a noble conclusion. Here the Lady does not fail to rise to the occasion of her last scene. She has a fine restraint, moving calmly and surely to a splendid end. There is no hesitation in her action; she knows what she should do, and she never falters. Her primary concern is for her lost love and her own soul, and her jealous husband receives no notice until her last words. Then her character has been so cleanly delineated that we cannot read the last quatrain as a shrewish accusation and ill-wish. Just as she calmly but firmly followed the only course of action which she felt was open to her, she calmly but firmly defines her attitude toward her husband. It is unnecessary to consider the implicit contradiction between her wilful suicide and receiving of the last Sacrament, for the theological considerations are not what interests the poet. He wants a dramatic conclusion to his narrative, and the Lady's death does not disappoint us or fail to make his didactic point.

A situation which lends itself readily to dramatic interplay is that in which there are differing opinions. A good example is in *Firumbras* after the death of Lucafer when there is much shifting of blame (Anthology, p. 176). This is inevitable because Lucafer was killed in his attack on the tower in which Roland and his men have been given shelter by Floripas, the Saracen leader's daughter. Balam is grieved and begins to lament, saying "Allas, that I was born!" He sorrows because a good counsellor is lost. Sokebrond does not spare Balam in his reply, accusing him of acting foolishly, casting his will and heart at his "taylend." Curiously, Balam, who is very hot-tempered, is not angered by his subordinate's charge, but admits his fault in trusting a woman, his daughter Floripas, and alters his sentiment to "Allas, that ever she was born!" He vows that within forty days he will be completely revenged. This heartens Sokebrond, who advises, however, that the first attack be delayed until the next day when more Saracen forces may be assembled. Balam agrees and, having thus planned his revenge, he returns to his lament. With another flurry of "Allas," Balam grieves for Lucafer, his best guardian, who has been lost through the incompetence of others; and again the pivotal phrase which holds the scene together is altered, "Allas, the wyle that eu*er* they were bore." Balam vows to Mahoun that he will never leave this field of battle until his revenge is accomplished, that is until the opponent knights have suffered foul deaths and Floripas has been burned. Sokebrond echoes the vow to Mahoun and adds that Balam's plan will be carried out through his own chivalry. The lament serves in the narrative a primary function of explaining the situation and of preparing for the long siege that follows, as well as being an acceptable tribute to Lucafer.

Moreover, the scene of lamentation gives some insight into characters. Balam's grief at losing Lucafer momentarily softens his ire and violence; he is even just enough to accept Sokebrond's judgment. The result is an impression that the Saracen leader is a man with some sensitivity and justice. This early association of good qualities makes the later Balam, who is almost insane with anger and frustration, more contemptible because he destroys himself through violent passion. Similarly, the impression we have of Sokebrond is helpful; he is very just, daring as readily to accuse the Sultan when he believes him wrong as to rally to him when he commands as a leader should. Sokebrond's role of rational adviser, who calms and soothes, is thus established early in the narrative. The scene of lamentation is like an early scene in a drama, for it not only sets out the main facts of the story, but it also establishes precisely one character (Sokebrond) and gives hints about another (Balam). Sokebrond is consistently a sane counsellor. Balam's outbursts are only a small indication of his potential chaos, and Sokebrond's accusation that Balam's wits are in his "taylend" (harsh comment for anyone, let alone a king) warns us that he is not a character of discretion, as is subsequently made clear.

The scene is very tightly unified through repetition of the phrase "Allas, that I was born" (with variations); and this exclamation focuses attention on Balam, who not only is grieved by the loss of a valuable and loyal follower and the betrayal of a beloved daughter, but also is concerned about the way in which he must react to gain revenge and maintain his dignity as leader. There is always some tension between a commander and his lieutenant, and the interplay between Balam and Sokebrond gains intensity by taking place at a moment of heightened emotion, at a scene in which the death of an esteemed peer through betrayal by a loved one is accepted. Thus Lucafer's death is not simply commemorated; it provides an opportunity for the Saracen leaders to assess their situation and strength before continuing the battle, and we are presented with a memorably dramatic scene which prepares us for the explosive conclusion of the narrative.

An assembly of several characters to make a lament does not always produce a dramatically effective scene. In the *Foure Sonnes of Aymon* there is a fine opportunity; the surviving brothers lament over the body of Reynard, who has always been their leader, and whose death has produced a miracle (Anthology, pp. 176–77). There is, however, a certain lack of interest and vitality which results from a paucity of ideas. Alarde begins, "Alas, what shall we do?" This idea, which recalls laments of Charlemagne, is not one which wins our sympathy when the mourners are knights. Like other Charlemagne romances, the *Foure Sonnes of Aymon* has a lament in which the mourners are more concerned for themselves than for the person lost. Grief usually has some of this quality, but it is seldom more pronounced. Here Alarde suggests that much of his concern is over a loss, not of his brother as a person, but as the guardian of their strength and prestige. He queries who dared to slay his brother, for certainly no one who really knew him would have done so. Alarde continues, telling his brothers that it is right that they all be sorry for the loss of Reynard, who was all their "hope, trust, and comfort"—again stock epithets of praise. At this point, Richard begins with a rhetorical question to Reynard, "why had ye euer that courage for to habandoune vs as ye dyde/." There is no doubt that Reynard loved them, and yet he stole away at night to go among murderers who slew him. Richard repeats Alarde's sentiment that none who knew Reynard would have killed him, and certainly they could not have realized how much sorrow his death would cause. The lament is broken while the brothers weep, kiss the body, and swoon. Then Richard speaks again, saying "Alas" for the brethren who are now lost forever. And it is here that his ideas most definitely echo those of Charlemagne, for his first concern is that the sons of Aymon have lost honor, that they will command no more respect and fear than children. Thus he counsels suicide, for the three brothers ought not to live after the death of the fourth. This wish for death produces more contempt than sympathy, for it comes not from grief over the loss of a loved one, but from fear of going on without him. Within the twenty lines of this lament, then, there is some alternation of feeling. Alarde only hints at a selfish anxiety about how those yet living can go on, so that his comments might be regarded simply as expressions of distress and grief and praise. Even the "our hope, our trust, & comfort" phrase may be taken without question because it is so traditional; it is not necessary to realize how pointed these apostrophes are. Similarly Richard begins rather innocuously; his observations on Reynard's leaving may be taken merely as outbursts of grief. In light of his conclusion, however, they are, if not actually bitter recriminations, at least suggestively so. The balance of feeling is precarious; this lament wavers between genuine unselfish expressions of grief where concern is for the desolation of a life without the loved one and blatant, self-pitying distress where the loss of prestige is the principal cause for anxiety.

As a dramatic scene the mourning for Reynard is more a failure, with tantalizing hints at its unrealized possibilities, than a success. Throughout the narrative it is Reynard who dominates; he has energy and courage to make decisions and to act. His brothers tend simply to follow, so that their feeling of hopelessness and despair, if unpleasing and even contemptible, is not inconsistent. Earlier when Reynard left to become a hermit (574), Alarde and Richard made a similar lament with many exclamations of "Allas" and swoons, saying that it would have been better for Reynard, from whom all their honor and strength came, to slay them than to leave them alone. We cannot fail to recognize Reynard's worth, but we are sorry that his brothers could not have been more like him. At least one might have managed more than a whining sentiment. Even the narrator's judgment that observers would have wept to see the brothers' grief, suggests the limited achievement of the scene as it is written. Thus we have a scene of lamentation in wihch there is a recognition of a desired effect, and the possibility of achieving it, but there is no skillful handling of the available material.

There are two other laments in which a relationship of brothers is important, and both are more effective dramatically than the one above. Curiously, both turn on an unwitting slaying in battle. In *Ipomedon* Dreas kills his brother Candor, whom he did not recognize until after the fatal blow (Anthology, pp. 177–78). He cries out "Alas" for his woe and begs his brother to forgive him before he dies. Candor dies, and Dreas is mad with grief. He tears his hair and grasps his sword with an intention to kill himself, but he is stopped by Ipomedon. Dreas explains what he has done and thus how he has been led to violence. Ipomedon offers the consolation that it is better that one be dead than two. He tells Dreas to remount and to pray for his brother's soul. The basic ideas—grief, a wish for death, and religious consolation—are commonplace, but they are handled interestingly. Too often a character merely wishes that he were dead, so that we become inclined to accept the sentiment as a rhetorical flourish. Here Dreas actively tries to kill himself. The scene is well planned. Amid the chaos of battle Dreas realizes that he has killed his brother. In his remorse he forgets his duty as a knight and is preparing to kill himself. Dreas' commander Ipomedon rides up just in time to stop the self-slaughter by knocking his sword aside, exclaiming "Benedycyte!" This sobers Dreas, and Ipomedon's consolation is sufficient to make burial possible. It is a pity that Ipomedon's solution is made so facilely, for we lose the rich development which might have been possible in the scene. We are, however, impressed by Ipomedon's command, which cuts short a passionate expression of grief; and we remember a scene of notable warmth and intensity.

There is an almost identical situation, with consequent similarity of ideas, in *Valentine and Orson.* Failing to realize that Valentine is wearing the King of Inde's armor, the Emperor of Greece, who like all his force is disguised as a paynim, attacks his son. Valentine thus unwittingly slays his father and laments appropriately (Anthology, pp. 178–79). The idea that a son who slays his father is a most cursed creature is not unfamiliar, as we noted earlier in Blanchardyn's lament. Here having two brothers heightens the dramatic situation, for it is Orson, who, fighting on the side of the Emperor of Greece, recognizes Valentine and stops the battle, revealing that his brother has slain his father. Reynard and Myllon try to comfort Valentine, but he begins by declaring himself cursed and immediately wishing for death. He blames himself without mercy, believing himself to be unworthy to be sustained by the earth and nourished by the elements, because he has killed his father. This detail of natural phenomenon is appropriate because it is the "unnaturalness" of Valentine's killing which makes it so abominable. He laments the hour in which he was born to commit such a detestable deed. All previous hardships—and Valentine has had a fair share—seem trivial when compared with this. He curses the shield which created the deception. Unable to sustain himself any longer, Valentine turns to Orson and offers his sword, begging his brother to slay him as he slew their father. He asks that his head be cut off—an added indignity and another example of a single detail of physical violence heightening the feeling of a lament—repeating his avowal that he is unworthy to live on and should not be counted a knight.

All of this puts Orson in a tense position, and he replies with a perfect Christian attitude. He offers his distraught brother consolation, counselling him to avoid despair and trust in God, Who is mighty enough to pardon a sin far greater than this. Valentine should do penance, for whem soneone is dead there is no remedy. Prayers are better than excessive lamentation. Here greater length allows for a fuller development of ideas of grief, self-blame, a wish for death, and consolation in penance and prayer, than was possible in *Ipomedon*. Also, having the three principal characters—the dead man, his slayer and mourner, and the consoler—all closely related members of the same family heightens and intensifies.

The basic situation is the same that we found in *Ipomedon*, but it is handled with more imagination and perception. Ipomedon is too remotely involved in the slaying; he is the outsider who is brought in to pronounce a calm solution. In *Valentine and Orson* Reynard and Myllon serve this function. They offer a consolation, but the real play of feeling is that between Orson and Valentine. The writer has a fine touch when he makes Orson recognize the mistake, seeing his brother and his father's murderer, and he does not fail to develop this idea. He gives the scene with most feeling to those most intimately concerned. A little later, at the burial of the Emperor of Greece, Myllon appears again, and he repeats Orson's suggestion of prayer, offering consolation to both brothers: "Chyldren wepe no more but praye God for his soule, for he shall neuer bee the soner on lyue for your teares." (310). Shortly afterward Valentine vows to give up all pursuit of arms, believing that this sinful knowledge has made him slay his father. Thus an unwitting slaying is resolved in *Valentine and Orson* in much the same way as it was in *Ipomedon*, but the greater space devoted to it results in a more elaborate and convincing scene, where the author makes a genuine effort to vitalize his characters. Much of the point of the story is the effect of a tie of brotherhood, and here we see that tie most rigorously strained, so that a dramatic scene is almost inevitable.

Perhaps the finest dramatic scene built on a lament for the dead is the one with which the *Prose Life of Alexander* concludes. Alexander has been given poison and attempted to kill himself, but he was restrained by his wife Roxanna. Now he lies in bed, and his Macedonians have come before him. The succession has been settled, so that attention is focussed exclusively on Alexander's death (Anthology, pp. 179–80). Conventional ideas, such as the despair of those who remain, their anxiety about what can now be done, "Alas, that he was born," the disrepute which will follow loss of a great leader, questionings about why this had to be, a realization of loss so great that the wish for death predominates and merges into a statement that the death of the leader will kill the remaining followers, appear. What is striking about this lament is not so much its subject matter, however, but the manner in which it is presented. The alternation of comments between Alexander and his officers, the dialogue form, is quite unusual. The customary lament is simply a set-piece uttered over the body or when a letter or messenger has just announced a death. There are also several passages in medieval narrative in which the dying person laments himself. Here the two are fused. Seleucus expresses his grief, giving an added intensity by the reference to Philip of Macedon who had begun the empire. Then Alexander answers, but not as the usual dying man who is repentant for his life, warns against the pride which has brought about his end, or merely reconciles himself with the knowledge that all which lives must die. Instead Alexander voices the sentiment which is usually expressed by the mourners; he states that with his death his people and nation will diminish. This idea is restated by the followers, who add the inevitable wish for death. And Alexander repeats his importance. The brief enumeration of Alexander's successes is a kind of praise and also introduces the query about why Alexander must be lost, followed by a repetition of the wish to follow the king on this, his last invasion. The narrative explains that Alexander makes appropriate pagan preparations for his death; he sends jewels to temples of Apollo. Then he explains what he wants done with his body, giving directions for embalming and for constructing a special

tomb for burial at Alexandria. This done, Alexander dies. The rather
dramatic death procession, staged with Alexander, his crown on his
head, seated on his throne, pulled by twelve princes, is appropriately
splendid. A woeful Tholomeus leads the procession and makes a
lament, stating that by his death Alexander kills more than in all
his conquests. The group of followers conclude the scene with a
series of futile questions about how they can possibly continue alone
without the dead king's help.

Even though this lament for the dead is broken up into a dialogue,
it is more unified than most by the repetition of three key ideas
throughout the passage. The "What shall I do?" of the opening line
goes full circle, and the only answer to the question, that is, that
Macedoyne will no longer be great and, by implication, that there
is nothing to be done, is repeated several times. With Alexander
dead, there is no longer an opportunity for the conquests and dominance to continue. Consequently there can be no consolation. It is
this deficiency which also sets the lament apart from others; the
Christian element has not entered in. Thus frequent repetition of the
phrase "Full waa es me" is an appropriate way of tying the lament
together. There is a fine economy of time, for no interval occurs between the death and final procession, so that our interest is never
distracted. This is a magnificent last scene for Alexander, and the
author's final description and summary of his career are hardly necessary and come as an anti-climax. But there is no question that this
sequence is the most impressive in the narrative. All previous glories
are recalled and seem almost a preparation for the death scene, when
Alexander behaves triumphantly. Even in death he is a splendid
figure, sure of his powers and aware of his own greatness and the
relative insignificance of his followers. What is more, he controls
the scene with the sureness of a director in the theatre, exploiting
its magnificence and its emotional interplay.

Episodes such as these indicate that we can, if infrequently, find
in medieval narrative scenes where a clear and firm sense of the
dramatic is evident. A lamentation for death slows the endless account of adventures, so that there is an opportunity for development.
Then an attempt is made to interrelate characters; they are given
speeches which show an awareness of one another. At their best,
scenes of lamentation in medieval narrative are not very different
from those in drama of the sixteenth century; at their worst, they
still emerge distinctly from the bulk of the narrative to be noteworthy. That these laments are closely related to explicit dramatic

expression, may be indicated by their being scarcely distinguishable from those found in two rather unusual pieces of medieval drama.

Medieval drama does not characteristically conclude with a death scene as does Elizabethan tragedy, and its subject matter is largely religious rather than secular. Three illustrations from this religious drama, however, bear many similarities to the narrative scenes we have been examining and are thus pertinent to the tradition of the rhetorical death lament. There are two scenes which contain supposed deaths of young sons, and these are comparable to the lamentation in the beginning of *William of Palerne*.

Like William's mother Euphrosina believes that her son Adeodatus has been lost, and she laments in the most conventional phrases (Anthology, pp. 181–83). The drama is a St. Nicholas play, written in Latin, in four-line stanzas. Euphrosina's expressions of grief are answered by the Consolatrices, and certainly the author of the play was aware of a tradition of laments for the dead. The mother exclaims "Alas!" and asks "What shall I do?" She tries to understand the situation, but gives way to questioning why she was born and wishing for death. The comforters advise prayer and trust in God's mercy, but Euphrosina thinks only of her reversal in fortune, from joy to grief, and reiterates her wish for death. She is then advised that such sorrow is not prudent and that she ought to give of her wealth to clerics and the poor, asking St. Nicholas' mercy. At this point in the play, interest is shifted to prayers and service to St. Nicholas, who ultimately restores Adeodatus to his parents after seizing him from the King Marmorinus, who had stolen him from the church of St. Nicholas in Excoranda. Obviously the emphasis here is upon the miracle of a saint, but the occasion of a believed death is treated fully, "lamentabili voce." The boy's mother expresses the traditional grief and despair and self-blame with feminine helplessness. An attempt is made to assuage her anxiety by offering consolation. There is a rather highly stylized, formal tone to the expression, and not a great deal of dramatic interplay between characters; but *Adeodatus* does have an explicit scene of lamentation, and the similarities between this "drama" and medieval narratives, both characteristic ideas and elements of style, add much evidence for the existence of a widespread tradition of laments for the dead in medieval literature, ready to be adapted by Elizabethan dramatists.

Attention is placed on a young son whose death is eminent in another, and extraordinarily effective, piece of medieval dramatic writing, the Brome *Sacrifice of Isaac*. Actually the emphasis here is upon the interplay of father and son and God, the conflict of loves and duties. There is no extensive passage of lamentation, for the play is rather less highly stylized than many. The author's use of pathos and his skill in creating a climactic movement to the spectacular intervention of the Angel, have been frequently observed. The dramatic possibilities of the subject matter are obvious, and the significance of the material in Biblical narrative makes its appearance among the mystery plays almost inevitable. The success of the play is, however, extraordinary; and it ranks easily among the most significant pieces of medieval drama, not simply because of the unusual skill of the writer but also because the material itself is peculiarly suited to dramatic interplay of characters and exploitation of strong feeling, such as was to become the stock in trade of Elizabethan writers of tragedy. Here is a fine model in which grief, physical details of death, anxiety, pity, deep family feeling, religious devotion, and varieties of consolation—principal elements of laments for the dead—are investigated. There is a firm balance between two principal characters, the one not dominating the other, and tremendous audience sympathy is commanded.

Many similar effects are found in the Digby *Resurrection and Burial* (Bodley MS. E Museo 160), that most elaborate *planctus Mariae* which is extended to fill a whole play. The length and complexity of the lamentation (864 lines) would seem to strain our acceptance of the material, but the subject of the lament is Christ and the mourners are the Maries and Joseph of Arimathea, so that however protracted the expression of loss, it will remain inadequate. Indeed the power of this play lies in the author's skilled restraint, his tasteful blending of human and divine elements, and his consummate skill in varying the lamentation. The play begins with Joseph of Arimathea's expression of grief and distress at the death of the Innocent; then he introduces the Magdalene and the three Maries, who bewail the day. "O day of lamentation!/ O day of exclamatione!/ O day of suspiratione!/ Which Iewes shall repent!/ O day most doloruse!/ O day paynfull & tediose!" (62–67)—they cry, each uttering a single line (except lines 64–65) and thus defining more precisely the exclamation with which they began ["O most dolorose day! O tym of gretist sorowe!" (56)]. Rather appropriately the Magdalene emphasizes physical details of Christ's wounds and blood, and she repeatedly insists that Joseph look at His pitifully torn body. Joseph's many attempts to stop the Maries from mourning, succeed only when he diverts their attention to the Virgin Mary. Then the

Magdalene emphasizes her mother's grief, describing her participation in the Crucifixion scene. Recollection of Christ's thirst, "of charitee;/ For our faithe & fidelitee," (215–16) leads to a second stage of lamentation, the acceptance of responsibility for the death and resulting desire for comfort. Then the details of the Crucifixion are repeated by Joseph, who exhorts man to remember Christ's love. This leads the Magdalene to a fresh outburst in which she exclaims about her grief and wishes for death:

> Who saw eu*er* a spektacle more pitevs,
> A more lamentable sight & dolorus?
> A A! this wofull daye!
> Alese, this sorow that I endure
> W*ith* grete inwarde hevynes & cure!
> Alesse, þ*at* I do not dye,
> To see hy*m* dede, made me of noghte,
> And w*ith* his deth thus haves me boughte;
> O Cruell tormentrye!
> O dere mast*er*, be ye not displeasid
> Yf I might dy w*ith* yow/ my hart w*er* wel easid;
> O! ffaynt, & faynt it is
>
>   (322–33)

Joseph offers consolation in the Resurrection and urges a lessening of lamentation. She is adamant in her grief, but another Mary says, "Mawdleyne, yo*ur* mowrny*n*ge avaylis nothi*n*ge" (373) and turns to the immediate situation of taking Christ's body to the sepulchre. Nicodemus, who is to move the body with Pilate's consent, appears at this time; and he too laments the cruelty of Jesus' death and finds comfort in thoughts of the Resurrection. At the approach of the Virgin Mary, they all hurry to lower the body; she hastens to assist, but swoons immediately. Here there is a quickening in the dialogue, a series of short exclamations uttered by all present who try to revive Mary and comfort her, appealing to her to stop grieving.

Thus Mary's long lamentation is introduced. She appreciates the kindness of the Maries, Joseph, and St. John especially; but she is compelled to give full expression to her experience. Like the women of medieval narrative, the Virgin Mary begins with a sense of inadequacy:

> God reward yow of y*our* tend*er*nesse!
> I shall assiste you w*ith* all humylnesse;

But yit, or he departe,
Suffere me my mynd for to breke,
How be it full scantly may I speke
For faynte & febill harte:
A, A, Cosyn Iohn! what shall I saye?

(478–84)

As the next three hundred lines make abundantly clear, there is a
great deal to say in this lamentation, which is divided into four long
parts. Mary's words are interrupted first when she swoons and is
revived by the Magdalene and John, who urges her to stop lamenting; then later John tries to get her to leave by assuring her that
they will bury Christ. The third pauses occurs when Mary asks to
hold the body in her arms, and the others consent. It is when Mary
holds her son that she most explicitly laments his death (Anthology,
pp. 183–87) and finally turns to John and Magdalene to help her
when her expression of grief has totally exhausted her. The play
concludes with Mary's wish to be buried with her Son and a final
plea to see His face one last time after He is in the Sepulchre. Then
they depart severally, some comforting Mary, the Magdalene to buy
precious balms, and Joseph concluding:

Of this blessit beriall/ lat vs ane end make!
Here now is he gravid, & her lyes hee,
Which for loue of man, of his charite
Suffert bit*ter* passion.
Great comforthe it is vnto vs all,
That the thride day aryse he shall
In the most gloriose fassion.
The tyme drawethe fast, & approchis ner;
Schortly I truste sum gud tiding*es* to her.

(852–60)

The divisions of this lamentation are quite important, for they
signal progressive stages in Mary's reaction to Christ's death. At
first she simply emphasizes her mother's grief and contrasts this to
her initial happiness when the Angel Gabriel had appeared to her
and there had been no forewarning of her present grief. But Symeon
had warned her of the sufferings which now cause her to swoon.
In the second stage she accepts John's consolation, belief in the
Resurrection, but her attention focuses on the unkind Jews. In a
series of rhetorical questions, she rebukes Judas, contrasting his "pesyn

& infection" to Christ's "tend*er* gudnese," and wondering how Judas dares such treason. In her plea to hold the body Mary gives fullest praise to her Son, in language reminiscent of that found in secular laments made by ladies for their sons or lovers.

> Ye knaw well, her is my tresure,
> Whom I loue beste, whom all my plesure
> is & eu*er* be shall;
> Her is my likinge & all my loue;
> Why wald ye than me hens remoue?
> I pray yow hartly, cesse!   (571–76)

She further states the claim which Christ's love makes on the followers who are present. Thus four major ideas—grief, responsibility, praise, and love—are introduced in the passages which lead to the central lament, where they are more fully exploited with rich additions of specific details and variations of the main ideas.

Mary begins her fullest lamentation with appeals for pity, asking rhetorically how she will have sufficient tears to beweep such a sorrowful occasion. She gains considerable personal sympathy by her recollection of Christ's birth and circumcision and her own purification and flight into Egypt. Much emphasis is placed on the physical details of the first three events, and this is repeated in her description of His wounds, "Dere son! ye haue steynd y*our* face,/ Y*our* face so frely to behold./ Thikk bludy droppes ry*n*nes down a-pace," (642–44). Then Mary repeats her accusations of the Jews and adds a prediction of the curses to befall the race that has betrayed its own Redeemer. A specific enumeration of Christ's wounds follows, and again the Virgin must pause to weep. Inevitably the contrast between Christ's innocence and betrayal is reiterated. The author introduces several dramatic touches; for example, recollection of Judas' kiss leads to Mary's wish to kiss her Son. This psychological association of ideas is emphasized by the style when for seven lines (694–700) the poet very tightly holds his lines together by having each line repeat the word or phrase with which the preceding line concludes. And thus he offers a modulation into the next crucial stage of lamentation, the wish for death which is to dominate the rest of Mary's utterance. Her grief is given fresh expression with repeated questions that urge all to join in her sorrow and exclamations against the unkindness of the Crucifixion. The enormous significance of the Virgin's grief is made clear and constantly repeated through a skillful handling of the refrain "Who can not wepe, com lern at me!" This line appears in many of the verse paragraphs (669, 676, 682, 693, 701, 708, 716), often in a terminal position, so that emphasis is gained. Close variants of the line are also used (637, 658, 725) at widely distributed points. The effect of this refrain is to tie the whole passage very closely together through the echoing of the reason for the lamentation: all mankind can learn from the Virgin Mary how to lament the Crucifixion. The popularity of the idea is further demonstrated by the appearance of the refrain as the burden of an earlier lyric "Who can not wepe, com lerne of me." [1] The combination of distinctive ideas and the powerful refrain with more conventional generalized statements— "Now is my songe, alese, ales, my child!/ Now may I wayle, wringe my hand*es,* & wepe!/ Who shalbe my comforth? who shall me kepe." (720–22)—shows the range of the passage.

When the Virgin's personal anxiety is somewhat assuaged by her memory that Christ has given her care to John, she turns from her own concern to further praise of her Son. Like most women who are mourners, however, she soon returns to that helpless question 'What shall I do?' and repeats her wish to die, calling "crewell deth" both "welcome" and "acceptabill." She asks the Jews to crucify her, for she can have no greater loss than that of her Son. Then she prays to her Son, Who was so merciful to so many, to grant His mother's request for death. The last section of the lament exploits fully the mother-child relationship. There are several references to the mother's nursing the child (760, 773ff, 780ff) and the uniqueness of virgin's milk. A final contrast between the healthy baby and the wounded man is made, and Mary swoons again, thus ending her long formal lamentation. The play is soon concluded. Mary makes only a few brief speeches, always requests for death or for a few last moments with Christ. Joseph places the body in a grave and again expresses his faith in Resurrection. Mary Magdalene explains that she will buy "*preciose* balmes," and this reference serves as a transition to the second part of the play, "Christ's Resurrection." Here there is further lamentation, but none so splendidly imagined and sustained as that we have just been considering.

---

[1] See F. J. Furnivall's note in *Digby Plays, with Bodley Burial and Resurrection,* Early English Text Society, Extra Series, 70 (London, 1896), p. 171, which refers to his text of the poem in *Hymns to the Virgin and Christ,* Early English Text Society, 24 (London, 1867), pp. 126–27. The text also appears in *Early English Lyrics,* ed. E. K. Chambers and F. Sidgwick (London, 1921), pp. 144–45.

Indeed it would be difficult to imagine a lament for the dead which surpassed this in its full and rich handling of ideas and stylisitc effects and dramatic pauses. The author has an extensive knowledge of the genre; he is not only aware of the dramatic possibilities of laments for the dead, but also he relies upon these to carry the play. Here we have a lament used, not as a high point in a larger work, but as the essence of the large work. The Digby *Burial* is pure lamentation; the feeling, the effect, produced by the play, is derived from expression of grief and the difficulties of coping with loss through death. The language is highly rhetorical; it is full of exclamations and questions, has a fairly regular and distinctive verse and stanzaic pattern, uses repetition and refrain, and exploits highly emotional description and human compassion. The nature of the subject matter makes such relentless restriction of technique and direction of response highly appropriate, so that the effect of the play is unforgettable.

Later dramatists, who were writing about secular subjects did not so completely limit their material and technique; and the length of early Elizabethan plays is much greater than that of this late medieval mystery. It is perhaps no accident, however, that the rich resources of laments for the dead are called upon in *Gorboduc,* which is traditionally recognized as the earliest English tragedy.[2] Here a lamenting mother suggests a clear continuity in the tradition. Videna's lament for her son in Act Four scene one uses many of the ideas and elements of style which we have noticed in medieval literature. And the passage is given a prominent position, just as in earlier narratives and dramas. Further the scene is one of the most compelling in the play; for the skill of the rhetorical utterance and the handling of feeling about death gain and sustain emotion.

Videna begins by asking why she should go on living, and she considers several ways in which she might have died earlier, so that she would not have lived to face the present day of sorrow. She argues that a grave in the earth would have been more pleasing than having her "living breast remain the ryghtful tomb/ Wherein my heart, yelden to death, is graved." Videna, like William of

---

[2] Tudor interludes contain many examples of rhetorical death laments that are clearly in the medieval tradition. See, for example, the anticipatory lament of Eubulus and the Muses in Richard Edwards' *Damon and Pithias* (1564/5–1571), lines 1454–1507; and the laments for Sisamnes and Praxaspes' son, lines 460–70 and 573–601 respectively, in Thomas Preston's *Cambises* (c. 1560).

Palerne's mother, apostrophizes her dead son and asks rhetorically if he is really dead. Then she turns her fury against her other son, Porrex, who has traitorously slain his brother and her son. Treason against kindred, as we saw in *Valentine and Orson,* is the point which is emphasized. She expects an absolute revenge; her hand will be its instrument on earth, and the gods in hell will also release their anger. In a series of rhetorical questions Videna demands why Porrex could not have satisfied his lust for blood on someone other than Ferrex, who came from the same womb as he did. It would have been better to slay the mother who gave birth to Ferrex, who then would have been spared to be a delight of his father's old age. From this argument Videna shifts quickly to a renunciation of Porrex, who she avows is not her son but a changeling. This murderer was nursed by a tiger's milk, not a woman's. His heart is iron, not flesh and blood, and wild woods were his home. Videna concludes, as she began, with a series of rhetorical questions that make clear her determination to revenge Ferrex. This is a very elaborate lament for the dead, written in a consciously rhetorical style that uses many of the devices we saw in Geoffrey's lament for Richard I—rhetorical questions, repetition and emphatic reintroduction of words, alliteration, hyperbole, apostrophes, inversion of natural word order, affirmation followed by negation, and so on. Videna forcefully expresses her grief and indignation, particularly by using vivid descriptions, such as the various ways in which she might have died, the image of her breast as a tomb for her heart, sharp details of Porrex's blood-thirsty cravings, and play on specific imagery of her womanhood (her womb and nursing her child). Much of the effect of what she says comes from the contrast between her avowal of motherhood, which should produce softness and gentleness, and her actual manner, which shows fierceness of anger and determination to have full revenge. This is especially pointed since each of her professed attitudes is a result of feeling for her two sons. The exploitation of a mother's feeling and grief by Videna reminds us of the richness—though very differently employed—in the Digby *Burial.* There is little doubt about the use of Videna's lament in the drama; it summarizes the situation which has arisen in the first three acts and prepares for the catastrophe of the two final acts. By slowing the action through a rhetorical lament, the dramatist allows time for the parts of his tragedy to come together and be assimilated. And he provides a literary embellishment which is intrinsically interesting. The effect of Videna's soliloquy is like that in an elaborate lament in romance, such as the one for Roland in *Charles the Grete,* when the narrative is stopped so that grief may be expressed and revenge planned.

Videna's lament is a climax in the tragedy, but it is not the only instance of Sackville's use of the form.[3] Marcella's lamentations (IV, ii, 166ff.) have much the same tone as Videna's, for she speaks in rhetorical questions with an *ubi sunt* idea. She asks about lack of pity and wonders where to seek mercy when it is absent from a mother's breast. Videna's execution of her younger son to avenge her elder has made explicit the paradox which her lament suggested. Gorboduc cries "Allas" and asks the meaning of Marcella's plaint. She replies with the previous rhetorical vagueness, asking why she continues to live and wondering whether people will believe the horror which she must report. Then she reveals that she saw Porrex slain by his mother while he slept. Gorboduc's despair is complete, and he calls upon his faithful counselor Eubulus to slay him. Eubulus tries to suggest that there may be some chance that this heir still lives, but Marcella removes all doubt, describing how the dying Porrex called upon Videna for aid, was assisted by the ladies of the court, but died pitifully staring, sighing, looking towards heaven. Marcella prolongs her plaints (IV, ii, 228ff.) dividing attention between Porrex and the Queen, praising and expressing disbelief that Videna could destroy one so fair. Porrex's handsome looks, princely manner, valor in arms, and position as a son, should have produced mercy. Heaven, Marcella insists, will avenge this unnatural murder. Finally Marcella recalls a glowing vision of Porrex, in shining armor fighting well, which will never be seen again. There is no doubt that Marcella is more than a messenger who reports and describes a death. Although there is no mention of a personal relationship, Marcella's lament has a direct, personal quality which is not unlike that of Videna's. Arostus interrupts Marcella to point out that all plaints are vain, and he suggests that Gorboduc must be comforted. The Chorus conclude the act by reiterating the dreadful quality of what has happened and the possi-

[3] Thomas Sackville is generally regarded as the author of the last two acts of *Gorboduc.* See Baugh, p. 461 and *Elizabethan and Stuart Plays,* ed. Charles R. Baskervill et al (New York, 1934), p. 77. And he is also the author of the most memorable section of the *Mirror for Magistrates,* an Elizabethan narrative which not only has a structure much akin to rhetorical death laments, but also contains several notable laments for the dead within that structure. Thus his knowledge of the medieval tradition is explicitly clear.

bility of revenge, and they suggest that he who does not get involved is happy.

Because Porrex is a prince and a last heir he deserves worthy
lamentation, and he is a fit subject—in spite of his own transgres-
sions—because he was slain unnaturally by his mother. Sackville
gives Marcella much of the rhetorical skill which was Videna's. The
difference is that Marcella's lament is repeatedly interrupted by comments of others. This gives the passage a more dramatic effect, and
it lessens rhetorical fervor. Marcella never quite soars to Videna's
height (indeed her loss is a less worthy one), and she divides her
interest between grief at the loss and horror at the mother's crime.
Just as Videna's lament prepared for the action to follow, so Marcella's very carefully and specifically introduces the idea of revenge
which is the subject of the final act. This preparation for revenge
is more elaborate than that in most medieval romances, but the
feelings of Arthur for Gawain or Achilles for Patroclus, are no less
volubly expressed.

Just as Videna's lament recalls those of heroines in medieval
narrative, and the *planctus Mariae,* and Marcella's elaborates the
patterns of cries for revenge, so Arthur's lament when Modred's
body is brought on stage (Act V, scene i) in Thomas Hughes' *The
Misfortunes of Arthur* (1587) might well have appeared in a medieval Arthurian romance. Here Arthur both praises his son Modred,
in whom he had placed great hope, and accuses him, for his ambitious thoughts. Arthur blames himself, however, and wishes that
the Fates which led to his incestuous life might have produced a
greater affection between him and his son. Seeing the bloody corpse
makes Arthur think of his own approaching death, and he cries out
in emotional, carefully balanced lines:

> I see (alas) I see (hide hide againe:
> O spare mine eyes) a witnesse of my crimes:
> A feareful vision of my former guilte:
> A dreadfull horror of a future doome:
> A present gaule of minde. O happie they,
> Whose spotlesse liues attaine of dreadlesse death.
>
> (V, i, 98–103)

A comparison with Phaeton, who symbolizes ambitious youth, makes
Arthur recall his plight; he is a sire without sons. Arthur can only
regret his incestuous life and hope that it will serve as a mirror to
others. This lamentation leads to Arthur's death scene, which has

striking similarities to the conclusion of the *Life of Alexander*. Like other great heroes, Arthur himself reviews his victories, and his initial defiance of the Fates has an assured quality very like that of the other conquerors. Arthur's conclusion, however, is an exact antithesis. He gives no elaborate orders for his burial, but instead he hopes that his death will soon be forgotten. Actually he wants the news of his death suppressed, and there is to be no burial, so that Arthur will still be feared. The play ends with elaborate lamentations and moralizations on the death of Arthur, made by the Chorus and Gorlois, and an elaborate epilogue summarizes the transitory nature of all temporal things. Thus although Arthur's patriotic motives prevented his lament from reaching the full sweep of that of Alexander, there is still evidence that a need is felt for some expression that will produce the effect of a lament for the dead.

That this need was not restricted to lesser dramatists is shown by the plays of Marlowe and Shakespeare, whose indebtedness to medieval traditions has long been recognized. What the Renaissance dramatist was able to do with this material can be significantly illustrated by a few examples of laments for the dead in their plays. Both playwrights exploited the techniques of rhetorical lamentation in their earlier plays, yet both discarded later the more obvious treatment of the form. One of the most popular types of lament in narrative, as we have seen, is that made for a great warrior or king, a hero. Both Shakespeare and Marlowe wrote many of these, so that they form a good basis for comment.

The lament, rich in rhetorical qualities, was a particularly happy model for Marlowe; and the contrasts between laments made for Tamburlaine and Edward II typify the movement from rhetoric to feeling which is characteristic of the development of the death lament. The laments for Zenocrate and Tamburlaine are Marlowe's most elaborate, and together they occupy almost the whole of *Tamburlaine, Part II*. Tamburlaine's death is reminiscent of those of other warriors/kings, and an almost exact parallel of the scene is to be found in the *Prose Life of Alexander*. In each instance, the dying leader has dominated the action; and his great strength and importance are finally reiterated as he dies. Though he is surrounded by his heirs and followers, none is worthy to lament the hero, who must make his own complaint, thus completing the characterization of total dominance and confidence. No mere follower or heir may presume to comment significantly upon his end; all must simply listen, grieve, and accept the heir's succession, though he is unworthy of it. Marlowe is by no means slavish in his maintenance of this conventional scene, for although he retains the usual summary of the hero's career and conquests, he gains variety, for example, by the introduction of the messenger and by having Tamburlaine, in the tradition of the Cid, mighty even in death. Tamburlaine rallies sufficiently to confront his enemies, and the sight of him is something to make them flee. Similarly, the introduction of the death scene is highly dramatic; Tamburlaine is drawn in by the captive kings—and this only after the eloquent prologue, "Weepe heauens, and vanish into liqid teares." This careful preparation for a death scene recalls the attention given to dramatic details in such narratives as *Le Bone Florence of Rome,* and it enlivens what might have been simply a formal, conventional scene. Further, Marlowe has already begun to create sympathy for Tamburlaine in the laments for Zenocrate, which fill the earlier portion of the play. Even an egocentric figure like Tamburlaine forgets his own personal involvement sufficiently to praise the beloved who has died, and thus Marlowe places him in the long tradition of heroes, like Charlemagne and Arthur, who are characterized (notably gaining sympathy) by their elaborate utterances of grief. Tamburlaine's love for Zenocrate is the most appealing episode of his life; and by recalling this material, Marlowe defines more sharply the audience's reaction, bringing together a summary of impressions about him and suggesting a unity of action. The total impact is sufficient to leave one breathless with a sense of loss.

Just as there is a massing of ideas and dramatic techniques of laments, so the customary rhetorical embellishments are freely and richly used in *Tamburlaine, Part II.* In the lament for Tamburlaine Marlowe repeats the imagery of heaven, angels, and gods, which has often been used to praise his hero. There is also skillful repetition of words and phrases, careful parallelism, antithesis, and much exhortation and rhetorical questioning, as well as conventional personification of death and a heavy sprinkling of classical allusions and sonorous names. The rhetorical death lament is skillfully handled in this play, but it is not particularly subtle; and Marlowe was never again to use the form straightforwardly and with such obvious emphasis and delight in rhetoric, though he had learned well the many advantages of the form.

Edward II is generally considered Marlowe's most mature play, and certainly it contains his most subtle writing of laments for the dead. Most of the rhetorical bombast of *Tamburlaine* has disappeared, and laments are no longer obviously exploited. In fact, however, Marlowe uses a simplified version of lamentation as a principal device to shift the audience's sympathy so that Edward, who is initially weak and depraved, emerges as a praiseworthy man of some nobility.

The change in attitude toward Edward does not result entirely from Marlowe's use of the rhetorical death lament, for obviously devices like his brutal death, or the basic situation of betrayal by his wife, or the implications of treason against a king, are contributing factors. However, Marlowe uses laments for the dead in vital scenes— Edward's lament for Gaveston shows him for the first time as a person of determination; those of Spencer and Baldock introduce his final tragic death; Edward's laments for himself as king solidify our admiration; and his son's final tribute is a memorable ending. There is a quiet solemnity at this moment when grief is expressed after the accomplishment of revenge and provisions for the future are complete. The speech is not without stylistic embellishment; for example, the alliteration of the passage is effective, and the emblems of death are vividly introduced, particularly in the contrast between Edward's position as mourned and honored king and Mortimer's role as despised and dismembered traitor.

Thus in his most mature play Marlowe has freed himself of the rhetorical extravagance which is so characteristic of most laments for the dead. He has made this form of expression not a stylistic embellishment for which action stops, but an integral part of the drama, an indication of the main points and an emphatic statement of changing characterization so that sympathy can be shifted. Edward's character is a difficult one to render acceptable; however, by combining Edward's growing strength, his divorcement from purely selfish concerns through grief for Gaveston and other favorites, and his increasing awareness that nobility befits a king, with praise from those who observe the change, Marlowe makes Edward's fall tragic and lamentable. In *Tamburlaine* Marlowe used laments with rhetorical brilliance, and he learned that they could make up almost an entire play and contribute markedly to the delineation of a character. In *Edward II* he relaxes the "mighty line" and writes laments in the new, simple, dramatic language that is the strength of the play because of its clarity and crispness in presenting characters as individuals. The familiar ideas of "fall literature" are used, but they are not belabored. Fine flourishes have been lost, but in their place is a device whose simple directness makes its appearance less obvious and more significant. The excessively formalized quality, with its attendant dangers of exaggeration, has been replaced by a feeling of spontaneity and sincere conviction. When Edward laments and others lament for him, there is no impression that a pattern is being followed; people are simply saying what the situation requires, and they can do so without self-consciousness because Marlowe has totally mastered the techniques of the rhetorical death lament. He has brilliantly integrated the fundamental form with the meaning of the play.

Like Marlowe, Shakespeare in his early handling of the form, writes laments which are fairly stiff and traditional utterances. The Lady Anne's lament for her husband in *Richard III* (Act I, scene ii) is characteristic. Lady Anne recognizes specifically the form that her situation demands, for she orders the bearers to set down the corpse, "Whilst I awhile obsequiously lament," and again she says, "Rest you, whiles I lament King Henry's corse." Her words are very obviously rhetorical, for they are rich with repetition, parallel structure, figurative expressions, and exclamations. But even in this early play Shakespeare was unwilling to use a lament merely as a rhetorical embellishment, for the action brilliantly departs from the conventional scene with Richard's wooing and winning of the woman whom he has made a widow. Sometimes, of course, Shakespeare does not exploit and develop the possibilities of scenes of lamentation. Hal's farewell to Hotspur has dozens of precedents and no very individual touches. Lady Percy's lament for her husband is more distinctive, because it is much more than woman's grief. Kate, like many heroines of medieval narrative, is using her expression of grief to gain an end; she is trying to dissuade Northumberland from going to fight.

Perhaps the culmination of the genre of rhetorical death laments, is Antony's funeral oration, which is a climax both within the play and in the development of the tradition. No other lament more fully exploits the possibilities of this kind of expression, the subtlety and wit of argument, the deployment of rhetorical techniques of repetition and balance, reiteration of emotional appeals, the systematic playing on the feeling of the bystanders, are unsurpassed. Antony, like so many before him, knows precisely how significant a scene of lamentation may be, and he utilizes his opportunity to its fullest. Here is praise at its richest, but always tempered to avoid excess; here is no blatant cry for revenge, but a cunning argument to move others to this desired course of action. Antony knows the effect which "blood" and the sight of the corpse will produce, and he skillfully designs his argument to give prominence to these effects. He reports Caesar's concern about the fate of the public weal and produces the tangible evidence of the will at precisely the right instant to clinch his argument. There is a dynamic quality in this scene which has been clearly prepared for in earlier narratives and plays, but never so fully realized. We must admire Antony's forensic skill; indeed his lament for Caesar is a culmination of the calculated expression of grief since it irresistibly moves even the reader who recognizes its premeditation, as well as the hearers within the dramatic situation. Thus this most striking expression of "Renaissance" virtuosity proves, paradoxically, to be deeply rooted in a medieval tradition, one which had distinguished the most interesting scenes in the narratives of the preceding four hundred years.

When we turn to the later plays, we find that, again like Marlowe, having written a superb rhetorical death lament that exploited a host of conventions and introduced individual techniques as well, Shakespeare finds the form no longer suitable for his purposes. Marlowe in *Edward II* allowed feeling primacy over rhetoric, but in doing this he still retained a simplified kind of lament. In Shakespeare we find a more emphatic rejection of the early rhetorical lament, a rejection which reminds us of Chaucer's in the *Nun's Priest's Tale*. Macbeth explicitly refuses to make such a comment—"She should have died hereafter;/ There would have been a time for such a word." (V, v, 17–18). And Hamlet's comments develop from, "Thou wretched, rash, intruding fool, farewell!/ I took thee for thy better: take thy fortune;/ Thou find'st to be too busy in some danger." (III, iv, 31–33) to "Wretched queen, adieu!" (V, ii, 344). After this, it is difficult for laments to serve as more than lines to fill the time needed to carry bodies from the stage. The rich and varied tradition of rhetorical death laments comes then, it would seem, to a conclusion, its usefulness apparently ended. However, without the laments for the disguised Imogen in *Cymbeline* (Act IV, ii, 197 ff.) or the speeches of the Nuntius in *Sejanus*—"Then there begin your pity" (V, x, 399 ff.)—the attitude of the audience, the feeling, would be wrong. And thus the lament never ceases really, for the mourners, those present, must make a comment upon the occasion of someone's death. The Elizabethan and later material is outside my present scope; and it is important enough to require separate treatment, though I have included a few examples here simply to show the direction in which the tradition evolves.

ANTHOLOGY OF LAMENTS

FOR THE DEAD

Many romances have been printed by the Early English Text Society, so that it is usually not difficult to obtain some of the material; but others exist only in volumes not recently printed. Further, the laments I have chosen form, when collected together, a substantial authentication of the genre "laments for the dead," and they make an impressive comment on the treatment of death in medieval narrative. Laments in this anthology are arranged in the order in which they are discussed in the critical text. Each lament is headed by a short title of the work in which it appears and a reference in Arabic numerals for lines of verse and pages of prose in the narratives. Again large Roman numerals indicate parts of the narrative, small Roman numerals are for volumes of an edition, and manuscript references are given when this is necessary to avoid confusion. The short title reference is followed by a full bibliographical entry. An alphabetical index of short titles appears at the end of the anthology. I have preserved certain typographical forms, such as þ, Þ, ȝ, ȝ, and ð, but not π and η, which are more difficult to read and used only infrequently by editors. Similarly, ſ has not been retained.

Geoffrey de Vinsauf, *Poetria Nova*, 324–430.
[Edmund Faral, *Les Arts Póetiques du XIIᵉ et du XIIIᵉ siècle* (Paris, 1923), pp. 207–10.]

       Tempore successus, jocundi tempore fati,
Haec potes ore loqui, luctus praesaga futuri: 325
Anglia, regnorum regina, superstite rege
Ricardo, cujus laus est diffusio tanti
Nominis et mundi cui monarchia relicta

Est soli, secura fides sub regmine tanto.
Rex tuus est speculum, quo te speculata superbis;   330
Sidus, de cujus rutilas splendore; columna,
Per quam fulta viges; fulmen, quod mittis in hostes;
Laus, qua paene deum pertingis culmina. Sed quid
Singula? Non illo potuit fecisse priorem
Nec voluit Natura parem.—Sed viribus absit   335
Prorsus habere fidem: mors est quae fortia frangit.
Omnibus ne crede tuis; si tempore parvo
Illuxere tibi, mox sunt clausura serenum
Nubila fata diem, ducentque crepuscula noctem.
Jam cito rumpetur speculum, speculatio cujus   340
Gloria tanta tibi; sidus patietur eclipsim,
A quo fulges; nutabit rupta columna,
Unde trahis vires; cessabit fulminis ictus,
Unde tremunt hostes; et eris de principe serva.
Omina laeta vale tibi sunt dictura; quiescis,   345
Sudabis; rides, flebis, ditescis, egebis;
Flores, marcebis; es, vix eris.—Attamen istud
Unde scies? Quid ages? Volucrum rimaberis aure
Murmura? Vel motus oculo? Vel Apolline fata?
Tolle mathematicos! Est augur surdus, aruspex   350
Caecus et ariolus amens. Presentia scire
Fas homini, solique Deo praescire futura.
Non habet hic patriam; vetus ille repatriet error
Et pater erroris gentilis nutriat illum
Quem genuit, quia sana fides a lumine tollit   355
Ecclesiae tripodes Phoebi soliumque Sibillae.
Hoc unum praescire potes quia nulla potestas
Esse morosa potest, quia res fortuna secundas
Imperat esse breves. Si vis exempla, priores
Respice fortunas. Emarcuit illa priorum   360
Florida prosperitas: Minos subvertit Athenas,
Ylion Atrides, magnae Cartaginis arces
Scipio, sed Romam multi. Fuit alea fati
Tempore versa brevi. Brevis est distantia laeti
Ominis et maesti; nox est vicina diei.   365
Haec aliena docent, sed te tua fata docebunt.
　　　　Temporibus luctus his verbis exprime luctum
Neustria, sub clypeo regnis defensa Ricardi,
Indefensa modo, planctu testare dolorem;

Exudent oculi lacrimas; exterminet ora　　370
Pallor; connodet digitos tortura; cruentet
Interiora dolor; et verberet aethera clamor.
Tota peris in morte sua: mors non fuit ejus,
Sed tua. Non una, sed publica mortis origo.
O Veneris lacrimosa dies! O sidus amarum!　　375
Illa dies tua nox fuit et Venus illa venenum.
Illa dedit vulnus; sed pessimus ille dierum,
Primus ab undecimo, qui, vitae vitricus, ipsam
Clausit. Uterque dies homicida tyrannide mira.
Trajecit clausus exclusum, tectus apertum,　　380
Providus incautum, miles munitus inermem
Et proprium regem. Quid miles, perfide miles,
Perfidiae miles, pudor orbis et unica sordes
Militiae, miles manuum factura suarum,
Ausus es hoc in eum? Scelus hoc, scelus istud et ausus?　　385
O dolor! O plus quam dolor! O mors! O truculenta
Mors! Esses utinam, mors mortua! Quid meministi
Ausa nefas tantum? Placuit tibi tollere solem
Et tenebris damnare diem: scis quem repuisti?
Ipse fuit jubar in oculis et dulcor in aure　　390
Et stupor in mente. Scis, impia, quem repuisti?
Ipse fuit dominus armorum, gloria regum,
Deliciae mundi. Nihil addere noverat ultra,
Ipse fuit quicquid potuit Natura. Sed istud
Causa fuit quare rapuisti: res pretiosas　　395
Eripis et viles quasi dedignata relinquis.
Et te de, Natura, queror; quia nonne fuisti,
Dum mundus esset adhuc, dum nata jaceres
In cunis, in eo studiosa? Nec ante senectam
Destitit hoc studium. Cur sudor tantus in orbem　　400
Attulit hoc mirum, si tam brevis abstulit hora
Sudorem tantum. Placuit tibi tendere mundo
Et revocare manum, dare six et tollere donum.
Cur irritasti mundum? Vel redde sepultum
Vel forma similem. Sed non tibi suppetit unde:　　405
Quicquid erat tecum vel mirum vel pretiosum,
Huic erat impensum; thesauri deliciarum
Hic sunt exhausti. Ditissima facta fuisti
Ex hac factura: fieri pauperrima sentis
Ex hac jactura; si felix ante fuisti,　　410

Tanto plus misera quanto felicior ante.
Si fas est, accuso Deum. Deus, optima rerum,
Cur hic degeneras? Cur obruis hostis amicum?
Si recolis, pro rege facit Jope tua, quam tot
Milibus oppositus solus defendit, et Achon,   415
Quam virtute sua tibi reddidit, et crucis hostes,
Quos omnes vivus sic terruit, ut timeatur
Mortuus. Ipse fuit sub quo tuta tua fuerunt:
Si, Deus, es, sicut decet, fidelis et expers
Nequitiae, justus et rectus, cur minuisti   420
Ergo dies ejus? Potuisses parcere mundo:
Mundus egebat eo. Sed eum magis eligis esse
Tecum quam secum; mavis succurrere caelo
Quam mundo. Domine, si fas est dicere, dicam
Pace tua: posses fecisse decentius istud   425
Et properasse minus, dum saltem frena dedisset
Hostibus (et facta dilatio nulla fuisset:
Res erat in foribus): tunc posset honestius ire
Et remanere tibi. Sed in hac re suire dedisti
Quam brevis est risus, quam longa est lacrima mundi.   430

Dunbar, "Elegy on the Death of Bernard Stewart, Lord of Aubigny."
[*The Poems of William Dunbar,* ed. W. Mackay Mackenzie (London, 1932), pp. 133–34.]

Illuster Lodovik, of France most Cristin king,
    Thow may complain with sighis lamentable
The death of Bernard Stewart, nobill and ding,
    In deid of armis most anterous and abill,
    Most mychti, wyse, worthie, and confortable,   5
Thy men of weir to governe and to gy:
    For him, allace! now may thow weir the sabill,
Sen he is gone, the flour of chevelrie.

Complaine sould everie nobill valiant knycht
    The death of him that douchtie was in deid,   10
That many ane fo in feild hes put to flight,
    In weiris wicht, be wisdome and manheid.
    To the Turk sey all land did his name dreid,
Quhois force all France in fame did magnifie;
    Of so hie price sall nane his place posseid,   15
For he is gon, the flour of chevelrie.

O duilfull death! O dragon dolorous!
  Quhy hes thow done so dulfullie devoir
The prince of knychtheid, nobill and chevilrous,
  The witt of weiris, of armes and honour,   20
  The crop of curage, the strenth of armes in stour,
The fame of France, the fame of Lumbardy,
  The chois of chiftanes, most awful in airmour,
The charbuckell, cheif of every chevelrie!

Pray now for him all that him loveit heir!   25
  And for his saull mak intercessioun
Unto the Lord, that hes him bocht so deir,
  To gif him mercie and remissioun;
  And namelie we of Scottis natioun,
Intill his lyff quhom most he did affy,   30
  Foryhett we nevir into our orisoun
To pray for him, the flour of chevelrie.

Sir Ferumbras, 4207–21.
[*Sir Ferumbas,* ed. Sidney J. Herrtage, *EETSES,* XXXIV (London, 1879), p. 131.]

& "Alas!" said he, by-forn hem þar, "þat y euere y ʒut
        croune bar, þis is a deeful þyng!
þat suþþen myn barouns buþ þus y-slayn, & y thus wrecchedly
        schal torne a-gayn, Wiþ-oute wrech takyng:
Þar as y ha be arst mykel of tolde, For a coward y worþ
        y-holde, boþe in tour and bour.
Alas! Alas! cold ys my red; Why lybbe y now þat þay
        buþ ded, þat huld myn honour?
Alas! for Roland, my Cosyn dere; Were he lyues wiþ me
        here, A wolde noʒt suffry þys,
Þat y thus scholde me torne aʒene, Wiþ-oute ve[n]iaunce of
        my tene, Hit farþ now al a-mys:
For now y haue hym for-go, And myn oþre barons al-so,
        þorw my folye dede.
Whar-for certis me ys wo."

Morte Arthure, 4275–90
[*Morte Arthure, mit Einleitung, Anmerkungen und Glossar,* ed. Erik Björkman (New York, 1915), p. 126.]

  "Kyng comly with crowne,   in care am I leuyde;
All my lordchipe lawe in lande   es layde vndyre!

That me has gyfen gwerdons   be grace of hym seluen,
Mayntenyde my manhede   be myghte of thine handes,
Made me manly one molde   and mayster in erthe;
In a tenefull tym   this torfere was rereryde,
That for a traytoure has tynte   all my trewe lordys.
Here rystys the riche blude   of the rownde table,
Rebukkede with a rebawde,   and rewthe es the more!
I may helples one hethe   house be myn one
Alls a wafull wedowe,   þat wanttes hir beryn.
I may werye and wepe   and wrynge myn handys,
For my wytt and my wyrchipe   awaye es for euer.
Off all lordchips I take   leue to myn ende;
Here es þe Bretons blode   broughte owt of lyfe,
And nowe in þis journee   all my joy endys!"

Partenay, 2159–74.
[*The Romance of Partenay, or of Lusignen,* ed. W. W. Skeat,
EETS, XXII (London, 1866), p. 79.]

"Als! dede is," said, "my fader, my comfort;
    Fader ne moder haue I noght, perde!
    Here bide And dwell most, orpheline to se.
        What now willt thou don, woful Eglentine?
        To gret heuynesse off-fors moste thou incline;

For now I se here the destruccion
    Off all my regyon And Rewme roial.
Als! caytif! what shalt thou now don?
    In what maner forme gouerne the now shall?
    Thy contre shalt se put in exile all,
        Distroed, robbed, peled, and more wurse,
        By ille sarisins; god gife thaim his curse!   2170

I wote nere wat to do, neither what to say,
    Ne I may noght to it shappe remedy;
Me moste here-After our lord to renay,
    And in sarisine lau beleue fully!"

Hay's Buik of Alexander (The Forraye of Gadderis, fol. 46a), 7
[*The Taymouth Castle Manuscript of Sir Gilbert Hay's "Buik
of Alexander the Conqueror,"* ed. Albert Herrman (Berlin,
1898), p. 7.]

    "adew, moist vorthe king of price!
Adew, king Alexander of Dulariss!

Adev, my luif, adew quhom foir I die!
Nov vat I veill thow sall me neuer sie!
I am the caus of thair distructioune;
I am the caus of thair confusioune;
Fow thow me bad to tak of thy mein3e
Als monye as me list to tak vithe me,
And for my pryde and my hie arrogance
I did my vill and not thyne ordinance.
Now am I caus of all the perresching
Of all this pepill and of the nobill king.
God gif my lyf mycht succour all the leif
And I var dede and deip dovne in my grave!
Small tinsall var, suppois my deid var dicht;
Bot throv me vill sa mony vorthe knicht
This day or evin baithe lyfis and guidis forlorne.
Ane hard fortoune vas ordand me beforne.
Alace the day that I ever armes bere!"

Partenay, 269–310
[*The Romance of Partenay, or of Lusignen, otherwise known
as The Tale of Melusine,* ed. W. W. Skeat, *EETS,* XXII (London, 1866), pp. 17–19.]

"ha! alas! thou fals fortune," ther sayng,
    "To me hast thou be felonesly bent!   270
Goode to tho wykyd thou grauntest and lent;
    he is A more foole than Any mute best
    That trustith on the, or in thy behest!

Thou art no gudfader ne Godmodere!
    To on art thou swet, Another bitter to;   275
Non may on the trust, ne in thy fals gere;
    Off A smal man thou makest a kyng, lo!
    And of tho ful rych right pour men also.
    In the no wyl streine to helpe moste or lest;
    Thou on aydest, Another destroest!   280

Alas for sorow! thys in me to fynde!
    Thou here me hast destroed entierlie,
And perdurabelly dampned to mynde,
    But i*hesu* crist, the cheritable god hye,
    The trew, the swete, the piteful, of mercy   285
      Of my wery soule lust to haue pyte!"
      And *with* that Raymound zownyng dōn gan fle,

And wel nye an hour ryght so gan hym hold
    Without spech or loke; after cam agayne,
Ther begynnyng his sorowes manyfold.   290
    When he rewardyd hys lord souerayne,
    Whiche ther dede-cold lay, sore hym gan complayne,
        Rewfully sayng *with* scrychyng vois hie,
        "Come, deth! tarye noght, anon let me dye!

Comyng me to take, for time now it is;   295
    For loste haue I here both soule and bodye;
My souerayne lorde that dede here lith thys,
    By my grete mysdede here hym slayn haue I.
    Deth, come to me! season is trulye;
        Come forth here anon, or I shal me sle;   300
        But god shold me sle, I shold noght so me.

God wold noght, which is our chef fader hye,
    That any cristyn in dispeir be shold;
But the hour coursed that born was worly,
    Or that wreched lyf so long leuyng hold.   305
    Better had me be dede-born here vnfold,
        For then had I noght dampned ne lost be.
        Alas! my lord cousyn, gentile and fre,

LEsse worth am I then any sarysyne,
    Whiche is in beleue of sory mahound!"   310

Clariodus, III, 1557–92
[*Clariodus: A Metrical Romance* (London, 1830).]

Alleace! he said, quhat sall I do or say,
My warldis joy is [from me] reft for ay;
O now quhair sall I go or quhair sall I ryd,
Quhair sall I walke at evin or morrow tyd!   1560
Whairto for sleip sould I to bedis go,
Or quhairto ryse, I waits of nocht bot wo,
Or quhairto leive I, [now] thus myne allone,
When all my cumpanie is fra me gone;
O Death, cum slay me cative in distres,   1565
That never sall have ane day of mirrines!
Why lests my bodie, seing my heart is slaine,
Fairweill for ever all eardlie joy againe!
And this he said with sik ane pitious cheir,
It was ane paine him for to se or heir;   1570

And sorrow him tormentit so fellounlie,
Monie ane tyme he cryit God mercie,
Have mercie, Lord, that [wiselie] hes me wrocht,
Syne with thy daith so deir thow hes me bocht,
That I fall not in desperatioun;   1575
Thy woundis fyve be my salvatioun
That I do nocht that may my soul [eer] tyne;
I ask thé mercie, sweit Redemer myne,
Now of my grief and my impatience,
Who am bereft of all intelligence,   1580
And can no resoun have nor sufferance;
Whill daith upon me do his uterance;
And eike have mercie on ʒon fair Ladie,
Sen I hir lovit for no villanie,
As for the cryme scho stervit ane innocent,   1585
And pitiouslie with churlis all to rent,
And murtherit as ane theif without a judge,
Be thow hir ressait, succur and refuge;
And let thy woundis be for hir remeid,
That for hir sinnis oppinit war so reid;   1590
Among thy angellis resave hir in thy joy,
As thow that ar of mercie Prince and Roy.

Recuyell of the Historyes of Troy, 500–501

[*The Recuyell of the Historyes of Troy, written in French by Raoul Lefeore, translated & printed by William Caxton (c.A.D. 1474*), reproduced and edited by H. O. Sommer (London, 1894), pp. 500–501.]

/What haue I doo alas/ Alas what haue I doo. The most solempne man of men shynyng amonge the clerkes/ He that traversid the stronge marches amonge the fondementes terrestre/ that bodyly conuersid amonge the men/ And spirytuelly amonge the sonne the mone and the sterris And that susteyned the circomference of the heuenes is ded. by my cause and by my coulpe And with oute my culpe/ He is ded by my culpe ffor I haue sende to hym the sherte that hath gyue to hym the bytte of deth/ But this is with oute my culpe. for I knewe no thyng of the poyson/ O mortall poyson/ By me is he pryved of his lyffe. of whome I louyd the lyf as moche as I dide myn owne. He that bodyly dwellid amonge the men here in erthe And spyrituelly aboue with the sonne the mone and the celestiall

secretis. He that was fontayne of scyence/ by whom the Athen-
yens arrowsid and bedewyd their wittes and engyns. He that
made the monstres of the see to tremble in their abismes and
swalowis. and destroyed the monstres of helle. He confonded
the monstres of the erthe. the tyrantes he correctid. the
orguyllous and prowde he humelyed & meked The humble and
meke he enhauncyd and exaltyd. He that maad no tresour but
vertue. He that alle the nacions of the world subiuged and subdued with his clubbe/ And he that yf he had wolde by ambicion
of seygnourye myght haue atteyned to be kynge of the est. of
the west. of the sowth. and of the north/ of the sees and of
the montaynes. of all thise he myght haue named hym kynge
and lord by good right. yf he had wold. Alas alas what am I
born in an vnhappy tyme Whan so hyhe and so myghty a prynce
is ded by my symplesse He was the glorye of the men. Ther
was neuer to hym none lyke. ne neuer shall be/ ought I to
lyue after hym Nay certes that shall I neuer doo. ffor to the
ende that amonge the ladyes I be not shewid ne poyntyd with
the fynger/ And that I falle not in to strange hande for to be
punysshid of as moche as I haue of coulpe and blame in this
deth. I shall doo the vengeance to my self/ And with that she
toke a knyf. and sayng I fele my self and knowe that I am
Innocente of the deth of my lord hercules. And with the
poynte of the knyf she ended her dispayred lyf/

Otuel and Roland, 2505–10, 2520–40
[*Firumbras and Otuel and Roland,* ed. Mary I. O'Sullivan,
EETS, CXCVIII (London, 1935), pp. 137–38.]

"O roulond, the good conquer*our,*   2505
And the noblyst warry*our,*
That eu*er*-more schal be!
Now y haue the for-lore,
Dey y wylle the be-fore,
But god wyl saue!"   2510

                    .   .   .

"Roulond, now for the loue of the,   2520
Dede now wyl y be!
Of blys y am alle bare.

"Thow were strong as sampson,
And bolder thanne any lyon,

In batayle and eke in fyȝt.   2525
I may wepe for thy partyng,
So dude dauid the kyng,
ffor absolon the whyte.
Best me ys my self to sle,
ffor glad ne worthe y neuer mo,   2530
After thys ylke syȝt.
Thow were in were good and wys,
As was Iudas machabeus,
That was godys knyȝt."

The barouns beden hym let be,   2535
And sayde, "syre, þur charyte,
lete a-way thys ylke mornyng!
wel ȝe seth how it geth,
There nys no bote of mannys deth,
Take to the confortyng!"   2540

Guy of Warwick, Auchinleck MS., 4884–95
[*The Romance of Guy of Warwick,* ed. Julius Zupitza, *EETSES,*
XLIX (London, 1887), pp. 279–80.]

'A, leman Tirri,' quaþ sche þo,
'What, y se þi neb al blo,   4885
Þat so white of colour was:
Þi beter neuer y-born nas.
In wreched time mi bodi þou say,
When þou schalt for me day.
Dye ich-il forþ wiþ þe: 4890
For sorwe liues no may y be.
Bot y may dye ichil me quelle:
Leng to libbe is nouȝt mi wille.
Seþþen þou hast þi deþ for me,
For soþe dye ich-il for þe.'   4895

Buik of Alexander, II, 71–86
[*The Buik of Alexander, or the Buik of the Most Noble and
Valiant Conquerour Alexander the Grit by John Barbour,* ed.
R.L.G. Ritchie, *STSNS,* XII (London, 1921), pp. 110.]

Than to him said he, "shir, perfay,
At Gaderis endit hes that day
The best on ground that euer was borne,
Bot Alexander I tak beforne;

To him I mak na man compair, 75
King nor knicht na ʒit empeir;
And gif the King into bounte
Had ony peir, it micht be he.
For kynde had nurished him sa weill
Of all verteuis that man may feill, 80
For nocht was wantand in that wyse
That mycht put ony man to pryse;
For wise he was and debonare,
Hardy, kynd, courtes and fare,
To witnes dar I drawe Venus, 85
Mars, Neptune and Mercurius."

Malory, iii, 1259
[*The Works of Sir Thomas Malory,* ed. Eugen Vinaver (Oxford, 1947), III, 1259.]

'A, Launcelot!' he sayd, 'thou were hede of al Crysten knyghtes! And now I dare say,' sayd syr Ector, 'thou sir Launcelot, there thou lyest, that thou were never matched of erthely knyghtes hande. And thou were the curtest knyght that ever bare shelde! And thou were the truest frende to thy lovar that ever bestrade hors, and thou were the trewest lover of a synful man that ever loved woman, and thou were the kyndest man that ever strake wyth swerde. And thou were the godelyest persone that ever cam emonge prees of knyghtes, and thou wast the mekest man and the jentyllest that ever ete in halle emonge ladyes, and thou were the sternest knyght to thy mortal foo that ever put spere in the reeste.'

Guy of Warwick, Caius MS., 10, 976–11,022
[*The Romance of Guy of Warwick,* ed. Julius Zupitza, *EETSES,* LIX (London, 1891), pp. 623–25.]

'Lordyng*is*,' he seyd, 'thys ys *sir* Gye,
Of warwyke the Erle worthy.
He faught for me worthylye
At wynchester, ye all hyt sye,
And slow for Englondis ryʒt 10,980
Of all the world the strengest knyʒt.
Also he slow here in Englond
A dragon, for-soth, as I vndyrstond,
Full fer in the north contree:
All ye hyt know that here be; 10,985

So that twyse this blessyd knyʒt
Hath savyd Englond with hys myʒt
In all thys world ne was hys pere.
This gentyll knyʒt that lyeth here,
Yf he had coveyted honoure,   10,990
He myʒt have bene an Emperoure.
The Emperoure hym bad hys douʒter dere
With all hys landys ferre and nere
For hys douʒtynes of honde
That he provyd in hys londe.   10,995
Of all the world the grettest lord
With the Emperoure was a dyscorde,
Of babylon the hyʒe sowdan:
Thrytty kyngis hym omage done.
Sir Gye hym slow at hys bord: 11,000
All they ne durst speke on word.
He brought hys hed to the Emperoure.
Of Cristendom he was the floure.
He slow ameraunt, the bold paynym:
All the world was a-drad of hym.   11,005
He slow the Duke Otown of pavy
For hys treason and hys trechery,
And sethen berrard after hym:
He was a Geaunt styffe and gryme.
This gentyll Gye, of whome I talke,   11,010
Thorough all the world hath he hys walke.
All falshed and trechory
Euer-more he wold dystroye.
I may well hyt avow ryght,
That he was a trew knyʒt.   11,015
Vppon a boke he dyd me swere
At Wynchester no fer ne nere
That I shuld wrey hym tyll no man
Tell thys twelmoneth were a-gone.
I have holdyn myn othe parfaye: 11,020
Yesterday was the laste daye.
God assoyle the sowle ryʒt.'

Morte Arthure, 3866–85
[*Morte Arthure, mit Einleitung, Anmerkungen und Glossar*, ed.
Erik Björkman (New York, 1915), p. 114.]

"Knewe thow eu*er* this knyghte   in thi kithe ryche?
Of whate kynde he was comen,   beknowe now þe sothe;
Qwat gome was he,   this w*ith* the gaye armes,
With þis gryffou*ne* of golde,   þat es one growffe fallyn?
He has grettly greffede vs,   sa me Gode helpe!   3870
Gyrde down oure gude men   and greuede vs sore.
He was þe sterynneste in stoure,   that eu*er* stele werryde,
For he has stonayede oure stale   and stroyede for eu*er*."
    Than s*ir* Mordrede w*ith* mouthe   melis full faire:
"He was makles one molde,   mane be my trow[t]he;
This was s*ir* Gawayne the gude,   þe gladdeste of othire,
And the graciouseste gome,   that vndire God lyffede,
Mane hardyeste of hande,   happyeste in armes
And þe hendeste in hawle   vndire heuen riche;
Þe lordelieste of ledyng*e*,   qwhylls he lyffe myghte,
Fore he was lyone allossede   in londes inewe;
Had thow knawen hym, s*ir* kyn*ge*,   in kythe thare he lengede,
His konynge, his knyghthode,   his kyndly werkes,
His doyng, his doughtynesse,   his dedis of armes,
Thow wolde hafe dole for his dede   þe days of thy lyfe."
                                                          3885

Laud Troy Book, 11,330–418

[*The Laud Troy Book, A Romance of c. 1400,* ed. J. E. Wulfing, *EETS,* CXXII (London, 1903), pp. 334–36.]

And seyde: 'lordynges, my dere frende,   11,330
Wel auȝt vs to glorifie
Oure goddis that ȝeuen vs the Maystrie
Off oure enemy that we haue sclayn;
Ther-of we ben alle fayn
And gret worschepe & hono*ur* do,   11,335
For elles hadde we neu*ere* comen ther-to,
    Whil he hadde leued, to oure p*ur*pos.
But now may we wel suppos,
Sithen he is ded that hem defende,
That thei haue alle theire endyng ende,   11,340
And we schal lordis & maystres be
Off here godis & here Cite.
For whil he leued, myȝt we not spede,
So was he douȝti In his dede;
Vs myȝt no g*ra*ce for him by-falle,   11,345

For he on vndid vs alle.
   We hadde no let but him alon*e*,
But now is he ded & from vs gon*e*,
We schal that Cite lyghtly wynne
And alle that ben hit with-Inne;   11,350
For thei are now of no power
To kepe he*m* fro oure daunger,
Sithen he is ded & from hem went
That vs al day so foule schent.
It is to vs wel more a-vauntage   11,355
That he is ded & loken In cage,
Then we hadde sclayn In fight felle
Halff the men that with hem dwelle.
   For he sclow mo him-selff alone
Then alle that other did eu*er*ychone,   11,360
And we ben now—I vnderstande—
Mo then sixti hundred thousande
Off Mennes bodies gode and able,
That ben a-pert and defendable.
THe dedis of Ector ben wide y-kyd,   11,365
That thei may not wel be hid:
How fele kynges sclow he of oure
With his myȝt & his vigoure!
How he sclow In his reuery
The douȝti kyng Pr*o*thesaly!   11,370
   Patrodus also, Achilles cosyn,
In his strenghte sclow he him!
   How sclow he In his gret Ire
Kyng Mennon, that lordly sire!
We were echon of him a-dred.   11,375
How sclow he the gode kyng Ced!
So did he kyng Polenete.
He fond no man that to him was mete.
He sclow also kyng Alphynor,
And so he did kyng Pr*o*uenor   11,380
That was a kyng of gret genterie,
Off douȝtines and chiualrie.
   How sclow he with his force
The myghti kyng of douȝti Corce!
He died with dynt: so he gart   11,385
The noble kyng Piloȝenart.

He sclow also the kyng Yside.
No man durst him a-byde.
He did also to dethe sone
The douȝti kyng Letabone.   11,390
Ne sclow he not the kyng Humere?
I wist neu*ere* man that was his pere.
    He sclow oure kyng Archilogus,
And the kyng also Episcropus;
And so he did kyng Archomene,   11,395
And the hardy kyng Palymene.
Ne sclow he not the kyng Antipe?
And so he did kyng Sanxipe.
    He did vs moche sorwe and tene:
He sclow the gode kyng Philoxene;   11,400
He smot to dethe vndir his fete
The noble kyng Polibete,
Kyng Phiebete, and kyng Leankes,
Alle he sclow oure gret vnthankes,
He smot her bodyes euen In-two;   11,405
So did he other mo also.
We auȝt wele his bodi wary!
    He sclow kyng Fume & kyng Dary,
And Many duk and Amerelles;
He sclow oure lordes & robbed oure halles,   11,410
And bar a-wey coffre & chest.
He that him sclow mot be blest!
For now—I hope—he is ded
That did vs schame and qued,
That oure men so foule sclow,   11,415
And we he*m* alle schal Maystre now
With-Inne a while at oure wille.
But herkenes now! this is my skylle:

Buik of Alexander, IV, 9580–94
[*The Buik of Alexander, or the Buik of the Most Noble and
Valiant Conqueror Alexander the Grit by John Barbour,* ed.
R. L. G. Ritchie, *STSNS,* XXV (Edinburg, 1929), pp. 392–93.]

And said, "fle we! thare fleis anew!   9580
Sen that our lord is slane and deid,
That held all gude men ay at feid,
And of trechouris and of lossingeris

He maid his preue counsalers,
And now thay fle als wele as we,   9585
That he vplyfted throw maieste,
And reft our gude agane our will,
Bot now he is brocht thairtill,
That he na ȝarnes siluer na gold fyne,
He hes na mister of medecyne!   9590
We sould not greit, bot lauch full loud,
For men sould scarce men, hard and proud
And couetous, always despyse,
And helpe thare harme on alkin wyse!"

Buik of Alexander, IV, 9603–18
[*The Buik of Alexander, or the Buik of the Most Noble and
Valiant Conqueror Alexander the Grit by John Barbour,* ed.
R. L. G. Ritchie, *STSNS,* XXV (Edinburgh, 1929), p. 393
cont.]

"EME," said Marciane, "stout and bald,
That in great stour and battell wald
Alwayes with the formest be!   9605
Pride, inuy and skarsite,
Couatyce, reif and succudry,
And that gudemen and worthy.
And than defoulit and vntrew ay,
Hes brocht the now to thyne ending day!   9610
A! thow that lufit theuis and murderers
And hated all trew bachlers,
Now helpis the nocht thy great ȝarning
Of landis, rentis, and vther thing
That thow was wont to reif and ta   9615
Fra wedowes and fatherles barnes alsa,
Bot now the dede that spared nane
Hes the in his handis tane!"

Buik of Alexander, I, 2830–46
[*The Buik of Alexander, or the Buik of the Most Noble and
Valiant Conqueror Alexander the Grit by John Barbour,* ed.
R. L. G. Ritchie, *STSNS,* XVII (London, 1925), pp. 89–90.]

"Thair lyis pryse in defoulling!   2830
Men that ar wraith will nocht weill ta
In thank to be defoulit sa!

That hes thow feld in sum party!
Had thow nocht proud bene, sikkerly
Thow had bene of great vassalage,   2835
Now mon thow keip heir this passage,
And quhan marcat or fair sal be,
To thame that may pertene to me
Luke thow with thame na bargane ma!
Gaudifeir de Laris, thy fa.   2840
Hes heir acquentit him with the.
To-day my fleing sall not be
Lattit for the, I vnderta!
All quick to Gaderis sall I ga,
Bot gif that I vnhorsit be   2845
With ane better all out na the!"

Barbour's Bruce, V, 161–74
[John Barbour, *The Bruce: or the Book of the most excellent noble prince, Robert de Broyss, King of Scots,* ed. W. W. Skeat, *EETSES,* LV (London, 1889), pp. 110–111.]

"Allas!" he said, "for luf of me.
And for mekill gud laute,
*Th*ai nobill men and *th*ai worthy
Ar distroyit sa vilonisly!
Bot and I lif in lege pouste,   165
*Th*air ded sall ry*ch*t weill vengit be.
*Th*e king, *th*e quhe*thir,* of yngland
Thoucht *that th*e kinrik of scotland
Wes to litill to hym and me;
*Th*arfor I will it all myn be.   170
Bot of gud cristal of Setouñe,
*Th*at wes of sa nobill renouñe,
*Th*at he suld de war gret pite,
Bot quhar vorschip my*ch*t prufit be."

Morte Arthure, 4034–47
[*Morte Arthure mit Einleitung, Anmerkungen und Glossar,* ed. Erik Björkman (New York, 1915), p. 119.]

"I praye the, kare noghte, *sir* knyghte,   ne caste þou no dredis!
Hadde I no segge bot my selfe   one vndire son[n]e   4035
And I may hym see *with* sighte   or one hym sette hondis,
I sall even amange his mene   malle hym to dede,

Are I of þe stede styre   halfe a stede-lenghe.
I sall [stryke] hym in his stowre,   and stroye hym for euer,
And þareto make I myn avowe   devottly to Cryste   4040
And to hys modyre Marie,   þe mylde qwene of heuen.
I sall neuer soiourne sounde   ne sawghte at myne herte,
In ceté ne in subarbe   sette appon erthe,
Ne ʒitt slomyre ne slepe   with my slawe eygh[e]ne,
Till he be slayne, þat hym slowghe,   ʒif any sleyghte
    happen: 4045
Bot euer pursue the payganys,   þat my pople distroyede,
Qwylls I may par[r]e them and pynne,   in place þare me
    likes."

Laʒamon's Brut, MS. Cott. Calig. A. IX, ii, 460–61
[*Laʒamon's Brut, or Chronicle of Britain*, ed. Sir Frederick
Madden (London, 1847), II, 460–61.]

Wala wa walawa.'
Þat ich sparede mine iua.
Þat ich nauede on holte.'
mid hūgere hine adefed.
oðer mid sweorde.'
al hine to-swungen.
Nu he me ʒilt mede.'
for mire god dede.
ah swa me hælpen drihten.'
pæ scop pæs dæies lihten.
þer fore he scal ibiden.'
bitterest alre baluwen.
harde gomenes.'
his bone ich wulle iwurðen.
Colgim & Baldulf.'
beiene ich wulle aquellen
& al heore duʒeðe.'
dæð scal iðolien.
ʒif hit wule ivunnen.'
waldende hæfnen.
ich wulle wurðliche wreken.'
alle his wiðer deden.
ʒif me mot ilasten.'
Þat lif mire breosten.

& hit wulle me iunne.'
Þat i-scop mone & sunne.
ne scal nauere Childric.'
æft me bi-charren.

Sir Percyvelle of Galles, 539–68.
[*The Romance of Percyvelle of Galles* in *The Thornton Romances,* ed. J. O. Halliwell (London, 1844), pp. 21–22.]

"Allas!" he sayde, "that I was made
   Be day or by nyghte! 540
One lyve I scholde after hym bee,
That methynke lyke the,
Thou arte so semely to see,
   And thou were wele dighte!"
            XXXV
He saide, "and thou were wele dighte, 545
Thou were lyke to a knyghte
That I lovede with alle my myghte,
   Whilles he was one lyve;
So wele wroghte he my wille
In alle manere of skille, 550
I gaffe my syster hym tille
   For to be his wyfe;
He es moste in my mane,
Fiftene ʒere es it gane
Sene a theffe hade hym slane 555
   Abowte a littille stryffe!
Sythene hafe I ever bene his fo,
For to wayte hym with wo,
Bot I myʒte hym never slo,
   His craftes are so ryfe!" 560
            XXXVi
He sayse, "his craftes are so ryfe,
Ther is no mane apone lyfe,
With swerde, spere, ne with knyfe,
   May stroye hym allane,
But if it were syr Percyvelle sone; 565
Who so wiste where he ware done,
The bokes says that he mone
   Venge his fader bane."

Lydgate's Troy Book, III, 3823–69
[*Lydgate's Troy Book,* ed. Henry Bergan, *EETSES,* CIII (London, 1908, pp. 505–506.]

And of o þing moste is my greuaunce,
Whan I haue fully remembraunce,
And in my mynde considre vp & doun,   3825
How þou madist a diuisioun
Of me, allas! and of Patroclus,
So ȝonge, so manly, and so vertuous!
Whom I loued, as it was skyl & riȝt,
Riȝt as my silf, with al my ful myȝt,   3830
With as hol herte and inly kyndenes
As any tonge may tellen or expres.
Now hast þou made a departisioun
Of vs þat werne by hool affeccioun
I-knet in oon, of hertly allyaunce,   3835
With-oute partynge or disseueraunce—
So enteerly oure feithful hertis tweyen
I-lacid werne, and lokkid in o cheyne,
Whiche myȝt[e] nat for noon aduersite
Of lyf nor deth assonder twynned be,   3840
Til cruelly þou madest vs departe,
Whiche þoruȝ myn hert so inwardly [doth] darte,
Þat it wil neuer, in soth, out of my þouȝt.
And, trust wel, ful dere shal be bouȝt
Þe deth of hym, &, be no þing in were,   3845
Parauenture or endid be þis ȝere:
For vp-on þe, only for his sake,
Of cruel deth vengaunce shal be take,
I þe ensure, with-outen oþer bond;
ȝif I may lyue, with myn owne hond   3850
I shal of deth don execucioun,
With-oute abood or [long] dylacioun.
For riȝt requereth, with-outen any drede,
Deth for deth, for his final mede;
For I my silfe þer-on shal be wroke,   3855
Þat þoruȝ þe world her-after shal be spoke,
How Achilles was vengid on his foo,
For Patroclus þat he loued so.
And þouȝ þat I be to þe envious,

And of þi deth inly desirous,   3860
Ne wyte me nat, ne put on me no blame,
For wel I wote þou arte to me þe same,
And haste my deth many day desyred,
And þer-vp-on inwardly conspired:
And þus, shortly, as a-twen vs two   3865
Þer is but deth, wiþ-oute wordis mo,
Whan fortune hath þe tyme shape,
I hope fully þou shalt nat eskape —
Truste noon oþer, I seie þe outterly!"

Blanchardyn and Eglantine, 213
[*Caxton's Blanchardyn and Eglantine,* ed. Leon Kellner, *EETSES,* LVIII (London, 1890), p. 213.]

   'and is she gon, the comfort of my youth, the staffe of my age, the day of my night, the sonshine of my blisse, the sollace of my soule, and the life of my death? Ah! to to well I suspected (though alas I knew not the certentie) that my captiuitie would bring her callamity, and my imprisonment her death. But since all humane flesh is mortall, and nothing vnder the Sunne permanent, what auailes my sorowful grones and passions? to weake, alas, to recall her againe, or any way to remedie my misfortune!' with these or the like exclaimes, this silly aged King, panting betweene life and death, lay still a while, till finding his heart ouer charged with an other passion, he prosecuted his first complaint: 'O sacred Ioue, searcher of all secret thoughts, whose eternall dietie raigneth within the highest heauens, who from my cradle hast destined me to perpetuall miserie, now shew thy self a righteous judge, and reuenge my wronges vppon the accursed broode of infidels, who so irreligiously prophane thy blessed name, & suffer them not to escape they reuenging powre, but at thy pleasure consume and confound the workers of this my woe! and now dissolue my daies and weary life, & leade me through th' unknowne passages to my deere and sweetest wife, that though our daies on earth did finde small comfort, yet our soules in heauen may finde consolation!'

Sege of Melayne, 543–58
[*The Sege of Melayne,* ed. S. J. Herrtage, *EETSES,* XXXV (London, 1880), p. 18.]

"I sall neu*er* were the more,
Ne o*þer* habite for to bere,
Bot buske me bremly to þ ᵉ were,   545
    And lerene one slyke a lore.
A! Mary mylde, where was thi myght,
Þat þou lete thi men thus to dede be dighte,
    Þ*at* wighte & worthy were?
Art þou noghte halden of myghtis moste,   550
Full Conceyuede of þe holy goste?
    Me ferlys of thy fare.
            (47)
Had þou noghte, Marye, ȝitt bene borne
Ne had noghte oure gud men thus bene lorne?
    Þe wyte is all in the.   555
Thay faughte holly in thy ryghte,
Þat þus w*ith* dole to dede es dyghte,
    A! Marie, how may this bee?"

Firumbras, 1102–22

[*Firumbras and Otuel and Roland,* ed. M. I. O'Sullivan, *EETS,*
CXCVIII (London, 1935), pp. 36–37.]
"Lordynges," sayde charlys, "lysteneth to me!
Telleth me ȝoure counsayl, as ȝe be to me sworne.
Of my gode barons that y haue thus y-lore!
But y mowe on lyue haue hem agayn,   1105
By sent Denys now y schal ȝow sayn,
y schal to-day forsake myn heritage,
And ȝyld vp þe croun a-mong my baronage!
God and our*e* lady," sayde þe Emp*er*our.
"So saue hem, bothe Roulond & Oliu*er,* & send hem
    soco*ur*!   1110
And ȝyf hem myȝt and strengthe w*ith*-Inne a lyte space
To ou*er*-come her car*e* þoruȝ þyn holy gr*ace*!
ffor by þ*at* ylke lord, god omn*i*potent,
Be Roulond and Olyu*er* ou*er*come, cristendom ys yschent!
y ne schal suffre in fraunce, no bellys ryng,   1115
In Chyrch ne *in* chapel, no prest mas to synge,
Ne in none o*þer* plas halywat*er* to spryng,
No non bokes, godys name worchipyng,
The vygours and þe auta*r,* þat in holy chryche beȝth found,
I schal hem adoun falle and bete to þe grounde.   1120

Be my dussepers oue*r*com, to god a ʒyfte y ʒeue,
Ne schal I neu*er* worschyp god, whyles þat y leue."

Partonope of Blois, MS. Univ. Coll., Oxford, C. 188, 4585–4605

[*The Middle English Versions of Partonope of Blois,* ed. A.
Trampe Bödtker, *EETSES,* CIX (London, 1912), p. 168.]

"Allas, Partanope! thow were so nye   4585
My kynne and eke my gourernoure.
Now arte thow dede which were the floure
Of alle the knyghthode that longyth to Fraunce.
Allas! what happe or myschaunce
Was that this feelde so flasly   4590
Was kept; the hethen now trwly
Be forsworne wythouten nay.
The contrary they mowe not say,
For I myself was pr*e*sent for sothe,
Whan they toke her othe.   4595
Yet for Sornogoure I am ryght sory
That he shulde be founde in su[c]he vylany.
And yet I wote well he lakked no manhode.
I trusted eu*er* fully in his knyghthode
And in his gentell-nesse and suerte,
That such vntrouth wolde not he
Enforged ne neu*er* haue wrought.
I trowe therto he not co*n*sentyd in thought."

Foure Sonnes of Aymon, Chap. IX, 243–44
[*The Right Pleasant and Goodly Historie of the Foure Sonnes of
Aymon,* ed. Octavia Richardson, *EETSES,* XLIV (London,
1884), pp. 243–44.]

... and kyssed hym sore wepynge, and sayd/ 'Ha, fayre
brother/ It is grete pyte and dommage of you/ and of your
dethe/ For, certes, never man was worthe you; for yf ye had
come to mannys age/ never Rowlande nor Olyver were so prue
in knyghthode/ as ye sholde have be. Alas, now is loste our
beaulte and our youghte thorughe grete synne/ O, goode lorde/
who sholde ever a thoughte that ony treason sholde have entred
in to the herte of the kynge Yon/ Alas, my bother Richarde,
woo is me for your dethe/ For I am cause of it/ Alas, this daye
in the mornynge, whan we departed oute of Mountalban we
were four bretherne, all good knyghtes. Now are we but

thre, that ben worthe noo thynge, for we ben peryllously
wounded, and all vnarmed. Now god forbede that I sholde
scape, syth that ye be deed vpon the traytours. But I praye
god that I maye venge your deth vpon theym or ever I deceasse/
For I shall sette therto my gode wylle; and yf god wyll, it shall
be soo.'

Valentine and Orson, 161
[*Valentine and Orson, translated from the French by Henry
Watson,* ed. Arthur Dickson, *EETS,* CCIV (London, 1937),
p. 161.]

Alas now am I vsurped by bytter fortune on all sydes, and
all my Ioyes are well chaunged in to sorowe and dystresse whan
I haue loste my pryncipall frende the floure of all my comforte,
and the hope of all my lyfe. Alas my fayre broder Orson now
haue I loste you by the false sarazyns, for I knowe well that
your valyaunt[n]es and hardynes is cause of your dethe
shortynge. For I knowe so moche by you that you wyll ra|hter
dye valyauntly, than lyue in reproche and shame, Alas valyaunt
broder Orson in payne and in trauayl I conquered you in the
wodde and syth I haue kepte you in peryll and in daunger. And
nowe whan I purposed and thought to haue solace and myrthe
of you ye be separed and gone from me but syth that it is so
that I can haue no tydynges of you in no maner wyse. I swere
and promyse to god that I shall knowe shortlye where you are,
and fynde you quycke or deed, or youre loue shal be cause of
my dethe anone.

Guy of Warwick, Auchinleck MS., 1555–94
[*The Romance of Guy of Warwick,* ed. Julius Zupitza, *EETSES,*
LII (London, 1883), pp. 88–90.]

'Allas,' quod Gii, 'felawes dere!   1555
So wele doand kniȝtes ȝe were.
Al to iuel it fel to me,
Felice, þo y was sent to serue þe;
For þi loue, Felice, the fair may,
Þe flour of kniȝtes is sleyn þis day.   1560
Ac for þou art a wiman,
Y no can nouȝt blame þe for þan;
For þe last no worþ y nouȝt
Þat wimen han to gronde y-brouȝt.

Ac alle oþer may bi me,   1565
ʒif þai wil, y-warned be.
Allas, Herhaud, mi dere frende,
What þou were curteys & hende!
Who schal me now help in fiʒt
Neuer no was no better kniʒt.   1570
In ich fiʒt wele halp thou me,
Ful iuel ichaue y-ʒolden it þe;
For me þou hast þi liif forgon,
Of þe no tit me neuer help non.
How mai ich now fram þe wende?   1575
That y no mai dye þe hende!
Acursed be þe Lombardes ichon,
That slowen þe, and lete me gon!
& þat þai hadde y-slawe me,
& leten þe oliue be!   1580
Wharto lete þai me alon?'
Þus sir Gij biment his mone.
    'Allas! allas! Rohaut, mi lord,
Þat y no hadde leued þi word!
Þan hadde y nouʒt y-passed þe se,   1585
Ich hadde bileued at hom wiþ þe;
Þus yuel nere me nouʒt bifalle,
Y no hadde nouʒt lorn min felawes alle.
Who so nil nouʒt do bi his faders red,
Oft-siþes it falleþ him qued;   1590
For often ichaue herd it say,
& y me self it sigge may,
"Who þat nil nouʒt leue his fader,
He schel leue his steffadder."

Lydgate's Seige of Thebes, 3229–59
[*Lydgate's Seige of Thebes,* ed. Axel Erdmann and Elbert
Ekwall, *EETSES,* CVIII (London, 1911), pp. 133–34.]

And oftë sith she gan to seyn, "allas!
O wooful wrech/ vnhappy in this cas,   3230
What shal I don/ or whider may I tourne?
For þis the fyn/ ʒif I her soiourne,
I woot right wel/ I may not eskape
The pitous fatë/ þat is for me shape.
Socour is non/ nor ther may be non red,   3235

lich my desert/ but that I mot be ded;
For thorhe my slouth/ and my neclygence
I haue, allas! don so gret offence
That my gilt/, I may it nat excuse,
Shal to the kyng/ of treson me accuse.   3240
Thorgh my defaute/ *and* slouthë bothë two,
His sone is ded/ *and* his heir also,
which he louëd mor than al his good:
For tresour noñ/ so nygh his hertë stood,
Nor was so depë/ graue/ in his corage: 3245
That he is likly to fallen in a Rage
whan it is so, myn odyous offence
Reported be vnto his audience;
So inportable shal be his hevynesse.
    And wel woot I/ in *ver*rey sothfastnesse.
That, whan the quenë/ hath this þing espied,
To myn excus/ It may nat be denyed,
I doutë it not/ ther geyneth no pytè,
With-oute respit/ she wil avengëd be
On me, allas!/ as I ha deserued;   3255
That fro the deth/ I may not be *pre*serued
Nowther be bille/ ne supplicacio*n*;
For the rage/ of my transgressiou*n*
Requereth deth/ and noñ other mede."

Eneydos, 107–108

[*Caxton's Eneydos, 1490, Englisht from the French Liure des
Eneydos, 1483,* ed W. T. Culley and F. J. Furnivall, *EETSES,*
LVII (London, 1890), pp. 107–108.]

/"My righte swete suster, alas, what haste thou doo/ and
by what maner & rayson hast *t*hou broughte thi selfe thus to
eternall perdycyon/ and has deceyued me wyckedly & falsely
wyth a bytter deth/ whiche I wolde gladly haue suffred & endured wyth the/ Alas, what nede was it to me to make redy
the sacrifyces/ sith that a fyre for all other obsequyes & a
swerde well sharpe slyped, myghte haue broughte the two sus-
ters to deth bothe atones, wythout to haue be departed one
from the othre. Alas, what shalle I saye, ne what begynnynge
maye I now take for to make my mone/ Why haste you thus
dyspraysed me that am thy suster and true felawe? alle my
lyfe I haue honoured, worshiped, serued & praysed the/ and

eke moche loued the. For to folowe the, I haue alle haban-douned/ I haue knowen thy werke. I haue knowen thy wyll/ and also thy secretes thou wolde neuer hide from me/ Alas now, what furye hath taken the atte this nede/ whiche is the sorowe mortalle/ for to haue caste me thus abacke from thy presence/ by cause *that* I sholde haue had not knowen this faicte. "Alas! yf I myght haue knowen the same thynge, veraye trouthe I wolde haue deyed with the/ O what sorowe I doo supporte, whan I haue lost alle my force/ and noon ther is that me recomforteth; but of alle sydes is brought to me peyne & traueylle without mesure/ the grete wrathe and the grete care that wrongly, and magre myself, I doo endure, whan I me recorde of the Iniure that my suster hath falsly doon, not onely to me/ but hathe defyled vylaynsly the good name and the enchau*n*synge of the cytee that she hathe co*m*mysed, and sub-mysed to a grete vilete & shame; for alle tymes shalbe recyted the enormyte of this fowlle befalle, whiche euer shalbe imputed to a grete infamye, wherof they of cartage shalle haue a blame, *that* shalle torne vnto them to a grete diffamye. And moche more, bycause of theire good fame that was knowen/ that had be well entreteyned, and in grete worship susteyned/ yf my suster had mayntened and kept herself wythout dysperacyon/ Wherof alle hope/ as well to theym as to me, failleth, by her *that* hath extyncted oure goode renommee, & brought vs in a grete blame; & nowe be we without pastoure, as the sheep that is habau*n*douned! Now thenne, sith that it is thus come/ lete vs loke to her wounde, and in her face, yf she is thurghly passed"/

King Ponthus and the Fair Sidone, 125
[*King Ponthus and the Fair Sidone,* ed. F. J. Mather in *PMLA,* XII (1897), 125.]

And when the kyng and his doghtre sawe these *lett*res, it is not to aske of the grete sorowe and hevynes that they made. Sydone swoned often tymes and weped and whisshed aftre hym, the whiche myght not be oute of hir mynde. She drewe and rent hir fare here and made so grete sorowe that itt was grete petee to see. So the ladys and the courte wer in grete hevynes for hym and said, "Allas! What damege! What pitee! The flour of knyghthode, the flour of all gentyllnes, the myrro*ur* of all goode man*er*s be dystroyd." The toune, the burgesses, and all the comon people weped and soroed for theyr frendes and theyr kynesmen, for they trowed that they had ben all deyd.

Ther myght noo man comforth Sydone. "Allas!" sayd she. "He was that man in whom all bountee and trewth dwelled, and by (whome) I thoght to haue had all my ioye, and the which was so free and so trewe and loued me so wele and was so likly to haue holden the people in rest and peace. How has God soffred suche aventure agane hym and agane me? Allas sorofull wreche! What shall I doe?" So ther was noon so hard a hert bot that it wold haue had pitee of hir; and this sorowe endured more than viij days withoute cessyng.

William of Palerne, 125–161
[*The Romance of William of Palerne, otherwise known as "The Romance of William and the Werwolf,"* ed. W. W. Skeat, *EETSES*, I (London, 1877), pp. 4–5.]

La roine maine tel duel,	125
morte voudroit estre, son vuel;	
pleure sovent, et crie, et brait,	
a la beste son fil retrait.	
"fix, dous amis," fait la roine,	
tendre bouche, coulor rosine.	130
chose devine, espiritex,	
qui cuidast que best ne leus	
vos devorast! dix, quel eur!	
lasse! por coi vif taut ne dur?	
fix, ou sont ore ti bel oel,	135
li bel, li simple, sans orguel?	
tes frons li gens, et ti bel crin,	
qui tuit sambloient fait dor fin?	
ta tendre face, et tes clers vis?	
ha cuers! por coi ne me partis?	140
quest devenue ta biautes,	
et tes gens cors, et ta clartes?	
tes nes, ta bouche, et tes mentons,	
et ta figure, et ta facons,	
et ti bel brac, et tes mains blanches,	145
tes rains beles, et tes hanches,	
tes beles jambes, et ti pie;	
lasse! quel duel et quel pechie!	
ja devoies tu estre fais	

por devises et por sourhais!   150
or es a leu-garoul peuture,
li miens enfes, quele aventure!
mais je ne cuit, por nule chose,
beste sauvage soit si ose,
qui ton gent cors ost adamer,   155
plaier, sanc faire, ne navrer;
ne cuit que ja dame dieu place,
ne que tel cruante en face!"
Ensi la dame se demente,
ensi por son fil se gaimente,   160
ensi le ploure, ensi le plaint.

The queen makes such a mourning,   125
She would fain be dead, had she her will;
She weeps often, and cries and wails,
And demands back her child from the beast.
"Son, sweet love," saith the queen,
"Tender mouth, rosy colour,   130
Thing divine and spiritual,
Who could believe that beast or wolf
Could devour you? O God! what fortune!
Alas! wherefore live I or last so long?
Son, where are now thy beautiful eyes,   135
So beautiful, so innocent, without pride?
Thy fair forehead, and thy lovely hair,
Which seemed all made of fine gold?
Thy tender face, and thy clear looks?
Oh heart! wherefore hast thou not left me?   140
What is become of thy beauty,
Thy sweet body, and thy fairness?
Thy nose, thy mouth, and thy chin,
And thy form and fashion,
And thy fair arm, and thy white hands,   145
Thy fair reins, and thy thighs,
Thy fair legs, and thy feet;
Alas! what sorrow and what fault!
Thou oughtest only to have been made
For pleasures and for desires!   150
Now art thou food for the werwolf.
My child! what a mischance!

But I cannot believe, on any account,
A wild beast would be so daring
As to hurt thy tender body,   155
To wound it, make it bleed, or tear it;
I cannot believe that it would please our Lord God,
Or that He would do such cruelty to it."
Thus the lady is in despair,
Thus she laments for her son,   160
Thus she weeps, thus she complains for him.

The Fillingham Otuel, Ellis, ii, 353–54

[*The Fillingham Otuel,* quoted in George Ellis, *Specimens of Early English Metrical Romances* (London, 1805), II, 353–54.]

"O le bras dexte de mon corps! l'honneur des Gaules! l'espée de chevalerie! Hache inflexible, haubergeon incorruptible et heaulme de salut! Comparé à Judas Machabeus par ta valeur et prouesse, ressemblant à Sanson, et pareil à Jonatas fils de Saul par la fortune de la triste morte! O chevalier très aspre et bien enseigné à combattre! fort, plus fort, et très fort! génie royal! destructeur des Sarrazins! des bons Chrestiens défenseur! le mur et deffence des eleves! le ferme baston des orphelins et veuves! la viande et réfection des pauvres! la révélation des églises! langue sans avoir menti ès jugemens de toutes choses," &c. Chap. xxiv.

Charles the Great, 240–41

[*The Lyf of the Noble and Crysten Prynce Charles the Grete,* translated from French by William Caxton & printed by him 1485, ed. S. J. H. Herrtage, *EETSES,* XXXVI (London, 1881), pp. 240–41.]

'O comforte of my body, honour of frenssh men, suerd of Iustyce, spere that myght not bowe, hawberck that myght not be broken, helme of helthe, resemblyng to Iudas machabeus in prowesse, samblant to sampson in strengthe, & to Absalon in beaulte! O ryght dere neuew, fayr & wyse, in batyl ryal! O destroyer of the sarasyns, defendour of crysten men, walle of clergye, staffe to wydowes & of poure orphelyns, Releuer of chyrches, tonge of trouthe, Mouthe wythout lesyng, trewe in al Iugement, prynce of bataylle, conduytour of the frendes of god, Augmentour of the crysten fayth, & byloued of euery persone!

Alas! why haue I brought the in to a straunge contreye? wherfor am I not dede with the? O Roulland, wherfor leuest thou
me heuy & sorouful? helas! caytyf that I am, what shal I doo?
Alas! sorouful, whyther shal I goo? I praye to almygthy god
that he conserue the; I requyre thangellis of heuen that they
be in thy companye; I requyre the marters, of whom thou art
of the nombre, yᵗ they wyl receuye the in to the Ioye perdurable.
alway I shal remembre the wepyng, alway I shall fele thy de-
partyng, as dauyd dyd of natan & of absalon. Alas! Rolland,
thou goost in to lyf & Ioye perdurable, & leuest me in thys
world sorouful. Thou art in heuen in consolacion, & I am in
wepynges & tribulacions. Alle the world is euyl content of thy
deth, & thangellys hath brouʒt the in comforte.'

The Squyr of Lowe Degre, 929–66
[*The Squyr of Lowe Degre,* in *Ancient English Metrical Romances,* ed. Joseph Ritson (London, 1802), III, 184–85.]

Alas! than sayd that lady dere,	
I have the kept this seven yere,	930
And now ye be in powder small,	
I may no longer holde you withall.	
My love, to the earth i shall the brynge,	
And preestes for you to reade and synge.	
Yf any man aske me what i have here,	935
I wyll say it is my treasure.	
Yf any man aske why i do so,	
For no theves shall come therto:	
And, squyer, for the love of the,	
Fy on this worldes vanytè!	940
Farewell golde, pure and fyne;	
Farewell velvet, and satyne;	
Farewell castelles, and maners also;	
Farewell huntynge, and hawkynge to;	
Farewell revell, myrthe and play;	945
Farewell pleasure, and garmentes gay;	
Farewell perle, and precyous stone;	
Farewell my juielles everychone;	
Farewell mantell, and scarlet reed;	
Farewell crowne unto my heed;	950
Farewell hawkes, and farewell hounde;	
Farewell markes, and many a pounde;	

Farewell huntynge at the hare;
Farewell harte and hynde for evermare.
Nowe wyll i take the mantell and the rynge,   955
And become an ancresse in my lyvynge:
And yet i am a mayden for thee,
And for all men in Chrystentè.
To Chryst i shall my prayers make,
Squyer, onely for thy sake;   960
And i shall never no masse heare,
But ye shall have parte in feare:
And every daye whyles i lyve,
Ye shall have your masses fyve,
And i shall offre pence thre,   965
In tokenynge of the tryntè.

Partenay, 3887–3920
[*The Romance of Partenay, or of Lusignen, otherwise known
as The Tale of Melusine,* ed. W. W. Skeat, *EETS,* XXII (London, 1866), pp. 135–36.]

"Adieu, my lady, with heres yowlownesse!
Adieu, all debonerte for euermore!
    Adieu, I say you, my faire suete maistresse!
    Adieu, my ioy, my grace, And my richesse!   3890
        Adieu, my goodes and all my surete!
        Adieu commaunde, all the disporte of me.

Adieu, my iewell! Adieu, my solas!
    Adieu, you say, my lady preciouse!
Adieu, the fair whilom the prise gan purchas!   3895
    Adieu, my wife! Adieu, my trew spouse!
    Adieu, my lady verray graciouse!
        Adieu, I you say, my full doucet floure!
        Adieu, my lady of full gret valoure!

Adieu, suete throte of soundes clerenesse!   3900
    Adieu, fair Rose! Adieu, violet also!
Adieu, the tree of louers feithfulnesse!
    Adieu, I say my gentile lady vnto,
    Adieu, my glory! Adieu, my ioy, lo!
        Adieu, the fair that so hath loued me!   3905
        My goode days gon, shall I neuer you se."

Ryght this Raymounde bewaled and bement
    his noble wife, for whom he felt dolour,
Which thorugh the Air hir flight tho hent,
        Wherefor he hath A sory hert þat houre.   3910
        "Alas!" Raymound said, "wat do shall or labour?
      For certes I haue sorow ynow at hert,
        Neuer man had at the full so smert.

FOrwhy shold I noght be A plain man,
    yff I fele at hert noysaunce mondiall?   3915
Hit to declare good reson if I can,
        For the diche haue made whereon now I fall.
      Now Am I Acursed, to wo am made thrall,
        Now I am dolorous And full pensiffe
        More than Any goste felt in his life."   3920

Melusine, 298–99

[*Melusine, compiled 1383–1394 by Jean D'Arras, Englisht c. 1500,* ed. A. K. Donald, *EETSES,* LXVIII (London, 1895), pp. 298–99.]

'Halas, Melusyne,' sayd Raymondin, 'of whom all the world spake wele, now haue I lost you for euer. Now haue I fonde the ende of my Joye/ and the begynnyng is to me now present of myn euerlastyng heuynes/ Farwel beaute, bounte, swetenes, amyablete/ Farwell wyt, curtoysye, & humilite/ Farwel al my joye, al my comfort & myn hoop/ Farwel myn herte, my prowes, my valyaunce, For that lytel of honour whiche god had lent me, it came thrugh your noblesse, my swete & entierly belouyd lady. Ha/ a, falsed & blynd Fortune, aigre, sharp, & byttir/ wel hast thou ouerthrowen me fro the hyest place of thy whele vnto the lowest part of thy mansyon or dwellyng place, there as Jupyter festyeth with sorow & heuynes, the caytyf & vnhappy creatures/ be þou now cursed of god. by the I slough ayenst my wyll my lord, myn vncle, the whiche deth thou sellest me to dere. helas! thou had putte and sette me in high auctoryte thrugh the wyt and valeur of the wysest, the fayrest, & moost noble lady of al other/ and now by the/ fals blynde traytour and enuyous, I must lese the sight of her of whom myn eyen toke theire fedyng. thou now hatest/ thou now louest, thou now makest/ thou now vndost/ in the, nys no more surety ne rest than is in a fane that tourneth at al windes.

Helas/ helas! my ryght swete & tendre loue/ by my venymous
treson I haue maculate your excellent fygure/ helas! myn herte
& al my wele ye had heeled me clene of my first soore/ yl I
haue now rewarded you therfore. Certaynly yf I now lese you/
none other choys is to me/ but to take myn vtermost exill there
as never after no man lyuyng shall see me.'

Morte Arthure, 3956–4008
[*Morte Arthure mit Einleitung, Anmerkungen und Glossar,* ed.
Erik Björkman (New York, 1915), pp. 116–18.]

"Dere kosyn o kynde,   in kare am I leuede,
For nowe my wirchipe es wente   and my were endide.
Here es þe hope of my hele,   my happynge of armes,
My herte and my hardynes   hale one hym lengede,
My concell, my comforthe,   þat kepide myn herte!   3960
Of all knyghtes, þe kynge,   þat vndir Criste lifede,
Þou was worthy to be kynge,   þofe I þe corown bare;
My wele and my wirchipe   of all þis werlde riche
Was wonnen thourghe *sir* Wawayne   & thourghe his witt one!
Allas!" saide *sir* Arthure,   "nowe ekys my sorowe!   3965
I am vttirly vndon   in myn awen landes;
A! dowttouse derfe dede,   þou duellis to longe!
Why drawes þou so one dreghe?   thow drownnes myn herte!"
    Than swe[l]tes the swete kyng   and in swoun fallis,
Swafres vp swiftely   and swetly hym kysses,   3970
Till his burliche berde   was blody beronnen,
Alls he had bestes birtenede   and broghte owt of life;
Ne had *sir* Ewayne comen   and othire grete lordys,
His bolde herte had brousten   for bale at þat stownde.
"Blyne," sais thies bolde men,   "thow blondirs þi selfen,   3975
Þis es botles bale,   for bettir bees it neuer.
It es no wirchipe iwysse   to wryng thyn hondes;
To wepe als a woman,   it es no witt holden.
Be knyghtly of contenaunce,   als a kyng scholde,
And leue siche clamoure   for Cristes lufe of heuen!"   3980
"For blode," said the bolde kynge,   "blyn sall I neuer,
Or my brayne tobriste   or my breste oþer;
Was neuer sorowe so softe,   that sanke to my herte.
Itt es full sibb to my selfe,   my sorowe es the more;
Was neuer so sorrowful a syghte   seyn *with* myn eyghen,   3985
He es sakles supprysede   for syn of myn one!"

Down knelis þe kyng*e*   and kryes full lowde;
With carefull countenaunce   he karpes thes wordes:
"O rightwis riche Gode,   beholde thow this rewthe!
Þis ryall rede blode   ryn appon erthe,   3990
It ware worthy to be schrede   and schrynede in golde,
For it es sakles of syn,   sa *saue* me oure Lo[ue]rde!'
Down knelis þe kyng   *with* kare at his herte,
Kaughte it vpe kyndly   *with* his clene handis,
Keste it in a ketill-hatte   and coue*rde* it faire,   3995
And kayres furthe *with* þe cors   in ky*the* þare he lenges.
"Here I make myn avowe," q*uod* the *wye* than[e],
"To Messie and to Marie,   the mylde qwen*ne* of heuen,
I sall neu*er* ryvaye   ne racches vncowpyll
At roo ne [at] rayne-dere,   þat rynnes appo*ne* erthe;   4000
Neu*er* grewhownde late glyde,   ne gossehawke latt flye,
Ne neu*er* fowle see fellide,   þat flieghes *with* wenge;
Fawkon ne formaylle   appon fiste handill,
Ne ȝitt *with* gerefawcon   rejoyse me in erthe;
Ne reg*nn*e in my royaltez,   ne halde my rownde table,   4005
Till thi dede, my dere,   be dewly reuengede;
Bot eu*er* droupe and dare,   qwylls my *day* lastez,
Till Drighten and derfe dede   hafe don, qwate them likes."

Arthur of Little Britain, 516–17
[*The History of the Valiant Knight Arthur of Little Britain, A
Romance of Chivalry, Originally translated from the French by
John Bourchier, Lord Berners* (London, 1814), pp. 516–17.]

A! gentyl knightes hert, true and honorable to al people! alas!
that I haue thus lost you, certenly it forthinketh me. A! em-
perour! shame haue you, sith ye haue taken fro me my noble
& true compani͞o! Certenly I shal take vengeaunce on you as
sone as I shal se you. And as he was thus talkyng, there came
to hym the last messenger, and said: "Syr, yᵉ King of Orqueni
doth acertayne you that themperour is dead. And how is he
dead? quod the kyng. Certaynly, syr, quod the knight, whan
he herd of the deth of his broder, Kyng Floripes, and of his
other kings, and that his host was clene discomfyted, he dyed
for sorowe, as he that was sore sick before, becaus of his hurt
that he had in hys backe. Wel, quod the kyng, than I am re-
uenged on him for mi kyng: how be it, I would he were alyue
again, and al his, so that I had again my good Kyng of Mormal.

Richard Couer de Lion, 799–837
[*Der Mittelenglischen Versroman uber Richard Löwenherz,* ed.
Karl Brunner (Wien und Leipzig, 1913), pp. 122–24.]

A knyȝt sterte to þe kyng,
And tolde him þis tydyng,   800
Þat Rychard had hys sone jslon.
"Allas," he sayde, "now haue j non!"
Wiþ þat worde he fyl to grounde,
As man þat was jn woo jbounde.
He swownyd for sorwe at here ffeet,   805
Knyȝtes took hym vp fful skeet,
And sayde: "Sere, let be þat þouȝt!
Now is it don it helpes nouȝt."
The kyng spak þenne an hy.
To þe knyghtes þat stood hym by,   810
"Tel me swyþe off þis caas,
In what manere he ded was."
Stylle þay stood euerylkon,
Ffor sorwe þey myȝte telle non.
Wiþ þat noyse þer com þe qwene.   815
"Allas," sche sayde, "how may þis bene?
Why is þis sorwe *and* þis ffare?
Who has brouȝt yow alle *in* care?"
"Dame," he sayde, "wost þou nouȝt,
þy ffayre sone to depe is brouȝt!   820
Siþþen þat j was born to man,
Swylke sorwe hadde j neuere nan!
Alle my ioye is turnyd to woo,
Ffor sorwe j wole myseluen sloo!"
Whenne þe qwene vndyrstood,   825
Ffor sorwe, sertys, sche wax nygh wood.
Her kerchefs she drewe, her heer also,
"Alas," she sayd, "what shall j do!"
Sche cratched hereselff *in* þe vysage,
As a wymman þat was in rage.   830
Þe face fomyd on blood,
Sche rente þe robe þat sche *in* stood,
Wrong here handes þat sche was born:
"Jn what manere is my sone jlorn?"
Þe kyng sayde: "I telle þe,   835

Þe kynȝt here standes tolde it me.
Now tel þe soþe, . . .

Foure Sonnes of Aymon, Chap. I, 34–35
[*The Right Pleasant and Goodly Historie of the Foure Sonnes of Aymon,* ed. Octavia Richardson, *EETSES,* XLIV (London, 1885), pp. 34–35.]

And thenne the messager coude speke nomore/ but felle doun in a swoune, of the grete gryeffe and sore that he felte, bycause of his woundes/ And whan the kynge hadde herde these wordes/ he felle doun vpon the grounde for the grete sorow that he toke therof, and wrange his handes/ and pulled his berde/ and tare alle his heres, saynge, 'Ha, god that made heuen and erthe, ye haue broughte me in grete sorowe and sad tournement irrecouerable, that neuer shall ceasse wyth me/ so requyre I to you the deth humbly/ For neuer more desire I not to lyue'/The goode duke of Bauyre began to recomforte hym/ saynge, 'For goddis loue, syre, tourmente not your selfe/ but haue goode herte, and hope in god and recomforte your folke'/ And this wolde saye the duke Naymes for theym that he sawe wepe there for theyr kynnesmen and frendes that were ded wyth Lohyer. 'And do,' saye he to the kyng, 'late your sone be worshyfully buryed atte saynte Germayne of the medowes/ And thenne ye shall goo vpon the duke Benes of Aygremount, wyth alle your noble power and grete puyssaunce/ and shall dystroye hym and alle his lordes atte your playsure.' Thenne the kynge Charlemayne recomfortyd hym selfe/ and well he knewe that Naymes counseylled hym truly and lawfully/ Thenne sayd the kynge/ 'barons, make you redy/ and we shall goo ayenste my dere sone Lohier'/ And incontynente all the prynces and barons made theym selfe redy for to do the commaundement of the kynge/ And whan they were goon two myle oute of Parys, they mette wyth the corps/ And were there wyth the kynge, Naymes/ Ogyer, Sampson of bourgoyne, and many other grete lordes/ Thenne sayde the kyng Charlemayne whan he sawe the body of his dere sone Lohier/ 'Alas, how shamefully am I treated'/ he descended from his horse a foote, and toke vppe the clothe that was vppon the byere and byhelde his sone Lohier. Thenne sawe he the hede that was smytten of from the body, and the face that was alle to hewen/ 'Ha, god,' sayd he/ 'how well may I be madde now alle quycke. Well I oughte to hate that duke Benes

of Aygremounte, that thus hathe murdered my sone'/ he thenne
kyssed his childe alle bloody full often, and sayd in this wyse/
'Ha, fayre sone, ye were a talle man and a gentyll knyghte; now
praye I the puyssaunte god of glorye, that he take your soule
thys daye, yf it be his plesure, into his royame of paradyse'/
Grete sorowe made the kynge Charlemayne for the deth of his
sone Lohier;

Ywaine and Gawaine, 818–68

[*Ywaine and Gawaine,* in *Ancient English Metrical Romances,*
ed. Joseph Ritson (London, 1802), I, 35–37.]

And sone tharefter come the ber,
A lady folowd, white so mylk,
In al that land was none swilk;   820
Sho wrang her fingers, out-brast the blode,
For mekyl wa sho was nere wode,
Hir fayr har scho alto drogh,
And ful oft fel sho down in swogh;
Sho wepe, with a ful dreri voice.   825
The hali water, and the croyce,
Was born bifor the procession,
Thar folowd mani a moder son.
Bifore the cors rade a knyght,
On his stede that was ful wight,   830
In his armurs wele arayd,
With sper and target gudely grayd.
Than sir Ywayn herd the cry,
And the dole of that fayr lady,
For mor sorow myght nane have   835
Than sho had when he went to grave.
Prestes and monkes, on thaire wyse,
Ful solempnly did the servyse.
Als Lunet thar stode in the thrang,
Until sir Ywaine thoght hir lang,   840
Out of the thrang the wai sho tase,
Unto Sir Ywaine fast sho gase;
Sho said, Sir how ertow stad?
I hope ful wele thou has bene rad.
Sertes, he said, thou sois wele thar,   845
So abayst was i never are.
He said, Leman, i pray the,

If it any wise may be,
That i might luke a litel throw
Out at sum hole or sum window;   850
For wonder fayn, he sayd, wald i
Have a sight of the lady.
The maiden than ful sone unshet
In a place a prevé weket,
Thar of the lady he had a syght,   855
Lowd sho cried to god almyght,
"Of his sins do him pardowne,
For sertanly in no regyowne
Was never knight of his bewtè,
Ne efter him sal never nane be;   860
In al the werld, fro end to ende,
Es none so curtayse, ne so hende.
God grant the grace thou mai won
In hevyn with his owyn son!
For so large lifes none in lede,   865
Es none so doghty of gude dede."
When sho had thus made hir spell,
In swownyg ful oft-sithes sho fell.

Le Bone Florence, 794–843

[*Le Bone Florence,* in *Ancient English Metrical Romances,* ed.
Joseph Ritson (London, 1802), III, 34–36.]

And speke more of the Emperowre,
   How they on a bere hym dyght,   795
And how they broght hym to the towne,
Wythowten belle or procescoun,
   Hyt was a drery syght.
They layned hyt fro ther enmyes whyll they myght,
And fro Florence that worthy wyght,   800
   Hys own dere doghtur bryght.

Soone the standard yn they dud lede,
And baners bryght that brode dud sprede,
   The Romans lyked ylle.
And seyde they schulde upon the morne   805
Fyght wyth Garcy yf he had sworne,
   That hyely was on hylle.
Florence lay in a cornell,

And hur maydyns, as y yow telle,
   That was curtes of wylle;   810
They seyde men brynge yn a bere,
And that wyth a full mornyng chere,
   But all was hoscht and stylle.

Then can feyre Florence sayne,
Yondur ys be gonne an evyll bargayn,   815
   Y see men brynge a bere,
And a knyght in handys leede,
Bondynowre my fadurs stede,
   Then all chawngyd hur chere.
Sche and hur maystres Awdygon   820
Went into the halle alone,
   Allone wythowten fere,
And caste up the clothe, then was hyt so,
The lady swowned, and was full woo,
   Ther myght no man hur stere.   825

Allas, sche seyde, that y was borne!
My fadur for me hys lyfe hath lorne,
   Garcy may have hys wylle,
All my brode landys and me,
Thay y welde yn Crystyante!   830
   Ther myght no man hur stylle.
Lordys and ladys that there ware
Tyll hur chambur can they fare,
   Lorde that them lykyd ylle;
Knyghtes and squyers that there was   835
Wrange ther hondys and seyde, allas!
   For drede sche schulde hur spylle.

Dewkys and erles ther hondys wronge,
And lordys sorowe was full stronge,
   Barons myght have no roo: 840
"Who schall us now geve londes and lythe,
Hawkys, or howndes, or stedys stythe,
   As he was wont to doo?"

Guy of Warwick, Auchlineck MS., 6855–6941
[*The Romance of Guy of Warwick,* ed. Julius Zupitza, *EETSES,*
XLIX (London, 1887), pp. 362–64.]

In þe toun he herd belles ring,   6855
& loude crie, & miche wepeing,
Cloþes to-tere, her to-te:
More sorwe no miȝt non be.
'God,' quaþ þerl, 'lord fre,
Þis gret sorwe whi it be?'   6860
Into þe halle come þere
Tvai men, & a bodi bere:
Amid þe flore pai it leyden, y-wis.
Quaþ þerl Florentin, 'mi sone þis is,'
Torent his here, his cloþes he drouȝ: 6865
In his hert was sorwe anouȝ.
'Leue sone,' he seyd, 'who slouȝ þe?
Now wold god, þat is so fre,
Þat he were here in my beylie!
Nold ich it lete for al Romanie,   6870
Þat he no were anon y-slawe,
For-brent, & þat dust to-blowe.'
Þan seyd a squier biforne hem alle,
'Ichim se atte mete in þis halle,
He þat þi dere sone slouȝ.   6875
Ich it seye, wiþ-outen wouȝ.'
Anon þat þerl y-herd þis,
Fram þe bord he aros, y-wis:
An aundiren he kept in his honden þo,
Hetelich it haf, & seyd him to,   6880
'Traitour, þou schalt dye here.
Why slouȝ þou mi sone dere?'
Wiþ þat aundiren he þret sir Gij,
& wiþ gret hate, sikerly,
Ac þat din he feiled of him   6885
(Gij vp stert wroþ and grim):
Into þe wouȝ it fleye to fot & more.
'Merci,' seyd Gij, 'for goddes ore!
ȝif ich þi sone owhar a–slouȝ,
It was me defendant anouȝ.'   6890
Kniȝt anon about him þrong,
To slen him, boþe eld & ȝong.
Gij hent in hond anon riȝt
An ax þat was gode, apliȝt.
Bi þat on ende of þe halle he him drouȝ,   6895

& þer he werd him wele anouȝ.
Þai aseyld him strongliche,
& he him werd stalworþliche.
Wiþ þat com forþ þe steward liȝt,
A Brabasone he was, a wel gode kniȝt: 6900
A strok he smot to sir Gij,
& hewe on him ful felly.
Gij of him failed nauȝt:
Wiþ þe ax he haþ him rauȝt,
Þat his heued he him to-clef: 6905
Al to ded to ground he dref.
Þus Gij him wereþ manliche,
And hij him aseyle heteliche.
Þe kniȝtes he slouȝ þere,
Þe best þat in þat court were.   6910
  'Sir Florentin,' seyd sir Gij,
'For godes loue now merci!
Þou art y-hold so gode a man,
Hennes to Rome better nis nan:
& þou in þine halle me sle,   6915
For traisoun it worþ awist þe.
In edwite it worþ þe adrawe,
Swiche a man þou schust haue slawe,
When þou wiþ þi wille fre
Þe mete me ȝeue *par* charite.   6920
Were it wiþ wrong, were it wiþ riȝt,
For tresoun it worþ þe witt, apliȝt;
Opon alle þing a þing atte mete,
Þer ȝe ouȝt me to were fram hete.
For godes loue, sir, so michel do me,   6925
Þat ȝe þer-fore blamed no be:
Dome deliuer mi stede,
& lete me out at þe castel ride,
& seþþen þei y slawe be
No worþ ȝe nouȝt y-blamed in þe cuntre.'   6930
Þerl him wiþ drouȝ wiþ þat:
At his hert gret sorwe sat,
Þat he his sone seye ligge ded.
Of him no worþ him non oþer red.
'Sone,' he seyd, 'what schal y do,   6935
Whenne ich þe haue þus forgo?

Who schal now weld after me
Mine londes, þat brod be?
A man icham swiþe in eld:
Dye ichil, bi godes scheld.'
Opon þat bodi he fel anon:

The Knight of Curtesy and the Fair Lady of Faguell, 441–68
[*The Knight of Curtesy and the Fair Lady of Faguell*, in *Ancient English Metrical Romances*, ed. Joseph Ritson (London, 1802), III, 215–16.]

Your knight is dead, as you may se,
  I tel you, lady, certaynly,
His owne herte eaten have ye,
  Madame, at the last we all must dye.

When the lady herde him so say,   445
  She sayd, My herte for wo shall brast;
Alas, that ever i sawe this day!
  Now may my lyfe no longer last.

Up she rose, wyth hert full wo,
  And streight up into her chambre wente,   450
She confessed her devoutly tho,
  And shortely receyved the sacrament.

In her bed mournyng she her layde,
  God wote, ryght wofull was her mone:
Alas! myne owne dere love, she sayd,   455
  Syth ye be dead my joye is gone.

Have i eaten thy herte in my body?
  That meate to me shal be full dere,
For sorowe, alas, now must i dye:
  A, noble knight, withouten fere!   460

That herte shal certayne with me dye,
  I have received theron the sacrament.
All erthly fode here i denye,
  For wo and paine my life is spente.

My husbande, full of crueltè,   465
  Why have you done this cursed dede?
Ye have him slaine, so have ye me,
  The hie god graunte to you your mede!

Firumbras, 65–93

[*Firumbras and Otuel and Roland,* ed. M. I. O'Sullivan, *EETS,* CXCVIII (London, 1935), p. 5.]

"Allas," sayd Balam, "ye Lucafer alyfe?   65
My noble Covnsel*ou*r & my help I haue forlore.
Allas, that ylke tyme that eu*er* y was bore!"
"lorde," sayd socebrond, "the sothe for to mene,
thyn own cownsayl hyt hath y-do & that ys well sene;
ȝe cast all ȝo*ur* wyll and ȝo*ur* hert thouȝt   70
at ȝo*ur* taylend that schall vs brynge to nought."
"suche yt ys to tryst in wo*m*mans lore!
Allas, that ilke stovnd that eu*er* sche was bore!
but ȝyt here fourty dayes beȝt ful gone,
we schull be a-vreke of hem eu*er*ychon*e*.   75
Myn hornes & my bemes, doȝth hem swythe blowe!"
"syr," sayd sokebrond, "hyt schall be don a-throwe.
the day ys passyd, the sonne ys at declyne,
Dwells styll tyl to-morwe, that ys cownsell myn.
by that ȝo*ur* sarsyns wyl bene come that beyth fer & ner."   80
"Sokebrand," sayd balam, "of Covnseyll thou art cler."
"Allas, Allas, [for] Lucafer," sayd the Ameraunt,
"for he was my soco*ur* & my waraunt;
thoruȝ thes sory knyghtys y hym lore.
Allas, tha wyle that eu*er* they were bore.   85
By the soule that y owe to my god Maho*u*n to ȝelde,
schall y neu*er* hennys to tovne ne to felde,
Tyl the tour be take & w*ith* strenthe y-nome
And the knyghtys don to the foulest deþ that men conne,
And fflory*pe* for her loue schall be brent."   90
"by Maho*u*n," sayd sakebrond, "god om*n*ipotent,
lord, ȝo*ur* covnsell schall be don & the tour y-take,
w*ith* ȝo*ur* owne chyuallrye er he hennys schake."

Foure Sonnes of Aymon, Chap. XXVIII, 589–90

[*The Right Pleasant and Goodly Historie of the Foure Sonnes of Aymon,* ed. Octavia Richardson, *EETSES,* XLV (London, 1836), pp. 589–90.]

... the thre bredern comen agen to theymselfe/ and began to crye and fare as they had ben mad/ the*n*ne sayd alarde, all wepyng in thys maner, 'Alas, what shall we now caytyff knyghtes doo, pour of honour & of all wele, sith that we haue lost our broder, by whom we were so sore doubted & dred/ Alas, dere broder! who was soo hardy to laye honde on you? I byleve that he knew not your debonairte & kyndnesse/ for he wolde not have slayne you so cruelly'/ And thenne he torned him towarde his two bredern & sayd/ 'My fayr bredern, we ought well to be sory/ sith we have lost our broder reynaude/ that was all our hope, our trust, & comfort.' 'Alas,' sayd rycharde, 'broder reynaude, why had ye ever that courage for to habandoune vs as ye dyde/ seeng that ye loved vs somoche. Alas, ye stale awaye yourselfe by nyghte/ for to come amonge thandes of the murderers that have slayne you soo cruelly/ Alas, they wyste not the grete dommage that is of your dethe!' Whan the thre bretherne had wepte ynoughe, in grete, sobbynges and lamentacyons for the love of theyr dere broder Reynawde/ they went and [kissed] the corps on the mouthe, the one after the other; and wyth this thei felle doun agen in a swoune/ And whan thei were come agen to theymself/ rycharde began to crye, & saye/ 'Alas, fair bredern, now ben we lost for ever/ For we shall no more be set by, nother doubted nor drede more than children/ wherfore I saye that we shold slee ourself/ to the ende that we maye be wyth you, for we oughte not to live after your deth'/ Wyte it that who had be there, he sholde have had an harde hert, but he sholde have wepte for to see the thre bredern make theyr mone.

Ipomedon, 4465–90
[*Ipomedon in drei Englischen bearbeitungen,* ed. Eugen Kölbing (Breslau, 1889), p. 129.

Syghand, and sayd: "Alas,	4465
Dere broþer, woo ys mee,	
That euer I thy bane shuld bee,	
Mercy I the asse!"	
He lokyd vpe & lokyd hye,	
His eyne closude, & gan to dye,	4470
His soule away gan passe.	
Then hadde Dreas mekill care,	
He rent his clothis & drewe his hare,	
And oute a swerd drawethe he;	
The hylte downeward, þe poynte vp stode,	4475

He swere by god, that is good:
"Myne noune bane shall I bee!"
To hym prekkythe Ipomadon,
His swerd oute of his hond hathe tone
And sayd; "Benedycyte!"   4480
"Alas, syr, for sorwe & payne:
It is my broþer, that haue I slayne,
Therefore full woo ys me!"

"Ye, syr, lette this greffe ouergoo,
For better is oo man dede, þen tow,   4485
This is þe sothe, I saye!
Ye, so there is no more to kepe,
Agayne vp on your stede ye lepe
And for his soule do praye!
Dreas dyd, as he hym bade,   4490

Valentine and Orson, 308–309
[*Valentine and Orson, translated from the French by Henry
Watson,* ed. Arthur Dickson, *EETS,* CCIV (London, 1937),
pp. 308–309.]

The Emperou[r] of grece that had a hardey courage toke a
spere and came against his sonne that bare a shelde of a
sarazyn, so they recountred the one the other by suche force that
Valentyne perced his father throughout & smote him downe
dead to the earth without spekyng any worde. After he cryed
montioye viue grece, and Orson that vnderstode him knewe that
it was his brother that hade slayne his father, so he threwe
downe his shelde and hys/ spere, and lyfte vp hys helme. After
he cryed in weping Valentyne euill prowesses haue you doone,
for to daye you haue slayne the father that engendred you And
whan Valentyne vnderstood hym, he let hym selfe fall downe
of the hors to the earth. And Orson lyght downe and ranne and
colled hys brother, makyng soo great sorowe that non cant recount it. So there came toward them Reynarde of Prouaunce,
and Myllon of Dyion for to comforte them, and toke vp valentyne & sayd vn to hym. Knyght haue pacience for you can not
bye your father a gayne wyth wepynge, euen soo as it hath
pleased god the thyng is happened. Alas sayd Valentyne what is
be fallen me. I am a boue all the other *th*e moost cursed,

vnhappy, and euil fortuned. Alas death where arte thou that
thou comest not and take me for I am not worthy that the
earthe susteyne me, nor that none of the elementes lende me
nourisshinge whan that I haue commytted suche a dede before
god detestable, & to the men abhomynable. Alas vnhappy Valentine in what an hour was thou borne for to commete so vyllay-
nous a cause, and so vnnaturall murdre I haue suffred all my
lyfe paine, tormente and muche great thought, but aboue all
thinges I suffred now *th*e greatest dolour False kyng of ynde
cursed be thy shelde and hym that composed it for by it I haue
ben vnknowen of my father. Alas fayre brother Orson syth
that I haue put our father vn to death take my swerde and cut
of mi hede [f]or it is not reason that I liue ani more vpon the
earth, nor that I be put in the nombre of knightes. Brother said
Orson take comfort vn to you and kepe you from dyspayre,
be thynke you well swete brother *tha*t god is puyssaunte ynought
for to pardon a more greater thynge,/ retorne you towarde him
& aske him pardon for youre synne and promise to do penaunce,
for certes who *tha*t is dead, ther is neuer no remedye, so it
is better to praye for him than to wipe hys death so much.
Thus Orson comforted him that had hys hert right sorowfull,
and he dyd so muche with *th*e helpe of the other barons that
Valentyne mounted on hys hors, & as a man that careth not to
lyfe or dye, he entered in to *th*e battayle . . .

Prose Life of Alexander, 113–14
  [*The Prose Life of Alexander*, ed. J. S. Westlake, *EETS*,
  CXLIII (London, 1913), pp. 113–14.]

And þan he kyssede all þe lordeȝ & þe knyghtis of Macedoyne
ilkane aft*er* oþ*er*, and sighed and weped wonder sare. Þare was
þan so grete dole & wepynge, þat it was lyke a thonere. For men
Supposeȝ þat noȝte allanly men made Sorow for þe dede of
so worthy ane Emp*er*our, Bot also þe son and all þe oþ*er*
planetis and element*es* ware troubled.
   A prynce of Macedoyne stode nere Alex*ander* bedd þat
highte Seleuc*us*, & w*i*t grete dole & wepynge he sayd: 'A, A,
þou wirchipfull emp*er*our,' quoþ he, 'what sall we do when þou
ert dede. Philippe þi fader gouerned vs wele & alle oure rewme,
Bot þe gentilnes & þe largesse of the na tunge may tell.' And
þan Alex*ander* sett hy*m* vp in his bedd and gaffe hym selfe a

grete flappe on þe cheke and by-gan for to wepe riȝte bitterly,
and in þe langage of Macedoyne, he sayde on þis wyse:

'Full waa es me vuhappy wreche,' quoþ he, 'þat euer I was
borne to man. For now Alexander dyes and Macedoyne sall
waxe ay lesse & lesse and emenische day bi day.' Than all þe
Macedoynes wit an hye voyce and bitter wepynge sayd vn-till
hym: 'Better it ware till vs,' quoþ þay, 'for to dy wit þe þan
for to se þe dy in oure presence. For wele we wate þat, efter þe
dede of the, þe kyngdom of Macedoyne es vndone for euere.
Allas our wirchipfull Alexander, why lefes þou vs here and
wendeȝ away be thyn ane, withowten thi Macedoynes?' Than
kyng Alexander alway sighand & wepand said vn-to þam: 'A,
A, my dere Macedoynes,' quoþ he, 'fra this tym forwarde sall
neuer ȝour name hafe lordchipe ouer þe Barbarenes.' And þan
þe Macedoynes cryed and sayde: 'O wirchipfull lorde,' quoþ
þay, 'þou ledd vs in-to Perse, Arraby, Inde, and vn-to the
werldeȝ ende, and in-to what cuntree þat þe liste wende; why,
lorde, fleeȝ þou now fra vs? Lede vs wit the whedir so þou gase.'
Þan kyng Alexander sent to þe templee of Appollo in Athenes
many riche iowles, and on þe same wyse till all oþer temples.
And þan he commanded þat when he ware dede, þay schulde
enoynte his body and embawme it wit riche oynementes, þe
whilke kepis menes bodys in graues wit-owtten corupcioun. Þan
he badde Tholomeus þat he scholde [take] a c besantes of golde,
& þareoff gere make hym a tombe in Alexander. And onane as
he had commanded hym þus, one-seeand þam all, he swelt. And
þan his prynceȝ lifte vp his body, and did apon his clethynge
of astate and putt a riche coron on his heued, and sett hym in
þe emperours chayer, þe whilke twelue prynceȝ drewe wit
þaire bresteȝ fra Babiloyne till Alexander. Tholomeus went
alway bi-fore þe chayere wepande & sayande one þis wyse: 'Full
waa es me, My lord Alexander, waa es me. For in all thi lyfe
slew þou neuer so many men as þou dose nowe after þi dede.'
All Alexanders knyghtis also weped & made grete dole &
sayde on þis wyse: 'Waa es vs wreches! whatt schall wee now
do after þe dede of our lorde Alexander? Whedir sall we now
gaa or whate partye may we now chese? Whare schall we now
get any helpe till our lyfelade?' One þis wyse þay went wepand
after Alexander, till þay come till þe citee of Alexander. And
þare þay beryed hym in a toumbe þat was riȝte hye and wonder
curyouslye wroghte.

Adeodatus, 65–66

[*Adeodatus,* in *Chief Pre-Shakespearean Dramas,* ed. Joseph
Q. Adams (Boston, 1924), pp. 65–66.]

Interea Euphrosina, comperta oblivione filii, ad ecclesiam
Sancti Nicolai redit; cumque filium suum quesitum non in-
venerit, lamentabili voce:

> Heu! Heu! michi misere!
> Quid agam? quid queam dicere?
> Quo peccato merui perdere
> Natum meum, ultra vivere?

> Cur me pater infelix genuit?
> Cur me mater infelix abluit?
> Cur me nutrix lactare debuit?
> Mortem michi quare non prebuit?

Consolatrices exeant et dicant:
> Quid te juvat hec desolatio?
> Noli flere pro tuo filio;
> Summi Patris exora Filium,
> Qui conferat ei consilium.

Euphrosina, quasi non curans consolationem earum:
> Fili care, fili carissime,
> Fili, mee magna pars anime,
> Nunc es nobis causa tristitie
> Quibus eras causa letitie!

Consolatrices:
> Ne desperes de Dei gracia,
> Cujus magna misericordia
> Istum tibi donavit puerum;
> Tibi reddet aut hunc aut alium.

Euphrosina:
> Anxiatus est in me spiritus;
> Cur moratur meus interitus?
> Cum te, fili, non possum cernere
> Mallem mori quam diu vivere.

Consolatrices:
> Luctus, dolor et desperacio
> Tibi nocent nec prosunt filio;
> Sed pro eo de tuis opibus
> Da clericis atque pauperibus.
>
> Nicolai roga clemenciam
> Ut exoret misericordiam
> Summi Patris pro tuo filio,
> Nec falletur tua peticio.

In the meanwhile Euphrosina, having discovered that they had forgotten their son, returns to the church of Saint Nicholas; and when, after searching for her son, she fails to find him, let her say in a lamenting voice:
> Alas! Alas! Alas! O wretched me!
> What shall I do? What can I say?
> For what sin have I deserved to lose
> My son, and yet live after.
>
> Why did my hapless father beget me?
> Why did my hapless mother bear me?
> Why should my nurse have suckled me?
> Why did she not grant death to me?

Let the comforters go out [to her] and say:
> In what does this grief avail thee?
> Weep not for thy son:
> Pray to the Son of the Heavenly Father,
> That he bring succor to him.

Euphrosina, as if not regarding their consolation:
> O dear son! most dear son!
> O son, the greatest part of my soul!
> Now thou art the cause of grief to us
> To whom thou wert the cause of joy!

The comforters:
> Despair not of God's grace,
> Whose great mercy
> Hath given to thee this boy;
> He will restore to thee either this one or another.

Euphrosina:
>   My spirit is troubled within me.
>   Why does my death delay?
>   If, O son, I cannot see thee
>   I could prefer death to long life.

The comforters:
>   Sorrow, grief, and despair
>   Injure thee, and do not aid thy son.
>   But for him give of thy means
>   To the clerics and to the poor.

>   Ask the mercy of Nicholas,
>   That he may, by petition, obtain the pity
>   Of the heavenly Father for thy son;
>   And thy prayer will not fail.

Christ's Burial and Resuerrection, Bodleian MS. E. Museo, 160,
612–791.
[*Christ's Burial and Resurrection,* in *The Digby Mysteries,* ed.
F. J. Furnivall for The New Shakespeare Society, Series VII,
No. 1 (London, 1882), pp. 192–97.]

O sisters, Mawdelyn, Cleophe, & Iacobye!
Ye see how pitefull my son doth lye
Here in myn armys, dede!
What erthly mother may refreyn,   615
To se hir son thus Cruelly sleyn,
A! my harte is hevy os lede!
   Who shall gife me wat*er* sufficient,
And of distillinge teris habundance,
That I may wepe my fill w*ith* hart relent   620
Aft*er* the whantite of sorofull reme*m*brance?
   For his sak that made vs all,
Which now ded lyes in my lappe;
Of me, a mayd, by grace speciall,
He pleside to be born, & sowket my pape.   625
He shrank not for to shew the shape
Of v*er*reye man at his circu*m*cision,
And þ*er* shed his blude for ma*n*nys hape.
Al-so at my purification,

Of hym I made a fayre oblation,   630
Which to his fader was most plesinge.
For fere, than, of herodes persecution,
In-till egip[t]e fast I fled with hym—
His grace me gidid in euery thinge,—
& now is he dede! that changes my cher!
Was neuer child to moder so lovinge!
Who þat cañ not wepe, at me may lere.
    Was neuer deth so Cruell as this,
To slo the gyvere of all grace.
Son! suffer me your woundes to kisse,   640
& your holy blude spilt in this place!
Dere son! ye haue steynyd your face,
Your face so frely to behold.
Thikk bludy droppes rynnes down a-pace,
Speciosus forma, the prophet told.   645
    But alese! your tormentes so manyfold
Hase abatid your visage so gloriose!
Cruell Iewes! what mad you so bold
To commyt þis Crym most vngraciose,
Which to your-self is most noyose?   650
Now shall all the cursinges of your lawe,
Opon yow fall most myschevose,
& be knawen of vagabundes ouer awe.
    He & I com both of your kyn,
And that ye kithe vn-curteslye;   655
He com for to fordoo your syn,
But ye for-suke hym frowardly.
Who can not wepe, com sit me bye,
To se hym that regnyd in blisse,
In hevyn with his fader gloryoslye,   660
Thus to be slayn in all giltlesse.
    Son! in your handes ar holes wid,
And in your fete that so tender were;
A gret wounde is in your blessit sid,
Full deply drevyn with a sharpe sper;   665
Your body is bete & brussid here;
On euery sid no place is free:
Nedes muste I wepe with hevy chere.
Who can not wepe, com lern at me,
    And beholde your lorde, myn awn der son,   670

Thus dolfulye delt w*ith,* ose ye see.
Se how his hede w*ith* thornys is thronge!
Se how he naylit was till a tree!
His synows & vaynes, drawe so straytlee,
Ar brokyn sond*er* by paynes vngude!   675
Who can not wepe, com lern at me,
And be-holde hym here þ*at* hange on rude!
   Se all a-bowte the bludy streynes!
O man!   this suffert he for thee!
Se so many fell & bitter peynes!   680
This la*m*me shed his blude in full plentee:
Who can not wepe, com lern at mee!
Se all his frend*es* is from hym fled!
All is but blude, so bett was hee
Fro the sole of his fute vnto þe hed!   685
   O swete child! it was nothinge mete—
Saue yo*ur* sufferance, ye had no pere,—
To lat Iudas kisse thes lippes so swete;
To suffer a traytor to com so nere,
To be-tray his mast*er* myldist of chere.   690
O my swete child! now suffer yee
Me yo*ur* moder, to kisse yow here,—
Who can not wepe, com lern at me!—
   To kisse, & swetly yow imbrace;
Imbrace, & in myn armes hold;   695
To hold, & luke on yo*ur* blessit face;
Yo*ur* face, most graciose to behold;
To beholde so comly, eu*er* I wold;
I wold, I wold, still w*ith* yow bee;
Still w*ith* yow, to ly in mold,   700
Who can not wepe, com lern at me!
   My will is to dy, I wald not leve;
Leve, how suld I? sithen dede ar yee.
My lif were ye/ noght can me greve,
So þ*at* I may in yo*ur* presence bee.   705
Me, yo*ur* wofull mod*er,* her may ye se;
Ye see my dedly sorow & payn,—
Who can not wepe, co*m* lern at mee!—
To see so meke a lambe her slayn;
   Slayn of men that no m*er*cy hadd;   710
Had they no m*er*cy, I reporte me see;

To se this bludy body, is not your hart sadd?
Sad & sorowfull, haue ye no pitee,
Pite & compassion to se this crueltee?
Crueltee, vnkindnese! O men most vnkind!   715
Ye that can not wepe, com lern at mee!
Kepinge this Crucifixe still in your mynd!
   When ye war born, of me, a mayde myld,
I sange lullay to bringe you on slepe:
Now is my songe, alese, ales, my child!   720
Now may I wayle, wringe my handes, & wepe!
Who shalbe my comforth? who shall me kepe?
Save at your departinge ye segnyte to mee
Iohn, your cosyn, most virtuus & zepe,
Who that can not wepe, com & lern at mee!   725
   O derest childe! what falt haf ye done!
What was your trispace,—I wald knav it fayn,—
Wherfor your blessid blude is forsid forth to rone?
Haue murtherid any person or ony man slayn,
That your avn pepill þus to yow dose endeyn?   730
Nay/ nay/ nay/ ye neuer did offence!
Was neuer spote of syn in your cler conscience!
   And not-withstandinge their fell indignation,
Only of gudwill & inward charitee,
Also for loue, & mannes saluation,   735
ze haue suffert all this of your humylitee!
Of your large mercee, gret was þe whantite;
Grete was þe multitude of your merites all,
Thus for mannes sake to tast þe bitter gall.
   Soñ! helpe, help your moder in this wofull smarte!   740
Comfurth your wofull moder, þat neuer was vnkind!
In your Conception, ye reyoyet my harte;
But now of dedly woo/ so gret cawse I find,
That þe Ioy of my haylsinge is passit fro my mynd.
Yit suffere me to hold you her on my lape,   745
Which sumtym gafe you mylk of my pape.
   O swete, swetist child! woo be vn-to me!
O most wofull woman/ your awn moder, loo!
Who shall graunt it me/ with you for to dee?
The son is dede/ what shall the moder doo?   750
Where shall sho resorte? whider shall sho goo?
Yit suffere me to hold yow a while in my lap,

Which sum-tym gafe yow mylk of my pap!
O crewell deth! no lenger thou me spare!
To me thou wer welcom, & also acceptabill;   755
Oppresse me down at ons/ of the I haue no care.
O my son, my saueyour/ & Ioye most comfortabill,
Suffere me to dy/ with yow most merciabill!
Or at lest lat me hold you/ a while in my lape,
Which sum-tym gaue yowe þe mylk of my pape!
    O ye wikkit pepill, with-out mercy or pitee!
Why do ye not crucyfye & hinge me on þe crosse?
Spare not your nayles/ spare not your crueltee!
Ye can not make me to ron in greter losse
That to lesse my son þat to me was so dere!   765
Why sloo ye not þe moder/ which is present her?
    Dere sone! if the Iwes/ yit will not sloo me,
Your gudnes, your grace, I besech & praye,
So call me to your mercy, of your benignitee!
To youre mek suters ye neuer saide yit naye;   770
Then may ye not your moder, in this cavse delaye.
The modere, with the child desires for to reste;
Remembere myn awn son/ þat ʒe sowket my breste!
    Remember when your fleshe was soft os tender silke,
With the grosse metes then yow I wold not fede,   775
But gaue yow the licour/ of a maydyns mylke;
Till Egip[t]e in myne Armes/ softly I did you lede;
But your smylinge contenaunce I askit non other mede,
Then be content/ that I with yow may riste,
Remembere my der son/ þat ʒe sowkit my briste!   780
    At your natiuitee, remember, my dere son,
What vessell I brochit to your nobill grace!
Was þer neuer moder that brochit sich a ton!
From my virgyne pappes/ mylk ran owt a-passe;
To your godly power/ natur gaf a place;   785
Ye sowkit maydens milke/ & so did neuer none,
Nore her-after shall/ saue your-self alone/
    When ye sowkit my brest/ your body was hole & sound.
Alese! in euery place Now se I many wound!
Now, help me, swet mawdleyn/ for I fall to þe ground!   790
And me, wofull mary, help now, gud Iohn!

BIBLIOGRAPHY

This list is divided into four sections. a) List of Romances, arranged alphabetically by title. b) Other primary sources for medieval laments for the dead. These are divided into three sections: authors, anonymous works arranged alphabetically by title, and collections arranged alphabetically by editors. c) Rhetorical Treatises. d) Secondary Materials, which include general works and specific articles that are relevant to the tradition of laments for the dead.

a) List of Romances

Alexander and Dindimus, or the Letters of Alexander to Dindimus, King of the Brahams, ed. Walter W. Skeat. *EETSES,* XXXI. London, 1878.

[Alexander Fragments], "Vier Neue Alexanderbruchstücke," ed. Karl D. Bülbring, *ESt* XIII (1889), 145–56.

[*Alexander Fragments*], *Editio princeps des mittelenglischen Cassamus (Alexander fragments) der Universitäte-bibliothek Cambridge,* ed. Karl Rosskopf. Erlangen, 1911.

Alexander, The Prose Life of, ed. J. S. Westlake, *EETS,* CXLIII. London, 1913.

Amis and Amiloun, ed. Mac Edward Leach. *EETS,* CCIII. London, 1937.

Arthour and Merlin, ed. Eugen Kölbing. Leipzig, 1890.

Arthur, ed. F. J. Furnivall. *EETS,* II. London, 1854.

Arthur of Little Britain, The History of the Valiant Knight, A Romance of Chivalry, Originally translated from the French by John Bourchier, Lord Berners. London, 1814.

Athelston, ed. A. McI. Trounce. *EETS,* CCXXIV London, 1951.

Avowynge of King Arthur, Sir Gawan, Sir Kaye, and Sir Bawdewyn of Breton, The, in *Three Early English Metrical Romances,* ed. John Robson. London, 1842.

Awyntyrs off Arthure at the Terne Wathelyne, The, in *Scottish Alliterative Poems,* ed. F. J. Amours. *STS,* XVIII. London, 1891–2.

Beryn, The Tale of, ed. F. J. Furnivall and W. G. Stone. *EETSES,* CV. London, 1887.

Blanchardyn and Eglantine, Caxton's, ed. Leon Kellner. *EETSES,* LVIII. London, 1890.

Bone Florence, Le, in *Ancient English Metrical Romances,* ed. Joseph Ritson. 3 vols. London, 1802.

Buik of Alexander, The or *The Buik of the Most Noble and Valiant Conquerour Alexander the Grit by John Barbour,* ed. R. L. G. Ritchie. *STSNS,* XII, XVII, XXI, XXV. London, 1921–29.

"*Buik of King Alexander the Conqueror,*" *The Taymouth Castle Manuscript of Sir Gilbert Hay's,* ed. Albert Herrman. Berlin, 1898.

Charles the Grete, The Lyf of the Noble and Crysten Prynce, translated from the French by William Caxton & printed by him 1485, ed. J. H. Herrtage. *EETSES,* XXVI. London, 1880.

Cheuelere Assigne, The Romance of the, ed. Henry H. Gibbs. *EETSES,* VI. London, 1868.

Clariodus; A Metrical Romance. London, 1830.

Duke Huon of Bordeux, The Boke of, done into English by Sir John Bourchier, Lord Berners, ed. S. L. Lee. *EETSES,* XL, XLI, XLIII, L. London, 1882–87.

Duke Rowlande, Þe Romance of, and of Sir Ottuell of Spayne, ed. S. J. Herrtage. *EETSES,* XXXV. London, 1880.

Erle of Tolous, The, in *Ancient English Metrical Romances,* ed. Joseph Ritson. 3 vols. London, 1802.

Eger & Grime, in *Bishop Percy's Folio Manuscript,* ed. J. W. Hales and F. J. Furnivall. 4 vols. London, 1867.

Emaré, The Romance of, ed. Edith Rickert. *EETSES,* XCIX. London, 1906.

Eneydos, Caxton's, 1490, Englisht from the French Liure des Eneydes, *1483,* ed. W. T. Culley and F. J. Furnivall. *EETSES,* LVII. London, 1890.

Firumbras and Otuel and Roland, ed. Mary Isabelle O'Sullivan. *EETS,* CXCVIII. London, 1935.

Foure Sonnes of Aymon, The Right Pleasant and Goodly Historie of the, ed. Octavia Richardson. *EETSES,* XLIV, XLV. London, 1884–86.

Floris and Blancheflour, ed. A. B. Taylor. Oxford, 1927.

Gamelyn, The Tale of, in *The Complete Works of Geoffrey Chaucer,* ed. W. W. Skeat. 7 vols. Oxford, 1894.

Generydes, ed. W. A. Wright. *EETS,* L, LXX. London, 1873–78.

"*Gest hystoriale*" *of the Destruction of Troy, The: an Alliterative Romance translated from Guido de Colonna's "Hystoria Troiana,*" ed. G. A. Panton and David Donaldson. *EETS,* XXXIX, LVI. London, 1869–74.

Godfrey of Boloyne, or the Siege and Conqueste of Jerusalem, by William, Archbishop of Tyre, translated from French by William Caxton and printed 1481, ed. Mary Noyes Colvin. *EETSES,* LXIV. London, 1893.

Golagras and Gawane, The Knightly Tale of, in *Scottish Alliterative Poems,* ed. F. J. Amour. *STS,* XVIII. London, 1891–97.

Grene Knight, The, in *Syr Gawayne; A Collection of Ancient Romance-Poems,* ed. Sir Frederic Madden. London, 1839.

Guy of Warwick, The Romance of, ed. Julius Zupitza. *EETSES,* XLII, XLIX, LXIX. London, 1883–91.

Havelok the Dane, The Lay of, ed. W. W. Skeat. *EETSES,* IV. London, 1868.

Helyas Knight of the Swan, The History of, translated by Robert Copland. New York, 1901.

Holy Grail, The History of the, Englisht c. 1450 by Henry Lonelich, ed. F. J. Furnivall. *EETSES,* XX, XXIV, XXVIII, XXX. London, 1874–78.

Horn Childe and Maiden Rimnild, in *Ancient English Metrical Romances,* ed. Joseph Ritson. 3 vols. London, 1802.

Ipomadon, in *Ipomedon in drei Englischen bearbeitungen,* ed. Eugen Kölbing. Breslau, 1889.

Ipomedon, in *Ipomedon in drei Englischen bearbeitungen,* ed. Eugen Kölbing. Breslau, 1889.

Ipomydon, The Lyfe of, in *Ipomedon in drei Englischen bearbeitungen,* ed. Eugen Kölbing. Breslau, 1889.

Jason, The History of, translated from the French of Raoul le Fevre by William Caxton, c. 1477, ed. John Munro. *EETSES,* CXI. London, 1913.

Jeaste of Syr Gawayne, The, in *Syr Gawayne: A Collection of Ancient Romance-Poems,* ed. Sir Frederick Madden. London, 1839.

Joseph of Arimathie, ed. W. W. Skeat. *EETS,* XLIV. London, 1871.

Joseph of Armathy, The Lyfe of, ed. W. W. Skeat. *EETS,* XLIV. London, 1871.

Joseph of Armathia, Here begynneth the lyfe of, ed. W. W. Skeat. *EETS,* XLIV. London, 1871.

Kyng Alisaunder, ed. G. V. Smithers. *EETS,* CCVII. London, 1952.

King Horn, Floriz and Blauncheflor, The Assumption of our Lady, re-ed. G. H. McKnight. *EETS,* XIV. London, 1901.

King Ponthus & the Fair Sidone, ed. F. J. Mather, Jr. in *PMLA,* XII (1897), i-lxvii, 1–150.

King of Tars, and the Sowdan of Dammas, The, in *Ancient English*

Metrical Romances, ed. Joseph Ritson. 3 vols. London, 1802.

Knight of Curtesy, and the Fair Lady of Faguell, The, in *Ancient English Metrical Romances,* ed. Joseph Ritson. 3 vols. London, 1802.

Knight of La Tour-Landry, The Book of the, ed. T. Wright. *EETS,* XXXIII, rev. ed. London, 1906.

Lancelot of the Laik, The Romance of: A Scottish Metrical Romance (c. 1490–1500), ed. W. W. Skeat. *EETS,* VI, London, 1865.

Laud Troy Book, The, A Romance of c. 1400, ed. J. E. Wulfing. *EETS,* CXXI, CXXII. London, 1902–03.

Launfal (Rawlinson Version), ed. G. L. Kittredge in *AJP,* X (1889), 1–33.

Lay le Freine, ed. H. Varnhagen in *Anglia,* III (1880), 415–23.

Lybeaus Disconus, in *Ancient English Metrical Romances,* ed. Joseph Ritson. 3 vols. London, 1802.

Melusine, compiled 1383–1394 by Jean D'Arras, Englisht c. 1500, ed. A. K. Donald. *EETSES,* LXVIII. London, 1895.

Merlin, or the Early History of King Arthur, ed. Henry B. Wheatley. *EETS,* X, XXI, XXXVI, CXII. London, 1865–99.

Morte Arthure mit Einleitung, Anmerkungen und Glossar, ed. Erik Björkman. New York 1915.

Morte Arthure, Le, ed. J. D. Bruce. *EETSES,* LXXXVIII. London, 1903.

Octavian zwei mittelenglische bearbeitungen der sage, ed. Gregor Sarrazin. Heilbronn, 1885.

Oliver of Castile, The History of, ed. Robert Graves. London, 1898.

Otuel, ed. Sidney J. Herrtage. *EETSES,* XXXIX. London, 1882.

Otuel and Roland, in *Firumbras and Otuel and Roland,* ed. Mary Isabelle O'Sullivan. *EETS,* CXCVIII. London, 1935.

Paris and Vienne, ed. M. Leach. *EETS,* CCXXXIV. London, 1957.

Partenay, The Romance of, or of Lusignen: otherwise known as The Tale of Melusine, ed. W. W. Skeat. *EETS,* XXII. London, 1866.

Partonope of Blois, The Middle English Versions of, ed. A. Trampe Bödtker. *EETSES,* CIX. London, 1912.

Rauf Coilyear, The Taill of, ed. Sidney J. Herrtage. *EETSES,* XXXIX. London, 1882.

Recuyell of the Historyes of Troy, The, written in French by Raoul Lefeore, translated & printed by William Caxton (c. A. D. 1474), reproduced and ed. by H. O. Sommer. 2 vols. Oxford, 1894.

Richard Löwenherz, Der Mittelenglischen Versroman über, ed. Karl

Brunner. Wien und Leipzig, 1913.

Roberd of Ciseyle, ed. Richard Nuck. Berlin, 1887.

Roberte the Deuyll, A Metrical Romance from an Ancient Illu-minated Manuscript, ed. I. Herbert. London, 1798.

Robert the Deuyll, in *Early Prose Romances,* ed. Henry Morley. London, 1889.

Roland, Fragment of the Song, ed. Sidney J. Herrtage. *EETSES,* XXXV. London, 1880.

Roswell and Lillian, The History of, in *Early Scottish Metrical Tales,* ed. David Laing. London, 1889.

Rouland and Vernagu, ed. Sidney J. Herrtage. *EETSES,* XXXIX. London, 1882.

Sege of Melayne, The, ed. Sidney J. Herrtage. *EETSES,* XXXV. London, 1880.

Seige of Thebes, Lydgate's, ed. Axel Erdmann and Eilbert Ekwall. *EETSES,* CVIII, CXXV. London, 1911–30.

Sege of Thebes, The, ed. F. Brie, in "Zwei mittelenglische Prosa-romanze: The Sege of Thebes and The Sege of Troy," *Archiv,* CXXX (1913), 269–285.

Seege of Troye, "Zwei mittelenglische Bearbeitungen der *Historia de excidio Trojae des Phrygiers Dares,"* ed. A. Zietsch, *Archiv,* LXXII (1884), 11–58.

Sege of Troy, The, ed. F. Brie, in "Zwei mittelenglische Prosa-romanze: The Sege of Thebes and The Sege of Troy," *Archiv,* CXXX (1913), 269–85.

Seven Sages of Rome, The, ed. Killis Campbell. New York, 1907.

Seven Sages of Rome, The (Southern Version), ed. Karl Brunner. *EETS,* CXCI. London, 1933.

Sir Amadace, in *Three Early English Metrical Romances,* ed. John Robson. London, 1842.

Sir Beues of Hamtoun, The Romance of, ed. Eugen Kölbing. *EETSES,* XLVI, XLVIII, LXV. London, 1885–94.

"Sir Cleges, Eine Mittelenglische Romanze," ed. A. Trichel, in *ESt,* XXII (1896), 345–89.

Sire Degare, a Metrical Romance of the end of the Thirteenth Century, ed. David Laing. Edinburgh, 1849.

Sir Degrevant, The Romance of, ed. L. F. Casson. *EETS,* CCXXI London, 1849.

Sir Eger, Sir Graham, and Sir Gray-Steel, The History of, in *Early Scottish Metrical Tales,* ed. David Laing. London, 1889.

Sir Eglamour, ed. Gustav Schleich, in *Palaestra,* LIII (1906).

Sir Ferumbras, ed. Sidney J. Herrtage. *EETSES,* XXXIV. London, 1879.

Syre Gawene and the Carle of Carelyle, in *Syr Gawayne: A Collection of Ancient Romance-Poems,* ed. Sir Frederick Madden. London, 1839.

Sir Growther, ed. Karl Breul. Oppeln, 1886.

Sir Isenbras, in *Select Pieces of Early Popular Poetry,* ed. E. V. Utterson. 3 vols. London, 1817.

Sir Lambewell, in *Bishop Percy's Folio Manuscript,* ed. J. W. Hales and F. J. Furnivall. 4 vols. London, 1867–69.

Sir Lamwell, in *Bishop Percy's Folio Manuscript,* ed. J. W. Hales and F. J. Furnivall. 4 vols. London, 1867–69.

Sir Launfal, Thomas Chestre, in *Ancient English Metrical Romances,* ed. Joseph Ritson. 3 vols. London, 1802.

Sir Orfeo, in *Fourteenth Century Verse & Prose,* ed. Kenneth Sisam. Oxford, 1937.

Sir Percyvelle of Galles, The Romance of, in *The Thornton Romances,* ed. J. O. Halliwell. London, 1844.

Syr Tryamoure, The Romance of, ed. J. O. Halliwell. London, 1846.

Sowdone of Babylone, The Romance of the The, and of Ferumbras his Sone who conquerede Rome, ed. Emil Hausknecht. *EETSES,* XXXVIII. London, 1881.

Squyr of Lowe Degre, The, in *Ancient English Metrical Romances,* ed. Joseph Ritson. 3 vols. London, 1802.

Three Kings of Cologne, The, ed. C. Horstmann. *EETS,* LXXXV. London, 1886.

Three Kings Sons, The, ed. F. J. Furnivall. *EETSES,* LXVII. London, 1895.

Titus & Vespasian, or the Destruction of Jerusalem, ed. J. A. Herbert. London, 1904.

Torrent of Portyngale, ed. E. Adam. *EETSES,* LI. London, 1887.

Tristan-Sage, Die Nordische und die Englische Version der, ed. Eugen Kölbing. Heilbronn, 1878–83.

Troy Book, Lydgate's, ed. Henry Bergen. *EETSES,* XCVII, CIII, CVI. London, 1906–10.

Trojanerkrieges, Barbour's Des Schottischen Nationaldichters Legendensammlung nebst den Fragmenten seines, ed. C. Horstmann. Heilbronn, 1882.

Turke and Gowin, The, in *Syr Gawayne: A Collection of Ancient Romance-Poems,* ed. Sir Frederick Madden. London, 1839.

Valentine and Orson, translated from the French by Henry Watson, ed. Arthur Dickson. *EETS,* CCIV. London, 1937.

Wars of Alexander, The, ed. W. W. Skeat. *EETSES,* XLVII. London, 1886.

Weddynge of Sr Gawen & Dame Ragnell, in *Syr Gawayne; A Collection of Ancient Romance-Poems,* ed. Sir Frederick Madden. London, 1839.

William of Palerne, The Romance of, otherwise known as The Romance of "William and the Werwolf," ed. W. W. Skeat. *EETSES,* I. London, 1877.

Ywaine and Gawain, in *Ancient English Metrical Romances,* ed. Joseph Ritson. 3 vols. London, 1802.

b) Other primary sources

i. Authors

Barbour, John, Archdeacon of Aberdeen, *The Bruce; or the Book of the most excellent noble prince, Robert de Broyss, King of Scots,* ed. W. W. Skeat. *EETSES,* XI, XXI, XXIX, LV. London, 1870–89.

Chaucer, Geoffrey. *The Poetical Works of Chaucer,* ed. F. N. Robinson. 2nd. ed. Boston, 1957.

Dunbar, William. *The Poems of William Dunbar,* ed. W. Mackay Mackenzie. London, 1932.

Gower, John. *The English Works of John Gower,* ed. G. C. Macaulay. *EETSES,* LXXXI, LXXXII. London, 1900–01.

Hawes, Stephen. *The Pastime of Pleasure,* ed. William E. Mead. *EETS,* CLXXVIII. London, 1928.

Laȝamon. *Laȝamon's Brut, or Chronicle of Britain,* ed. Sir Frederick Madden. 3 vols. London, 1847.

Lydgate, John. *Lydgate's Fall of Princes,* ed. Henry Bergen. *EETSES,* CXXI–CXXIV. London, 1924–27.

Lyndesay, Sir David. *The Monarche and Other Poems,* ed. Fitsedward Hall. *EETS,* XI, XIX. London, 1865–66.

Marlowe, Christopher. *The Works of Christopher Marlowe,* ed. C. F. Tucker Brook. Oxford, 1910.

Malory, Sir Thomas. *The Works of Sir Thomas Malory,* ed. Eugen Vinaver. 3 vols. Oxford, 1947.

Shakespeare, William. *The Complete Works of Shakespeare,* ed. Hardin Craig. Chicago, 1951.

ii. Anonymous works

Brut of England, The, ed. F. Brie. *EETS,* CXXXI, CXXXVI. London, 1906–08.

Chester Plays, ed. Thomas Wright. 2 vols. London, 1843–47.

The Digby Mysteries, ed. F. J. Furnivall. The New Shakespeare Society, Series VII, No. 1. London, 1882.

Ludus Coventriae or The Plaie called Corpus Christi, ed. K. S. Block. *EETSES,* CXX. London, 1922.

Pearl, The, ed. E. V. Gordon. Oxford, 1953.

Sir Gawain & the Green Knight, ed. J. R. R. Tolkein and E. V. Gordon. Oxford, 1930.

Towneley Plays, ed. George England with notes and introduction by A. W. Pollard. *EETSES,* LXXI. London, 1897.

York Plays, ed. L. T. Smith. Oxford, 1885.

iii. Collections

Adams, J. Q. *Chief Pre-Shakespearean Dramas.* Boston, 1924.

Brown, Carleton. *English Lyrics of the XIIth Century.* Oxford, 1932.

Brown, Carleton. *Religious Lyrics of the XIVth Century.* Oxford, 1924.

Brown, Carleton. *Religious Lyrics of the XVth Century.* Oxford, 1939.

Chambers, E. K. and F. Sidgwick. *Early English Lyrics Amorous, Divine, Moral & Trivial.* London, 1921.

Cunliffe, J. W. *Early English Classical Tragedies.* Oxford, 1912.

Hammond, E. P. *English Verse between Chaucer and Surrey.* Durham, N. C., 1927.

Horstmann, Carl. *Altenglische Legenden.* Paderborn, 1875.

Horstman, Carl. *Altenglische Legenden, Neue Folge.* Heilbronn, 1881.

Manly, J. M. *Specimens of the Pre-Shakespearean Drama.* 2 vols. Boston, 1925.

Robbins, J. R. H. *Secular Lyrics of the XIVth and XVth Centuries.* Oxford, 1955.

Robbins, J. R. H. *Historical Poems of the XIVth and XVth centuries.* New York, 1959.

Wright, Thomas. *Political Poems and Songs from the Accession of Edward III to that of Richard III.* 2 vols. London, 1859–61.

Wright, Thomas. *Political Songs of England from the Reign of John to that of Edward III.* London, 1839.

c) Rhetorical treatises

Aristotle. *The Art of Rhetoric,* in *The Works of Aristotle,* XII, trans. W. R. Roberts. Oxford, 1946.

Cicero. *Brutus,* with trans. by G. L. Hendrickson, in *Orator,* with trans. by H. M. Hubbell. Loeb ed., London, 1949.

Cicero. *De Inventione, De Optimo Genere Oratorum, Topica,* with trans. by H. M. Hubbell. Loeb ed. London, 1949.

Cicero. *De Oratore, I and II,* with trans. by E. W. Sutton and H. Rackham. Loeb ed. London, 1942.

Cicero. *De Oratore, III, together with De Fato, Paradoxa Stoicorum, De Partitone Oratoria,* with trans. by H. Rackham. Loeb ed. London, 1942.

[Cicero]. *Ad C. Herennium de Ratione Dicendi,* with trans. by Harry Caplan. Loeb ed. London, 1954.

Geoffrey de Vinsauf. *Poetria Nova,* in Edmound Faral, *Les Arts Poétiques du XIIᵉ et du XIIIᵉ Siècle.* Paris, 1923.

John of Garland. *Poetria,* ed. G. Mari, in *Romanische Forschungen,* XIII (1902), 883–965.

Quintilian. *The Institutio Oratoria of Quintilian,* with trans. by H. E. Butler. 4 vols. Loeb ed. London, 1922.

d) Secondary materials

Atkins, J. W. H. *English Literary Criticism: The Medieval Phase.* Cambridge, U. K., 1943.

Babcock, R. W. "The Medieval Setting of Chaucer's *Monk's Tale,*" *PMLA,* XLVI (1931), 205–13.

Baker, Howard. *Induction to Tragedy.* Baton Rouge, La., 1939.

Baldwin, C. S. *Ancient Rhetoric and Poetic.* New York, 1924.

Baldwin, C. S. *Medieval Rhetoric and Poetic (to 1400).* New York, 1928.

Baugh, A. C. and others. *A Literary History of England.* New York, 1948.

Bennett, H. S. *Chaucer and the Fifteenth Century.* Oxford, 1948.

Chambers, E. K. *English Literature at the Close of the Middle Ages.* Oxford, 1947.

Chambers, F. K. *The Medieval Stage.* 2 vols. Oxford, 1903.

Charlton, H B. *The Senecan Tradition in Renaissance Tragedy.* Manchester, 1946.

Crane, Ronald S. *The Vogue of Medieval Chivalric Romance During the English Renaissance.* Menasha, Wis., 1919.

Cunliffe, John W. *The Influence of Seneca on Elizabethan Tragedy.* London, 1893.

Faral, Edmond. *Les Arts Poétiques du XIIᵉ et du XIIIᵉ Siècle.*

Paris, 1923.

Farnham, Willard. *The Medieval Heritage of Elizabethan Tragedy.* Oxford, 1956.

Hibbard, Laura. *Medieval Romance in England.* New York, 1924.

Ker, W. P. *Epic and Romance.* 2nd ed. London, 1908.

Ker, W. P. *Essays on Medieval Literature.* London, 1905.

Lucas, F. L. *Seneca and Elizabethan Tragedy.* Cambridge, U.K., 1922.

Manly, J. M. "Chaucer and the Rhetoricians," *Proceedings of the British Academy.* London, 1926.

Mendenhall, J. H. *Aureate Terms: A Study in the Literary Diction of the Fifteenth Century.* Lancaster, Pa., 1919.

Paetow, L. J. *The Arts Course at Medieval Universities.* Urbana-Champaign, Ill., 1910.

Patch, Howard. *The Goddess Fortuna in Medieval Literature.* Cambridge, Mass., 1927.

Peter, John. *Complaint and Satire.* Oxford, 1956.

Stratmann, F. H. *A Middle English Dictionary,* rev. by Henry Bradley. London, 1891.

Stuart, Duane. *Epochs of Greek and Roman Biography.* Berkeley, Calif., 1928.

Taylor, G. C. "The English *Planctus Mariae*," *MP,* IV (1907), 605–37.

Ward, H. L. D. and J. A. Herbert. *Catalogue of Romances in the British Museum.* 3 vols. London, 1883–1910.

Wells, J. E. *A Manual of the Writings in Middle English 1050–1400.* New Haven, Conn., 1916.

Young, Karl. "Chaucer and Geoffrey of Vinsauf," *MP,* XLI (1944), 172–82.

Young, Karl. *The Drama of the Medieval Church.* 2 vols. Oxford, 1933.

INDEX